# DOING BUSINESS IN ASIA'S BOOMING "CHINA TRIANGLE"

## Christopher Engholm

**PRENTICE HALL**
Englewood Cliffs, New Jersey 07632

Prentice-Hall InternationaL, Inc., *London*
Prentice-Hall of Australia Pty., Ltd., *Sydney*
Prentice-Hall Canada, Inc., *Toronto*
Prentice-Hall Hispanoamericana, S.A., *Mexico*
Prentice-Hall of India Private Ltd., *New Delhi*
Prentice-Hall of Japan, Inc., *Tokyo*
Prentice-Hall of Southeast Asia Pte., Ltd., *Singapore*
Editora Prentice-Hall do Brasil, Ltda., *Rio de Janeiro*

**Library of Congress Cataloging-in-Publication Data**

Engholm, Christopher.
    Doing business in Asia's booming "China triangle" / Christopher
Engholm.
      p.    cm.
    Includes index.
    ISBN 0–13–125188–0
    1. China—Commerce.  2. Investments, Foreign—China.  3. China—
Economic conditions—1976-  4. Taiwan—Commerce.  5. Investments,
Foreign—Taiwan.  6. Taiwan—Economic conditions—1975-  7. Hong
Kong—Commerce.  8. Investments, Foreign—Hong Kong.  9. Hong Kong—
Economic conditions.  10. Intercultural communication.  I. Title.
HF3836.5.E53  1994
332.6'732251—dc20                    94–21176
                                                CIP

**ISBN 0-13-125188-0**

**PRENTICE HALL**
Career and Personal Development
Englewood Cliffs, NJ 07632

Simon & Schuster, A Paramount Communications Company

PRINTED IN THE UNITED STATES OF AMERICA

# DEDICATION

*This book is for Joshua, Bryant, and Matthew—
friends always, however far apart.*

---

# ACKNOWLEDGMENTS

Writing a book such as this is an enormous task, and it would not have been possible without much patience and perseverance on the part of all the persons who responded to questions and assisted in the research.

I am particularly indebted to China specialist Scott Grimes, a graduate student at the University of California, San Diego Graduate School of International Relations and Pacific Studies, for his expert assistance during the research and writing of this book. My gratitude also extends to David Fletcher, V.P. of Marketing at The Engholm Group for his editorial and production assistance, Li Wo Hing, managing director of Tianjin Economic-Technological Development (Hong Kong) Ltd., Dr. Jack Lewis at the University of California, Yi Ping, Zhong Ding, James Wen, David Lehr, Chris Beck, Scott Warmuth, Simon Yung, Dean and Eva Ho, David Day, Daphne Zheng, John So, Tsang Wai Keung, Husheng Xie, Pi Qian Sheng, Liu Huiwen, Lisha Zhou, Robert B. Young, Taylor Claussen, Diane E. Long, Domiano Georgino, and my agent, Julie Castiglia.

I especially want to thank my friends in the People's Republic, who, in their continuing quest to transform their country into a more economically prosperous and technologically advanced nation, have instilled in me deep admiration and respect for the Chinese people as a whole.

# PRENTICE HALL'S EMERGING WORLD MARKETS SERIES

Exports were the number one source of new job creation in America from 1985 through the early 1990s and the largest engine of economic growth. As part of the Clinton Administration's National Export Strategy, the U.S. Department of Commerce recently issued a report about the so-called "Big Emerging Markets" or BEMs. The report stated that the large industrialized nations of the world economy "will continue to be the largest U.S. markets for decades to come."

Yet the *emerging* economies of the world hold "far more promise for large incremental gains in U.S. exports." That is, our traditional markets in Canada, Japan, and the European Union will remain important for U.S. exporters; however, they are mature markets that will remain flat in terms of growth. Toward the century's end growth in exports will be seen in countries such as China, Indonesia, South Korea, Mexico, Argentina, Brazil, South Africa, Poland, and Turkey. This is the "A" list of Big Emerging Markets, chosen by the Commerce Department from over 130 of the world's developing economies.

Nearly three-fourths of world trade growth is to come from developing countries over the next twenty years. The countries in the "A" list above—all of which feature large populations, high growth, and untapped markets—will account for one-half of that growth. BEMs already purchase about one-fourth of America's exports, well over $100 billion worth each year. American companies are a perfect match to supply the needed production equipment, business services, engineering expertise, computer hardware and software, health products, and—once wages climb in them—consumer goods to the world's emerging nations. Our effort is warranted because by 2010, the top 10 BEMs will import more than the European Union and Japan combined. They already account for over 40 percent of world imports, not including the United States.

Each country's emergence will act as a locomotive pulling along neighboring economies in its tracks. For instance, the emergence of China has fueled growth in Hong Kong, Taiwan, and in the Russian Far East. India's participation in the world economy will affect Sri Lanka, Pakistan, and perhaps Myanmar, which was formerly Burma. Poland, the first Central European country to achieve positive economic growth since the fall of the Berlin Wall, will pull along neighboring Hungary, Belarus, and provide a consumer market that will benefit the adjacent Czech and Slovak Republics.

The key to success is to set up a corporate presence in these so-called regional economic drivers and expand in each region as the country emerges. The purpose of the Prentice-Hall Emerging World Market Series is to both encourage companies to make an early commitment to this endeavor, and assist them in adroitly navigating their way.

Will succeeding in the BEMs be tough for U.S. companies?

Yes. There is nothing fast or easy about dealing with countries that share positive as well as negative commercial characteristics. These are countries in transition, both economically and politically. They are undergoing structural reforms of their commercial and legal systems which are tectonic in scope. Naturally, the risks to foreign companies pioneering in these countries are manifold. Yet the wait-and-see approach pursued by many U.S. corporations may be even more risky given the tangible advantages which earlycomers eventually wield in emerging economies like China's. Infrastructure projects are planned and decided upon early in a BEM's development, and foreign vendors chosen. Widespread brand name awareness can be achieved overnight before the competition drives up advertising costs. The limited number of capable indigenous business partners who run the best-endowed enterprises tend to go fast as Japanese and European companies race to tie up agreements along with their American competitors. To be sure, the future battlegrounds in the U.S.-Japan industrial competition will be decided in the Big Emerging Markets.

The ultimate objective of this series is to be a contributor to the process by which corporate America designs and implements its strategies to meet the tough challenges ahead. The series will prepare you to enter these volatile markets with your eyes open, aware of the mistakes your corporate brethren have made in them already, and how to approach them with the right information and enough savvy to keep the cost of the effort under control while enhancing your chances for long-term success.

# ABOUT THE AUTHOR

CHRISTOPHER ENGHOLM is founder of The Engholm Group in La Costa, California, a company that specializes in public relations and company representation in Asia. The company has marketed products and technology to Chinese customers since 1985, and currently represents the Tianjin Economic–Technological Development Area (TEDA) in the United States.

As an associate with Rowland & Associates, Inc., an international training company in San Diego, Engholm has conducted corporate seminars on Asian business practice and protocol for numerous Fortune 500 companies and trade groups.

He has authored five other books, including *The China Venture: America's Corporate Encounter with the People's Republic of China; When Business East Meets Business West: A Guide to Practice and Protocol in the Pacific Rim;* and *The Asia and Japan Business Information Sourcebook.*

He is currently at work on the next two titles in this series which focus on doing business in the emerging markets of Vietnam and Mexico.

# TABLE OF CONTENTS

# Introduction

## THE NEW CHINA—PROFILE OF AN EMERGING MARKETPLACE

*"To get rich is glorious."*
Deng Xiaoping

Westerners have been trying to get rich in China for 150 years. Yet few of them have successfully penetrated the "market of one billion." With sweeping economic reform in the People's Republic, and the merging of Hong Kong, Taiwan, and China into a financial and manufacturing powerhouse called Greater China, an increasing number of firms from the West now reap profits there, including H.J. Heinz, Avon Products, McCall's, Bausch & Lomb, and scores of others. In fact, Avon projects its sales to China to skyrocket from $1.5 million in 1991 to $1 *billion* annually in the near future. This book shows how any businessperson willing to prepare and persevere can also profit in the China Triangle. The book's purpose is to encourage business people in the West to take advantage of commercial opportunities in this genuinely dynamic region, while preparing them to do so successfully.

The book is divided into four sections. **Section One** provides an overview of the region's economic and political scene, as well as Chinese cultural origins. **Section Two** covers trading opportunities, appropriate market entry strategies, and what you must know to buy and sell with the Chinese. **Section Three** provides a complete guide to investing in China, setting up ventures there, and managing a factory. **Section Four** is a manual for communicating and negotiating with the Chinese in commercial settings, with special instructions on how to conduct oneself when socializing, dining, giving gifts, and so on.

This series of books uses a unique approach to helping business people find the information that they need. Like the other titles in its series, the book is set up to be used as a business advisor—a consultant—on the topic of doing business in Greater China. Most of the chapters are set up in a question-and-answer format so you can quickly find the information you are looking for. This book is designed to be either read or used as a desktop reference. The table of contents is divided into the four sections mentioned earlier. Secondary titles will lead you to specific topics. Also, the index has been made as complete as possible to help out as well. For readers setting out to conduct business research on the countries of Greater China, I encourage you to make use of the business information sources listed in the appendix.

Good luck in your Greater China endeavors!

*Christopher Engholm*
*La Costa, CA*

# GLOSSARY

**FOREIGN INVESTMENT.** In this book, the term "foreign investment" refers to investment by foreign firms in equity-based ventures such as joint ventures and wholly foreign-owned subsidiaries, in addition to "joint" business arrangements including joint development of resources, compensation trade, and cooperative ventures. Processing and assembling arrangements, on the other hand, are treated as service contract arrangements between Chinese and foreign entities rather than foreign investment.

**FOREIGN-INVESTED ENTERPRISE.** A "foreign-invested enterprise" (FIE), denotes any business entity in China in which a foreign company controls some, or all, of the equity. In this book, an FIE can be an equity joint venture, wholly foreign-owned venture, cooperative venture, or a compensation trade arrangement, but not an agreement for joint development of resources or processing and assembling.

**EQUITY JOINT VENTURE** (hezi jingying). A "limited partnership" company that is jointly owned and operated by foreign firm(s) and Chinese entities. Partners share risks, and profits, according to equity position; that is, liability is limited to the capital each partner invests. The venture is led by a board of directors.

**COOPERATIVE VENTURE** (hezuo jingying). Often called a contractual joint venture (qiyeshi heying), this business arrangement usually involves foreign firm(s) and a Chinese entity cooperating in the manufacture of a product or service operation. In most cases, the Chinese side provides the land, building, and workforce, while the foreign firm supplies the technical know-how, capital, and equipment. Output is usually shared, but it is not divided up according to an equity-based formula. Rather, it is shared according to the terms of a negotiated contract.

**WHOLLY FOREIGN-OWNED VENTURE** (duzi jingying). In essence, this venture is a wholly owned subsidiary wherein a foreign entity uses its own capital and technology to establish an enterprise in the People's Republic. The firm controls all of the venture's equity and its output, assuming all risks and rewards. To some extent, this business form allows the foreign firm to manage its production independent of any overseeing Chinese organization. The Chinese government sometimes uses an interchangable term: foreign-invested venture, or FIV.

**JOINT DEVELOPMENT** (hezuo kaifa). Agreements concerning the joint development and exploitation of China's resources are entered into by foreign and Chinese entities under guidelines spelled out in special Chinese laws and regulations. Usually involving two stages, the foreign firm typically assumes the initial costs and risks of exploration and/or development of oil or mineral resources; later, the risk and cost of resource exploitation is shared by all partners. Though all parties share in the distribution of output according to the terms of their contract, the Chinese have also utilized joint development arrangements to acquire foreign technology, equipment, and expertise, which they pay for with discovered resources.

**COMPENSATION TRADE** (buchang maoyi). Under this agreement, the Chinese side acquires technology and equipment from a foreign firm on credit, and pays back the principal and interest with goods produced using the technology and equipment and/or labor ("direct compensation"). In some cases, payment is made with products from a third source within China ("counter purchase"). The foreign firm then markets the goods outside China.

**PROCESSING AND ASSEMBLING** (lailiao jiagong, laijian zhuangbei). These two business arrangements are merely labor contracts in which the foreign company delivers raw materials and/or components to the Chinese factory to be assembled or manufactured into finished goods. Often, the foreign firm supplies processing equipment that is later purchased by the Chinese side with production output. All goods produced are controlled by the foreign firm, which simply pays a fee to the Chinese enterprise for work completed.

CHINESE CURRENCY EXCHANGE RATE

US$1 = 8.7 Rmb (yuan)

(1994)

# PART ONE

## The China Triangle

*"Growing economic links between China, Hong Kong, and Taiwan may eventually reshape East Asia."*

THE CHINA BUSINESS REVIEW

# CHAPTER 1

# WHAT *IS*

# GREATER CHINA?

*F*ormer Communist Party Secretary, Zhao Ziyang, coined the term "Greater China" to refer to a reunified China of the future—Hong Kong, Taiwan, and the People's Republic merged into one interdependent MegaChina. In 1997, Hong Kong and the Mainland will indeed unite; but Taiwan will remain politically independent from the Mainland into the foreseeable future. The three China's *are* uniting commercially, however, and the entrepreneurial synergy generated by that unity fuels economic growth that is now unsurpassed in the world. (Guangdong Province in South China, for instance, has sustained an astounding 12.5 percent annual economic growth rate since 1985.)

Political and commercial divisions between China's Three Dragons are rapidly disappearing. "The border between China and Hong Kong has been removed five years early," said a Hong Kong lawyer to the author recently. "People on each side are coming together." The Chinese town of Shenzhen, a coastal fishing village ten years ago, now features a skyline crammed with office towers financed by Hong Kong banks, with flashing neon corporate logos written in classic Chinese characters, the written language of Nationalist Taiwan, rather than the simplified characters of Communist China. Guangdong's surging real estate and stock markets, stoked by overseas Chinese investment from around the globe, have turned many Southern Chinese teenagers into tycoons, and school teachers into land developers.

The three China's now exist in permanent symbiosis. Mainland Chinese labor sustains Hong Kong's continued expansion as a locus of entrepôt trade—a "classroom for laissez-faire capitalism" based on its British legal tradition. Hong Kong firms employ an estimated 5 million workers in South China and supply 70 percent of the foreign investment flowing into Guangdong Province. Taiwanese companies now dot Southern China too, after a decade of conducting "invisible" trade across the Taiwan Strait, and indirectly into China through trading companies in Hong Kong. The island's (now politically-correct) exports to China ballooned from $3 to $6 billion annually in 1991 alone.

Most important to the readers of this book, the China Triangle now dwarfs other high-growth regions of the world as a market for Western goods and services. The commercial needs of the Three Dragons differ markedly. Hong Kong strives to upgrade its financial, transportation, and telecommunication infrastructure so it can compete with Taiwan and Singapore and remain Asia's financial and trade hub. The "Pearl of the Orient" seeks Western technical services in civil engineering, high-tech computing, and communications.

Taiwan, on the other hand, strives to move up the world's production technology ladder, seeking from Western suppliers state-of-the-art manufacturing know-how and patent licenses for sophisticated products and processes. The Taiwanese have been increasingly willing to part with their $80 billion in cash reserves to carry forward this effort; annual imports to Taiwan have tripled in the past 8 years to *$72 billion*. (Hong Kong imports $124 billion worth of goods each year.)

Finally, the vast People's Republic of China continues to expand its share of world export markets, from which it earns an ever-increasing amount of foreign exchange with which to carry forward its industrial modernization program underway since 1978. The People's Republic seeks help to privatise its massive socialist enterprises, upgrade technology, and satisfy legions of product-starved consumers. As part of the bargain, China offers its limitless supply of inexpensive, yet increasingly skilled, labor force to offshore export manufacturers.

## GREATER CHINA'S FABLED MARKET OF "ONE BILLION"

Ten years after the Boston Tea Party, in 1784, the United States became a participant in the Old China Trade when the Empress of China sailed into Canton harbor carrying furs, porcelain, and bundles of ginseng, the restorative herb grown in New England. Another American ship, the Harriet, was sent to China a year before, but had been intercepted at the Cape of Good Hope by British traders aghast that America was devising ways to compete with them in the Orient. The captain of the Harriet forsook his place in history and sold his China-bound cargo of ginseng to the Britishers at a sizable profit. Thus began America's trade relationship with the oldest civilization on earth.

From the outset, China trade fed the imaginations of early American entrepreneurs with its exotic handicrafts, textiles, teas, and vast market potential. Profit was not the only magnetism of the China market; Americans were also drawn by the romantic exoticism and ineffable mystique of the country. And there was the distinctly American pioneering spirit of the time, the notion of seeking out distant lands and building up a legacy of commercial success.

Unfortunately, China's ancient and uncanny will to be economically self-reliant cut short America's pecuniary fantasy of market share in the Orient. China's merchants were simply more interested in trading among themselves than with barbarians from across the great waters. The Chinese habitually neglected foreign merchants; hence Sino-American trade never amounted to more than 2-4 percent of America's total trade. But this was better than the British could claim, at least until they initiated the trading of opium to China and waged two wars to ensure its continuation.

By 1900, the mythical China market had become synonymous with unfulfilled expectations. Yet the image of China's vast market had been firmly implanted in the hearts and minds of America's new industrialists. James B. Duke (1865-1925), the American tobacco tycoon, learned of the invention of the cigarette machine in 1881, and said, "Bring me an atlas." He found China to have a population of 430 million and, pointing to the odd-shaped country, declared, "That is where we are going to sell cigarettes." By 1916, Duke's company held the lion's share of the cigarette market in China, selling $20.75 million worth of cigarettes in that year alone. Under his aegis, the Shanghai branch of the British-American Tobacco Company—one of the first multinational corporations to enter China—made large-scale investments there, transferring cigarette processing technology and managerial techniques, setting up a wide distribution network, and training Chinese labor. Thus, America's corporate encounter with China began.

Throughout the first half of the twentieth century, China was considered a relatively important export market until the United States placed a trade embargo on China during the Korean War (1950). All Sino-American trade had ceased until Richard Nixon reopened relations with China in 1972 by signing the Shanghai Communique with China's premier, Zhou Enlai. In that year, the first sale of U.S. grain was made to China, and U.S. firms were included in the Canton Trade Fair for the first time, then the only conduit for product promotion in the People's Republic. Between 1973 and 1979, communication between Washington and Beijing was initiated via office representation while U.S. companies M.W. Kellogg, Coca-Cola, and Arco, signed contract deals with China in the fields of ammonia manufacture, soft drink distribution, and offshore seismic surveying, respectively. Although economic contacts between China and the United States grew slightly during the 1970s, it was not until 1979, when China abruptly opened its doors to foreign companies in an effort to obtain foreign technology and direct investment, that economic intercourse between the two countries began to achieve momentum. The first Sino-U.S. joint venture was signed in 1979 between the ES Pacific Development Corporation and China International Travel Service to construct and manage the Great Wall Hotel in Beijing; in 1982, Foxboro and Shanghai Instrument Industrial Company signed the first Sino-U.S.

manufacturing joint venture agreement; in 1984, the 3M company formed the first wholly foreign-owned subsidiary in the People's Republic. In 1980, the United States granted China "most favored nation" status and in 1983, U.S. export controls regarding China were relaxed. Today, it is commonplace to find Chinese trade promoters traveling the United States and the rest of the industrialized world pronouncing the great economic and investment opportunities in the China market.

## U.S.-China Trade Comes of Age

The inauguration of China's opening and the lure of the market have given rise to two general attitudes among U.S. corporations. The first dates back to the old philosophy of China being the last and largest untapped market in the world, a notion epitomized in the 1840s when Great Britain promulgated the idea of lengthening the coats of every Chinese by one inch and thus, saving the British textile industry from imminent collapse. Unfortunately, there were no wool coats in China at the time. Another pursuer of the untapped China market was John D. Rockefeller, who at one time anticipated selling substantial quantities of oil to China to fuel the lamps in the homes of its huge populace. Today, this attitude is found in marketing executives who dream of exponential sales growth—10 trillion razor blades a year, 5 billion cans of cola a week, millions of telephones a year, or thousands of automobiles a month.

The other prevailing view of China's potential market is connected with broader corporate global initiatives. As part of their regional or product-based strategies, many companies now consider establishing an office and/or subsidiary in China as an opportunity to become acquainted with its emerging economic and technology-related capabilities. In this way, a corporation could develop sales through its market presence, and simultaneously network inside China with an eye to linking up with the firm's other operations in the Asia-Pacific region. By looking at China with this somewhat more complex and long-term view, companies are better able to gauge China's potential and appraise its investment climate while leveraging their Chinese contacts to enhance their global competitive position.

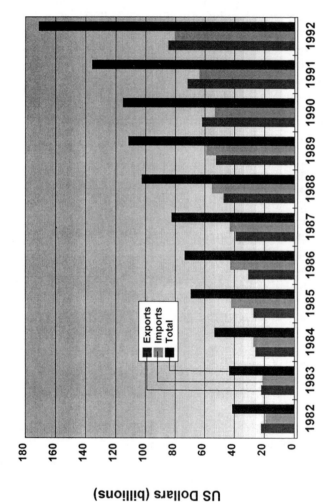

China's Total Trade, 1982-1992

US Dollars (billions)

Source: *The Economist Intelligence Unit.*

Spurred into action by the pronounced immediacy that the Chinese attached to their open-door policies, U.S. corporations entered China in large numbers. By the time of the Tiananmen Uprising in 1989, they had made direct investments in well over 250 joint ventures worth US $1.7 billion. As part of their global strategy, the U.S. partners in these early ventures accepted comparatively strict operating requirements in order to gain a foothold in China. In contrast to the strategies that many of these American firms have pursued in Taiwan, Japan, and South Korea (that is, export-oriented manufacturing), they licensed newer technology, trained more managers and workers, and set up factories in China with the overriding goal of selling to the Chinese domestic market. With the fading of memories about Tiananmen, and China's increasing willingness to allow foreigners to sell directly to better-endowed Chinese consumers, U.S. firms' trickle of investment in the PRC began to pour. By the end of 1993, U.S. firms were involved in 5,500 projects with an estimated value of $5.6 billion, over 75 percent more cumulative U.S. investment than made in 1992. By mid-1994, the figures show that U.S. companies have invested a total of $14.4 billion in approved investment in over 10,000 China ventures: 300,000 jobs in the U.S. now depend on U.S.-China business.

**THE OPENING OF THE CHINA MARKET.** Foreign corporations, realizing that China is steadily emerging as an important new player in world commerce (China trade makes up 5 percent of total world trade), also see the Chinese as fresh buyers of foreign equipment and expertise. China's total foreign trade reached almost $74 billion by 1986; by 1993, the figure had rocketed to $158 billion and is estimated to reach $293 billion by 1998, not including the additional trade of Hong Kong to be part of China at that time. China purchased $83 billion worth of goods from foreign suppliers in 1993; the figure is estimated to reach $150 billion by 1998.

Many American companies believe they are well positioned to offer China the much-needed technology and expertise its economic modernization will require. In effect, U.S. industries have approached the Chinese market with the belief that China will perceive American technology as the most advanced in the world. At the same time, however, they are aware that China does not intend to depend on one source or one country to meet all its modern-

## PRC Regional Trade Patterns
Including % Share of Total Trade (1992) and
Total Two-way Trade in US$ billion

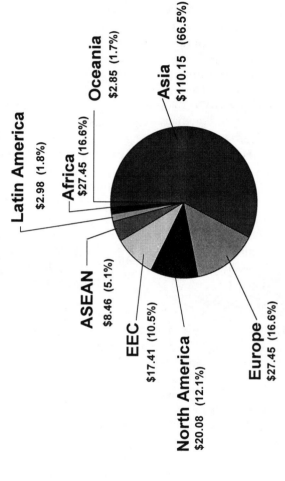

Oceania
$2.85 (1.7%)

Asia
$110.15 (66.5%)

Latin America
$2.98 (1.8%)

Africa
$27.45 (16.6%)

ASEAN
$8.46 (5.1%)

EEC
$17.41 (10.5%)

North America
$20.08 (12.1%)

Europe
$27.45 (16.6%)

Source:  *China's Custom Statistics, The Economist Intelligence Unit.*

ization needs. Though price is an important criterion in Chinese commercial decisions, China has been known to deal with so-called noncompetitive firms in order to avoid excessive dependence on one or two technology suppliers. This tendency, along with what Americans have been told (by the Chinese themselves) of Beijing's unwillingness to get too close to Japan, has attracted many U.S. firms that see potential niches in the Chinese market open to them.

**THE U.S.-CHINA TRADE PARTNERSHIP.** After the fall of the Gang of Four (1976) and diplomatic recognition of China by the U.S. in 1979, trade between the U.S. and China began to take off. Between the years of 1973 and 1987, the total volume of U.S.-China trade grew more than ten-fold, from $805 million to over $10 billion. By 1993, two-way trade between the countries reached $20 billion. Agricultural products traditionally accounted for more than half of U.S. exports to China, but this is changing. For example, U.S. exports of grain, cotton, and agricultural products to China amounted to 70 percent of U.S. total sales there in 1978; in 1979, the figure had dropped to 58 percent; and in 1993, it stood at 20 percent.

As total trade between the two countries has increased, the U.S. has been hard pressed to export to China as much as it imports. At present, the U.S. is experiencing a huge trade deficit (over $15 billion) with the People's Republic as the Chinese expand their efforts to bolster and diversify exports.

**MARKET SHARE.** The Japanese have traditionally maintained the largest proportion of the China market—around 25 percent—though that figure is down to 22 percent in 1993 as Tiawan's share has climbed from nil to 13 percent in the past decade. The U.S. share of the China market stood at around 12 percent throughout the 1980s, but has fallen since to 10 percent in 1993. Hong Kong's role as a trading partner as well as an entry port trade conduit for U.S., South Korean, and Taiwanese goods entering China has sustained its market share in China at 10 percent since the mid-1980s. By official accounts, U.S. companies trade over $5 billion worth of goods to the People's Republic via Hong Kong each year.

In terms of specific China market sectors, the U.S. position as a leading vendor of technology and primary products is holding ground against intensifying competition from Japan, Europe, and other Chinese countries. The U.S. market shares of scientific equipment (35%), telecommunications (5%), power generating equipment (22%), and transport machinery (18%) have remained roughly steady since the early 1980s. In computer sales, the U.S. share has increased from 40 percent in 1983 to 50 percent in 1993.

# CHAPTER 2

# COUNTRY PROFILES:

# CHINA, TAIWAN,

# HONG KONG

*O*pen almost any book about running a business and you find the cardinal requirement for entrepreneurial success: Know Your Customer. How can we pretend to know our customers in China when we hardly understand the Chinese as a people. Our collective cultural illiteracy of the Pacific Rim leaves many of us to rely on stereotypes and myth when dealing with the Chinese. As recently as 1980, a majority of Americans polled believed that people in China had a higher standard of living than people in Singapore, South Korea, and Taiwan.

In a Gallop pole in 1980 drawn upon a national sample of Americans, the most common descriptions of Asia were: "crowded with too many people," "undeveloped," a place of "political unrest," and "dirty, with poor sanitation." Only 4 percent of the respondents thought Asians were "peace-loving" and only 3 percent of them thought they were "well dressed." It took the West a long time to acknowledge that the East was even capable of progressing toward modernity. The old European adage seemed to color our thinking: "Nothing changes in the East. Better fifty years of Europe than a cycle of Cathay."

## GETTING TO KNOW YOUR CHINESE CUSTOMERS

There's little mystery as to the origin of our warped perceptions of the Chinese. The "ingenious Chinese" were, at first, respected as the inventors of paper, pasta, gunpowder, the compass, and houses that sway in the event of an earthquake. But they were also a "Yellow Peril," a threat to American labor. "The 'little yellow man' is…working ruin and desolation all over this great empire" recorded the minutes in the House of Representatives in 1886. The "Chinaman". smoked opium, played the lottery, and stole jobs. Yet American business employers and traders (to their credit) thought him honest, upright, hard working, frugal, peaceful, and industrious—in short, the "Chinaman" was good for business!

Hollywood took over from there. Chinese were portrayed as working in restaurants and laundromats, wearing their hair in a pigtail, having big buck teeth, and gambling like fiends. They looked alike. They were daft, superstitious, lazy, and unmanageable in movies like *The Good Earth* and *Red Dust* (starring Clark Gable), but unlike the ruthless and cunning Japanese, they were redeemingly cute and harmless. Their country, China, also represented an easy customer—hordes of them!—for American products, as portrayed in the 1939 film, *Oil for the Lamps of China*. Charlie Chan personified Confucian "wisdom," which he propounded in nongrammatical English. In the end, the Chinese were labeled "inscrutable" by Westerners who found it too much trouble to get to know them.

Nowadays, among North American business people, the Chinese suffer the stereotype of being unwilling or unable to pay (in cash) for the things they desire to buy. Mainland China's propensity for pushing for countertrade and barter arrangements to finance purchases has worsened their condescending perception. I was a participant in a meeting at which an American executive—a marketing representative of Science Applications

International Corporation—asked, in the presence of a Chinese businessperson, "How are the Chinese going to pay for this technology—with rice or what?" I answered the question by saying China's economy was the fourth largest in the world and a letter of credit for $1.5 million could be easily obtained.

## THE HUMAN LANDSCAPE IN GREATER CHINA

The human geography of Mainland China consists of an estimated 1.2 billion citizens, 90 percent of whom are ethnic Han Chinese, who are in the majority in every province of the country except for Tibet and Xinjiang. Fifty-five minority groups, each with its own customs and dialects occupy the land, though all of these peoples use only the Chinese written language primarily. The Muslim populations of Xinjiang read and write Arabic as well. Other than the Han Chinese, the most populous groups are the Manchus, the Chuang, the Uighurs, and the Tibetans. Government policy toward minority groups in China has been, for the most part, enlightened and accommodating. Minority groups such as the Hui, Kazakh, and 14 others live in "autonomous regions" located throughout the country but are concentrated in the South.

Conducting business in China, you will rarely deal directly with someone of non-Han descent, unless you are doing business in an autonomous zone. In Taiwan, besides the dominant Han Chinese, you will see indigenous islanders in some areas, called "mountain people" by many locals; again, it is rare for foreign business people to deal directly with this minority group in Taiwan. One key point to make here is that the Han Chinese have their own cultural subdivisions: the Mandarin of the North, the Cantonese of the South, the Sichuanese of the Southwest, and the Shanghaiese of the Yangtze River Delta area.

Han Chinese all read and write the Chinese language, but they speak different dialects of the Chinese language. Most can understand the Mandarin's dialect—called the "common language" and taught in schools throughout the country since Mao declared it China's language for the purpose of unifying the country. But Cantonese Chinese spoken in Hong Kong and Guangdong Province of China is more complex than Mandarin and mutually unintelligible. Shanghaiese and Sichuanese are unique dialects as well. In Hong Kong, Cantonese is the language of commerce though many Chinese there speak English as well. Moreover, many Chinese business people working in Hong Kong hail from regions inside the mainland, and thus, speak one of the other mainland dialects that I have mentioned. We will speak later about the importance of hiring an interpreter who speaks not just Mandarin Chinese, but also the matching dialect of your Chinese counterpart.

## THE RISING POWER OF THE OVERSEAS CHINESE

Chinese influence is not limited to Greater China. In fact, Chinese have created what the Los Angeles Times has called an "ethnic Chinese rim around the Pacific Basin." Chinese make up 10 percent of the population of Thailand, 2.5 percent in Indonesia, and 80 percent in Singapore. Some of the richest people in the world are overseas Chinese. Li Ka-shing, the richest man in Hong Kong, owns Canada's 12th largest oil company and owns Hong Kong International Terminals, controlling half of the shipping traffic through Hong Kong harbor. Y.K. Pao is from Hong Kong and is a shipowner and real estate financier who purchased the Omni Hotel chain in the U.S. for $135 million in 1988. Y.C. Wang from Taiwan owns Formosa Plastics Group which had sales of 5.8 billion dollars in 1988. Y.Z. Hsu from Taiwan is a textile king pin. Overseas Chinese from Hong Kong and Taiwan own 10% of downtown San Francisco.

Over a thousand years ago, the "sojourn" of overseas Chinese, called the *Nanyang,* began. Now, there are 50 million overseas Chinese living outside of mainland China. The great majority of overseas Chinese come from southeastern provinces of China, mostly Cantonese, Hakka, and Teochius peoples. Throughout Southeast Asia the Chinese invested in farms, rubber estates, copra plantations, timber, shipping, and merchandizing. They quickly gained the dominant economic position wherever they settled. They maintained their own better schools, and separated themselves as much as possible from local populations. In Malaya, they entered into trade, supplied most of the labor in the mines, soon owning a third of them, and became well positioned in nearly every other industry as well. In Thailand they worked in tin and tungsten mines, on rubber plantations, and as shopkeepers and traders. In both Thailand and Indonesia the Chinese came to control retail districts.

For more than a century, overseas Chinese investors have been critical to Mainland China's economy. They currently account for an estimated 80-85 percent of total foreign investment in the PRC, focused primarily along China's southern coast where the early overseas Chinese originated. Fujian province, for instance, is the ancestral home of 8 million overseas Chinese (80 percent of all Taiwanese trace their roots there) which virtually guarantees Fujian's economic development fueled by outside Chinese investment.

## COUNTRY PROFILE: PEOPLE'S REPUBLIC OF CHINA

China's name, Zhong Guo Ren, means "the people of the Middle Kingdom." Their collective world view places the Chinese at the center of "all below heaven" (tian xia), at the apex of civilization, surrounded by barbarian cultures that occupy the periphery.

### CHINA AT A GLANCE

| | |
|---|---|
| *Population:* | 1.16 billion |
| *Religions:* | Buddhist, Taoist, Moslem, Christian |
| *Government:* | Communist Party/Socialist |
| *Language:* | Putonghua (Mandarin Chinese); Various Dialects |
| *Currency Name:* | Renminbi (RMB) |
| *Trade (1993):* | $75.2 billion in exports; $83.1 billion in imports. |

## CHINA'S CHANGING SOCIETY

Social conditions in China are in great flux at the moment as increasing numbers of Chinese benefit from economic growth and modernization. Wages are still low overall, though with "moon-lighting" at second and third jobs, many Chinese can afford nicer apartments, home appliances, and fashionable clothing. Political restrictions on the common person have loosened significantly in the early 1990s as making money has become the prime focus for most working people. China's leaders learned the hard way during the Tiananmen Uprising that politics in China is economic: if the country's standard of living can be raised for everyone—not just well connected Party members—renewed protests will be unlikely. Changes in employment have been dramatic, with the communes and townships being dismantled slowly and the "iron rice bowl" philosophy of paying everybody's way being substituted by the "contract responsibility" system wherein a worker must agree to clearly stated performance clauses or risk dismissal. Finding a job has become tougher as companies restructure for competitiveness or close down because they are redundant. Though China is home to more than a million millionaires, there are 200 million Chinese who can't find work. In fact, China is home to more people out of work than any other country, with 3 percent unemployed in urban areas (up from 2.6 percent in 1993), out of a total urban workforce of 200 million. One hundred and thirty million farmers are jobless and 15 million people traverse the countryside as migrant workers. In addition, the government plans to pink slip 2 million local level civil servants in the near term.

All of this explains the growing thousands of young people who have crowded into coastal cities seeking work far from home. It also explains why so many young people are skipping the traditional stage of working for a state company and are setting up private businesses, or as they say, "xiahai jingshang"—across the ocean to do business! Obtaining a university education in China remains something for the very studious and well connected. Only one young person out of a thousand can attend college due to the scarcity of openings. A whole new generation of young people is maturing who are avoiding formal training of any kind to move directly into business; many of these 20-25-year-olds already have acquired the luxuries of the West as well as a palpable attitude problem, say Chinese a few years older and above. Many young Chinese capitalists are arrogant about their early success, decedent by every definition, and improvident in not investing their earnings in viable businesses but spending crazily in karaoke bars, casinos, and the expanding numbers of brothels.

**POVERTY ON THE DECREASE.** With economic growth has come a reduction of the number of Chinese living in "absolute poverty," down from 270 million in 1978 to 100 million in 1985, the latest statistic available. As Deng Xiaoping has told the Chinese, some regions of the country must get rich before others. Many inland cities and rural areas have not yet been able to attract foreign investment, international loans, or export-oriented businesses to participate in China's take-off as of yet.

**THE CHANGING ROLE OF WOMEN.** The self-perception of Chinese women is perhaps the most noticable psychological change in China since the Open Door reform program was started. "Girls are now very open," says a Chinese women visiting China after living in the United States for three years. "They don't trudge around with their heads lowered. They wear bright fashions and speak their minds to men and elders. Chinese women aren't waiting around for a successful man to come to them. They seek him out in the hotel discos and karaoke bars. They're looking for a man who can get them out of here." The role of women in China changed dramatically when Mao equalized the sexes immediately following communist victory in 1949. Many women were instrumental in the fight to liberate the country from the nationalists and from foreign domination, and thus many women were prominent in the party and in the state administration throughout the country. Chinese women hold positions as factory workers and managers in significant numbers, though it is still seldom that a woman will be a general manager or board member of a state enterprise or a director of a Chinese institution or agency. A growing number of women, however, have become entrepreneurs, often in conjunction with a job at a state-run firm or collective. One can predict growth in the number of private enterprises owned by women, and well run by them given that they are not as prone to lose sight of the need to invest in their future as many young Chinese men appear to be.

Chinese women are, however, under immense pressure to give birth to only one child. The one-child policy, first made a social policy in 1975 to control the growth of China's population,

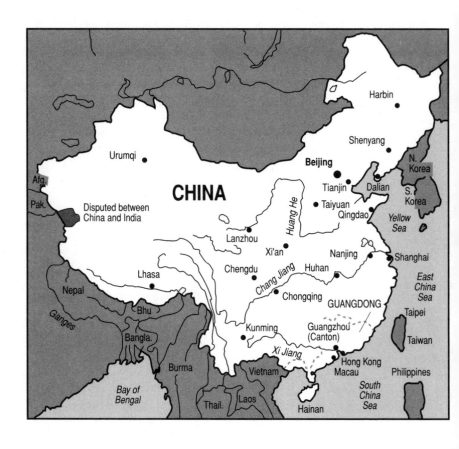

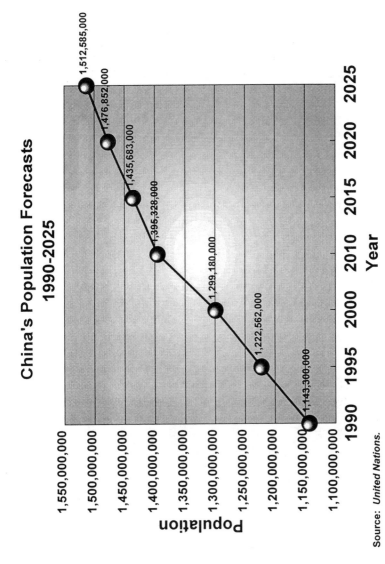

China's Population Forecasts 1990-2025

Source: *United Nations.*

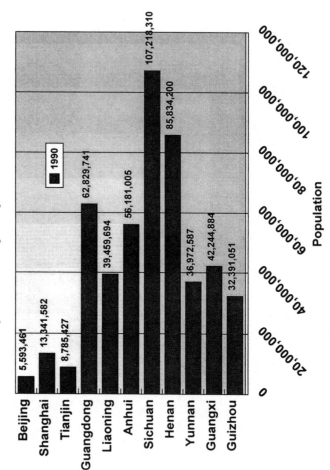

**China's Population by Key Cities and Provinces**

■ 1990

| | Population |
|---|---|
| Beijing | 5,593,461 |
| Shanghai | 13,341,582 |
| Tianjin | 8,785,427 |
| Guangdong | 62,829,741 |
| Liaoning | 39,459,694 |
| Anhui | 56,181,005 |
| Sichuan | 107,218,310 |
| Henan | 85,834,200 |
| Yunnan | 36,972,587 |
| Guangxi | 42,244,884 |
| Guizhou | 32,391,051 |

Source: *Chinese Statistical Yearbook.*

is enforced today through a woman's employer. Should a woman become pregnant with a second child, she faces having her pay docked. Each enterprise has a quota for births issued by the government. A person needs a license and permission from one's company to have a child. Those who want to have a second child face ostracism as well as pressure to terminate the pregnancy. A second child is not issued a *houkou,* an identification book, for a few years after birth, making them noncitizens for that period and depriving them of their share of rationed goods, not to mention basic rights as a legal person. Not only must a woman obtain a signed contract from her employer to have a child, she may face mandatory sterilization after she has given birth to her first child. She might also be fired should she proceed with a second pregnancy. If the workplace is not responsible for enforcing the one-child policy, a neighborhood committee will normally fill the role.

**CHINA'S NEW "SOCIALIST MAN."** The new Chinese "socialist man" must live up to a new set of criteria. I spent a day in Shanghai with Cai Guang Tian, one of China's outspoken new capitalists and a member of the National Committee of the Chinese People's Political Consultative Conference. Mr. Cai retired at age 61 and planned to live out his days in his small house with his 100 yuan pension. Now he owns 21 English-language schools in China and has a net worth of between 30-40 million yuan. He owns and operates 12 companies. "Only the fit survive here," he says of the new China. "If you're powerful you can make money." Mr. Cai was criticized during his first prosperous years from 1988 to 1991 by "jealous officials" and others who thought his wealth was made at the expense of students who should not have to pay dearly for an education in the English language. I asked what he meant by "those who are powerful will make money." He became angry and affirmed that he had taken advantage of no government connections in making his fortune, and had no political background. This is his list of "secrets" for young Chinese to follow in order to succeed in business: Wisdom, Knowledge, Diligence, Imagination, and Boldness. These secrets, says Mr. Cai, "must spread across China or China's future is hopeless."

A few of China's new capitalists that Mr. Cai speaks of, whom the author has worked with, include:

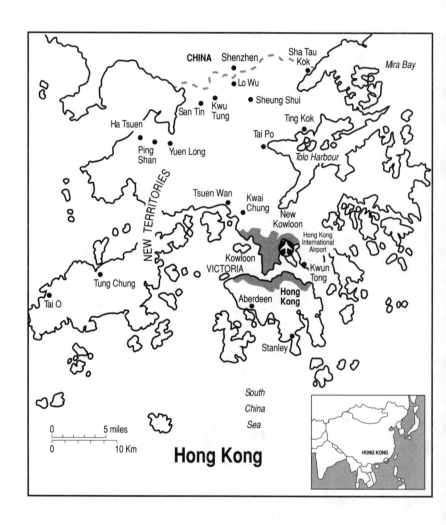

**Hong Kong**

**Quincey Wang:** Harvey just turned 23, and runs a private company called Power Investment Limited in Shenzhen. He's a stock broker selling Shenzhen- and Shanghai-listed stocks to Chinese citizens. He has already made a million in the market. Now he invests in real estate in America, and seeks a foreign partner to open a subsidiary in the West to sell stocks to foreign clients. His company isn't even legal yet, but within a year it will be because others like it are popping up all over the city.

**Sheila Liu:** She's 31 and worked for the Shenda Telephone Company for ten years. Two years ago, she used her savings to open a shop selling telephones. It flourished. Now she has a chain of stores in South China, plays the stock market avidly, and invests in Shenzhen real estate. She currently seeks Western suppliers to expand her product offerings.

**Cheng Yuanshi:** Hailing from Chongqing, he used to be a spy stationed in Washington, D.C. where he spent his days copying public domain documents at the National Technical Information Library to be sent back to a technology institute in China. Now he lives in South China, and has built up a database of Chinese industrial end-users which he sells all over the world. Mr. Cheng drives last year's Mercedes and, when you sit with him at lunch, has to break off conversation every two minutes to take a call on his cellular phone. He recently moved into arbitrage.

## COUNTRY PROFILE: HONG KONG

Hong Kong, which translates "fragrant harbor," rose upon a foundation of trade in "foreign mud," that is, opium. In its 100-year history it has become the world's greatest entry port trading center and the third largest financial center in the world, with more Rolls Royces per hectare than in anywhere else in the world. The Island possesses the second largest futures market on the planet, and the second busiest port. About the size of New York City, with 40,000 mostly small-sized enterprises, Hong Kong is, as the cliché goes, a schoolroom for the study of free market capitalism. There is duty on only five commodities coming in and no duty on goods going out.

Hong Kong was the destination for Cantonese and Fukienese Chinese fleeing war, famine, and political reprisal in Mainland China, especially during the years of civil war in China that culminated with Communist victory. Historically, these were some of China's hardiest capitalists, and they found fertile ground for cultivating enterprise in British-run laissez-fare Hong Kong. The British found Hong Kong, with its deep water harbor, perfect for mooring their large clipper ships. China gave the Island to England as a victory prize after the Opium War in 1842, a gesture which Queen Victoria's Foreign Secretary, Lord Palmerston, accepted with derisive laughter. Of course, it was not with laughter that Margaret Thatcher relinquished Hong Kong to China in a treaty signed in 1984.

### HONG KONG AT A GLANCE

| | |
|---|---|
| *Population:* | 5.8 Million |
| *Religions:* | Buddhist, Taoist, Christian, with small numbers of Moslems, Hindus, Jews and Sikhs. |
| *Languages:* | English and Cantonese; Mandarin is on the increase. |
| *Trade (1993):* | $119.5 billion in exports; $123.8 billion in imports |

Hong Kong has an affluent society and a service-oriented economy where the per capita GDP exceeds $13,500. With the ongoing economic growth throughout Asia, Hong Kong has benefitted as a trade and financial hub, channeling, for example, over $1 billion every year of Taiwanese investment into South China. It's similar role vis-a-vis Vietnam has just begun. Hong Kong is the gateway to the China market; between 4 and 6 million people are now employed by Hong Kong-invested enterprises in Guangdong Province. Thirty to 40 percent of China's foreign exchange income comes from, or through, Hong Kong to the PRC. However, the former British colony will soon be a Special Administrative Region of the People's Republic of China. No city or country on Earth lives under a heavier onus of uncertainty than Hong Kong, a city, as Chinese poet Han Su-yin wrote in Life magazine in 1959, "on borrowed time in a borrowed place."

Every Hong Kong business person has prepared, in his or her own way, for 1997. During the last three years, 150,000 Hong Kong professionals and skilled residents have fled for safe haven abroad. Most were pessimistic about Hong Kong's future in the months following the Tiananmen Massacre in 1989. At that time only 25 percent of people in Hong Kong were confident about the policy of "One Party, Two Systems" being preserved in the Basic Law. Seventy percent believed China would not honor it after 1997. However, since the spiralling of real estate and stock values in Hong Kong in 1989-90, the economy has rebounded, in large measure due to the much accelerated opening of the China market since. Large numbers of Hong Kong people now earn their living in businesses directly dependent on China trade and investment. While Christopher F. Patten, the governor of Hong Kong—"the last of Britain's viceregal figures, in the last of its major Crown Colonies" as reporter John Newhouse calls him—goes about trying to inject a bit of pluralism into Hong Kong's legislative system, the person-on-the-street is decidedly against the British upsetting relations with their primary business partner by forcing democracy down their throats in the eleventh hour of British rule. A friend and business associate summed up the feeling one hears more and more among Hong Kong Chinese: "Hong Kong people don't want democracy. They never had real freedom under the British, and the British now want to 'give back' Hong Kong by forcing it to be a pluralistic democracy." My friend then asks perceptively: "Do the British have to screw up every one of their former colonies so they can point to its problems later and say, 'now wasn't our system better?'"

Hong Kong's near-term future will not be without its bumps. One can expect months of uncertainty during the inevitable Deng succession, and intermittent tension with the mainland over social policies such as the language of education, welfare, and civil law. But the Hong Kong people—though they admit they are uncertain about their political future—realize how much they have to gain in their new relationship with the booming mainland. As of this writing, the "story" in Hong Kong is hardly how worried its citizens might be because the Chinese are coming, but how many citizens are ready to greet the future with pragmatic open arms.

## COUNTRY PROFILE: TAIWAN

Once called Formosa, Taiwan (population 20.8 million) is an island empire about the size of Holland and the twelfth largest trading nation in the world. Taiwan is the second most cash-rich country after Japan, and Japan has six times as many people. An economic powerhouse with a timid demeanor, the Taiwan stock market does as much business as both the New York and Tokyo exchanges. One hundred and twenty countries of the world don't recognize Taiwan diplomatically, yet Taiwan exports to virtually all of them.

### TAIWAN AT A GLANCE

| | |
|---|---|
| *Population:* | 20.8 million |
| *Religions:* | Buddhism, Confucianism, Taoism, Christianity |
| *Languages:* | Mandarin (official), Taiwanese, Hakka, as well as English and Japanese among many business people. |
| *Trade (1993):* | $81.5 billion in exports; $72.0 billion in imports. |
| *Currency name:* | New Taiwan (NT) Dollar |

The Taiwanese live under an authoritarian government, still run by Chinese Nationalists who fled the mainland before the bayonets of the Communists in 1949. (Martial law was only lifted in 1987 after being in force since 1949.) The Mainland's mandarinate that ran the KMT up until its defeat at the hands of the Communists, started arriving on the island of Formosa in the mid-1940s before the final fall of Chiang Kai-shek. Taiwan's Old Guard has been in control of Taiwan ever since. Although reforms in the 1980s broke the dictatorship in Taiwan, animosity between Mainlanders and Taiwanese has never faded completely even as Taiwan's population grew from 8 million (including 2 million Mainlanders) in 1951, to 20 million in 1981. The U.S. subsidized loans, expertise, military protection, and grants fueled Taiwan's takeoff. America's role in Taiwan's economy can be expressed numerically: of Taiwan's $10.9 billion dollar trade surplus in 1992, $10.4 billion was with the United States. We will return to describe Taiwan's economic and business atmosphere in the next chapter.

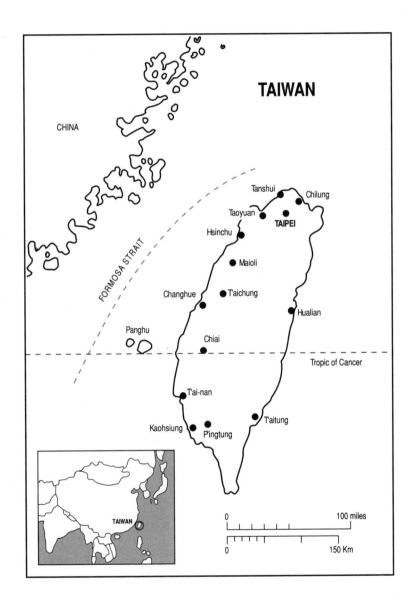

# CONFUCIANISM TO CAPITALISM—THE CHANGING CHARACTER OF THE CHINESE

The values and behaviors of the Chinese are shaped by the practical philosophies of China's earliest sages, including Zhougang, Mencius, and Confucius. What became known as Confucianism was never China's religion as one might think; rather, it is a practical code of conduct to follow in everyday life—a manual for managing human relationships harmoniously. Confucianism remains the founding philosophy behind Chinese behavior, attitudes, values, and mannerisms. One core rule states that there are superiors and inferiors and that superiors must act with virtue *(te)* and that inferiors must obey their superior. One should be dutiful toward one's parents and elders, reciprocal in one's obligations, respectful of human dignity, and fair toward all. Confucianism inculcated among its followers values such as servility, frugality, abstinence, and diligence. It recognized hard work, patriarchal leadership, entrepreneurial spirit, and devotion to family.

China's new professional class differs from the "Old Guard" in style and approach. Reemerging are the pre-socialist and quite non-Confucian values like individualism, independence, ambition, and faith. People are now more concerned with how they look than with how they think. Ideology has given way to status, conformity to individuality, Confucian-steeped traditions to the capitalist worship of cash. The attitude toward Westerners has reversed as well. Once burned in effigy in the streets, Westerners are now hailed as models to be imitated.

Remember, however, that in China there exist regional differences in behavior and manners; the degree of Westernization varies from region to region, even city to city. Even with change in China, a Chinese person may differ from a Westerner in crucial ways. What makes the *typical* Chinese person tick? Most Chinese—whether they are Taiwanese, Hong Kong Chinese, or Mainlanders—tend to be group-oriented, identifying strongly with the group to which they belong, be it their family kingroup, company, or ethnic group. The more traditional, the more they will judge themselves in terms of how much, or how little, respect they command from others—that is, their level of *mianzi*, or "face." One's "face" in Greater China is something to prize and to protect;

commercial relationships with high-level decision makers cannot be made or maintained by those of low status, those without face. The Chinese deal with others in a mode of reciprocity-seeking. They give and expect favors; as a business person in the region you will have to address the emotional needs of business counterparts as well as the commercial. Don't flinch when a Chinese person asks you to find a job for a relative; your business deal may depend on your coming through in nonbusiness ways.

The West likes to label the Chinese as cunning and even duplicitous. In fact, through their history of war, famine, and political reprisal, the Chinese have learned to keep their thoughts to themselves and their money in a mattress rather than a government-run bank account. Thus, the Chinese are usually verbally as well as socially cautious, as opposed to dishonest, while the typical Westerner in Asia is extroverted in comparison.

Though China is a developing country facing Third World problems, the Chinese person feels a deep sense of national and cultural pride. Historically, China was thought to be the "Middle Kingdom," a "Celestial Empire" surrounded by tribute states populated by barbarian peoples. China had a profound political and cultural influence on all of its neighbors, which it lorded over. Culturally, China is the mother of human culture in East Asia, spreading Confucianist philosophy, its exam-based education system, social organization, music, culinary practice, language, writing system, and government system to Korea, Japan, and throughout most of Southeast Asia. With 50 million overseas Chinese living outside China, and playing dominant roles in business communities in Thailand, Malaysia, Singapore, Indonesia, and the Philippines, the pervasive power and influence of the Chinese Mainland cannot be argued. In the hearts and minds of the Chinese people, this superior role as the source of regional cultural tradition and similar ethnic background with the powerful forces of overseas Chinese, lend the Chinese a deep, immovable, sense of pride. The current generation of Chinese read in the world press about China's unbelievable economic accomplishments, and about how China will have the largest economy on the planet by early in the next century.

China's sense of indelible pride plays a role in how the Chinese deal today with foreign business people and countries.

Theirs is the oldest continuous civilization on earth: the way Westerners do business, and "international standards of business" are of little concern to the majority of Chinese businesspeople. The pride of the Chinese has at times taken the form of cultural elitism, and has worked to isolate China while offending outsiders. The moral: to do effective business in China you must be willing to adjust to Chinese-style commerce, rather than waiting for the Chinese to suddenly adopt Western practices just because we think they should.

## The Chinese—Collective By Nature

The typical Chinese business person gains influence and empowerment through affiliation rather than independent action. Unconnected, individuals are powerless, especially in the realm of business. The ethos of groupism in the region goes back to darkest antiquity. The Chinese word for "everyone" is *daiya,* or big family. The Chinese word for "nation" is *gwojya,* or country family. A clan *(hsing)* was subdivided into families sharing the same surname. One's surname was one's group identification and it came first in one's name, before one's given name, as in the West. When a clansman died, they were worshipped as an expression of allegiance to the heritage of the clan group. In modern times, Chinese clans became secret societies and associations of people usually tied together by similar surname, which are still popular in Singapore and Hong Kong as well as other overseas Chinese communities. Business relationships among group members of these associations interlace all over the Pacific region, tethered together not by centrally located home offices, but by a web of personal and familial connections. You will find that as business opponents the Chinese are *team* players; tightly networked Chinese commercial groups are extremely difficult for Westerners to break into.

*Can a foreign company become an insider to Chinese business groups?*

Yes; in fact, your company *depends* on the business groups in China that it becomes a member. Commercial groups in the PRC are made up of comrades-turned-capitalists who share something in common; as you strategize for your gaining membership in a certain group, it is critical to find out the nature of the commonality. People often share affiliation in a local cell of the Communist Party or a division of the People's Liberation Army. Others share a familial bond or one based on town origin; people who speak the same regional dialect, such as Shanghaiese or Sichuanese, may experience instant familiarity. Common political experience has even bonded former Red Guards—the notorious Communist youths who terrorized intellectuals during the Cultural Revolution—into a network of aggressive, shrewd, and resourceful entrepreneurs.

As a newcomer in Chinese commercial culture you must observe its social customs and commercial rules if you intend to gain membership in the indigenous business community. Many foreigners make the mistake of openly criticizing local business procedures and decrying restrictions that seem illogical and inefficient; for example, the slowness of business decision-making in the country or its byzantine distribution system. Remember that business in China is a personal, in-group activity that until recently has been largely closed to strangers. Doors will not open quickly, but if you persevere, they will open eventually. Use a Chinese liaison at first to "front" your company and introduce you into appropriate business groups. And, by all means, don't run with the pack of foreign expats who populate the foreign hotels spending their evenings complaining about the terrible business environment in China. Socialize with Chinese who will bring you inside the business community once they've gotten to know you.

One last tip: respect the Chinese need to clarify and defer to status ranking. Egalitarian-minded Westerners often forget that Chinese culture places high priority on recognizing, and behaving in accordance with, a person's social standing. In business, a Westerner's insensitivity to shades of status gradation can have disastrous results. Take the case of the Taiwanese limousine. The Taiwanese often use both a limo and a van for transporting a delegation of business visitors from the West. The CEO of the Western company will ride in the limousine while the rest of his delegation will ride in the van. Such selective treatment backfired when an American delegation called on a company in Taipei. The American delegation eschewed the unequal treatment. Its members "rotated leaders" so each of them could have a ride in the limo. The Taiwanese, of course, were offended and thought such frivolity badly misplaced. Indeed, the blunder was an affront to the hierarchial system on which Chinese culture (and business) is founded. It made the American side look immature, insensitive, and thus, unaccountable.

# CHAPTER 3

# THE ECONOMIC

# LANDSCAPE

*"Only fast growth is socialism."*

—*Deng Xiaoping*

*T*o the surprise of the International Monetary Fund recently, China's economy vaulted from No. 10 in the world to No. 3, and its share of global output of the developing nations almost doubled. China is virtually guaranteed to be the largest economy on earth by the year 2020, should it sustain its current growth rate, whichis the fastest rate in the fastest-growing region of the world.

## CHINA'S INDUSTRIAL LANDSCAPE

Since 1979 China's economic system has evolved from total reliance on centralized state planning toward a structure that allows some market allocation and commercial competition: what the Chinese call "a new system of planned commodity economy." During this evolutionary process, the means of production are held by various collective bodies and individuals, in addition to state ownership. The overarching goals of the Chinese reform process were outlined in the early 1980s under the title of the "Four Modernizations." The Four Modernizations targeted four sectors of the Chinese economy—agriculture, heavy industry, light industry and defense—for focused and rapid development. In practice, the 1980s saw an initial reform of the agricultural sector, leading to the decentralization of decision making and a significant increase in peasant income. The major focus of reform was on light industry, as China consciously adapted the export-oriented manufacturing model of economic development previously pursued by the other newly-industrialized economies of East Asia.

The result of *gaige and kaifeng*—literally, "reform and opening up"—was a decade of unparalleled growth in China, with development becoming concentrated in China's coastal regions and newly-created Special Economic Zones. Regional disparities in growth and income were exacerbated by an infusion of foreign investment capital, which concentrated its investments in the coastal regions. China's growth has also experienced sectoral disparities, as light industry has progressed far beyond the capacity of supporting heavy industries and China's underlying infrastructure. Today the country is making a concentrated effort to upgrade and modernize its heavy industry and infrastructure sectors, while continuing light industry growth. In addition, the growth of the economy has created a new demand for services that far outstrips China's limited supply of service professionals.

### *Does China's state sector continue to be run by centrally controlled planning?*

China's state-owned sector remains under a partially planned system, but the scope of mandatory economic planning is narrowing as plans become guidelines or reference points, and market forces become more important determinants of production. The State Planning Commission is responsible for planning and plan implementation at the national level. Five-year economic plans establish general goals and priorities for capital investment, production, and supply. Annual plans set performance targets for state-owned industrial and commercial enterprises and govern allocation of state funds. As economic reform progresses, the Chinese government has sought to implement the plan through indirect economic levers—prices, taxes, credits, and market interest rates—instead of direct administrative controls. In the industrial sector, state-owned enterprises (SoEs) have been permitted to keep a portion of their profits rather than turning all earnings over to the government. Enterprise managers have been given greater authority in production planning, purchasing, marketing and pricing, determination of wages and bonuses, and labor management, and are increasingly responsible for enterprise profits and losses.

As a "commodity economy"—the Chinese term for a socialist style market economy—evolves in China, the annual and the five-year economic plans remain important indicators of government goals, and the planning cycle still influences investment and purchasing decisions. When indirect economic levers fail to achieve the results expected by the planners, or when the central authorities believe that too many resources are being diverted from goals in the plan, these authorities have tended to revert to direct controls and restrict the scope of enterprise autonomy.

## Economic Conditions in Mainland China

All eyes are on China as it continues to sustain rapid economic growth, increasing two-way trade and concern that its human rights performance may not improve sufficiently for the U.S. to continue to renew or conditionalize its Most Favored Nation status in 1995 and beyond. To these developments can be added the mystery and uncertainty surrounding the health and succession of Deng Xiaoping, China's paramount leader and helmsman since China began its Open-door reform program in the late 1970s.

China's average annual GNP growth rate of 10 percent during Deng Xiaoping's reform program starting in 1978 outstripped virtually every other country in the world. In 1993, China's real GNP grew by 10 percent, industrial output was up 18 percent, and foreign trade grew by 20 percent. (In Shanghai and Guangdong Province, 1993 GNP grew by 22 percent and 18 percent respectively.) And the Chinese continue to get richer. In prosperous East

China, 5 percent of the people are members of so-called 10,000 Yuan households, earning more than $2,700 a year. Retail price inflation, running at 4 percent in 1991, has jumped in the mid 1990s to 20 percent, signalling another cycle of economic overheating. Should this continue, austerity measures will be forced on the economy, as happened in 1986 and 1989, putting the brakes on growth.

Through its export drive, China amassed $44 billion in cash reserves by 1992. Combined with renewed lending from the World Bank and the Asian Development Bank since the Tiananmen uprising, this ensures that imports will grow rapidly in the coming years. Unfortunately, China runs a widening trade deficit, up to $12 billion in 1993 and to be reduced in 1994, hope China trade officials who point to a slight slowdown in foreign direct investment, tightened credit policies, and new restrictions on raw material imports by state firms. Imports, however, may continue to soar upward as the huge number of pledged investments are actually made; imports rose at an annual rate of 18 percent the first 5 months of 1994 while exports increased by 24 percent.

American companies selling aircraft, cotton, machinery, computers, wood, scientific equipment, iron and steel cannot ignore this burgeoning market. U.S. exports to China will increase 10-15 percent per year into the foreseeable future, barring major political upheaval in China. (At the same time, however, China will concentrate on expanding its export sales to the United States; should the trade imbalance continue to widen, chances increase for the U.S. Congress or President Clinton to put conditions on China's MFN status).

Another factor that could disrupt U.S.-China trade relations is China's continuing use of restrictive measures such as tariffs, import bans, import licensing requirements, import substitution policies, and unpublished directives to control its foreign trade. Should these practices continue alongside a growing trade imbalance, one can predict more section 301 investigations and increasingly tense U.S.-China relations in general.

As China approaches the next millennium, its leaders have clearly set a course toward continued opening and market-oriented reform, though the pace of the implementation of the reform is still a topic of debate. As larger and larger sectors of China's economy become marketized, and whole regions of the country look

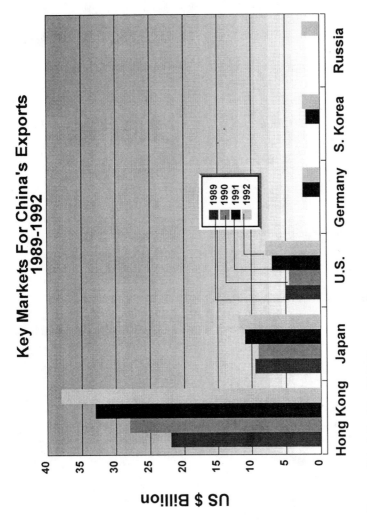

Source: *China's Customs Statistics.*

# China's Leading Export Commodities 1992

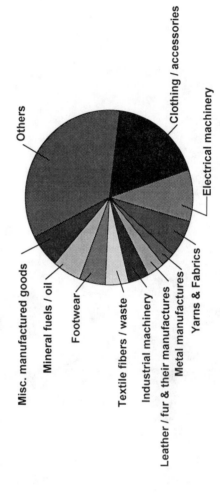

Others

Misc. manufactured goods

Mineral fuels / oil

Footwear

Textile fibers / waste

Industrial machinery

Leather / fur & their manufactures

Metal manufactures

Yarns & Fabrics

Electrical machinery

Clothing / accessories

Source: *China's Customs Statistics.*

increasingly capitalist in organization, the huge state sector continues to burden the economy. So does a growing budget deficit, a clogged and decaying infrastructure, and gross inefficiencies in production in all regions outside the Special Economic Zones of the South coast.

### What factors are responsible for China's tremendous economic growth?

China's growth is fueled by a number of sources, including the fast emergence of thousands of small- and medium-sized so-called Town and Village Enterprises formed as collectives but actually private companies formed under the auspices of local officials in partnership with local entrepreneurs and enterprises. Another source of growth is imported technology, which has empowered Chinese firms and FIEs alike to generate foreign exchange through exports. Thirdly, China's exploding capital market has provided growing numbers of Chinese companies with large infusions of capital with which to upgrade their production lines and thus export higher-quality products, earn more foreign exchange and increase overall output and efficiency. Lastly, foreign investment has generated growth in China, though to a lesser degree than the Chinese expected at first. In 1993 alone, the Chinese government approved an estimated 80,000 foreign-invested projects with an estimated total value of $105 billion, nearly equivalent to the total amount of approved foreign investment over the past 13 years since China first opened up to Western business. With tens of thousands of FIEs now in operation, most successfully exporting products from China, and all employing Chinese at higher than normal wages, the effect of foreign investment on increasing the overall growth of China's economy cannot be downplayed.

### What is the economic forecast for Mainland China during the next 5-10 years?

China's overall real GNP growth was 13.4 percent for 1993 and is expected to remain between 8-9 percent for the remainder of the decade, while industrial output will continue to grow in the double digits. The continued growth and reform of the PRC economy over the next 5 to 10 years, though halting at times, will compel U.S. firms in many industrial sectors to consider China as a strategically important market. U.S. firms should view seriously any country that has achieved a 65 percent increase in foreign trade during the last four years, and an average rate of real GNP growth of nine percent over the past thirteen years.

**INFLATION FEARS.** International economists expect that inflation, running at 23 percent in major cities, long the demon of China's economic reform program, will now stabilize over the course of the next several years. In the short-term, China's inflation rate is expected to dip as domestic demand is reduced by curbs on speculation and nonproductive investment. While the Chinese government was forced to end its temporary tightening on the economy in the summer of 1993, this inevitable slowdown is expected to be instituted sometime in 1994. By the end of the century China's inflation rate is predicted to rise again slightly. Overall inflation in the country should not be confused with the rate of price increases in urban areas, particularly in the rapidly growing coastal regions. Record rates of economic growth have driven up worker wages and disposable income, which in turn has spurred price increases in everything from building materials to consumer goods. As foreign investment and economic development continues to be disproportionately focused on urbanized and costal areas, foreign companies should expect to encounter higher prices across the board for their business and investment activities.

### INFLATION FORECAST

| | 1994 | 1995 | 1996 | 1997 | 1998 |
|---|---|---|---|---|---|
| Urban consumer price inflation (rate of increase) | 25% | 9% | 12% | 10% | 10% |
| Average urban wages (rate of increase) | 13% | 8% | 12% | 8% | 8% |

*Source:* The Economist Intelligence Unit

### *What economic reforms will China enact in the near future?*

Vice Premier Zhu Rongji, also known as China's economic czar (a title he eschews for its non-collective ring), has made public a blueprint for converting the country's economy into a "market economy based on public ownership." His program boils down to three initiatives: (1) overhaul the country's state-owned industrial sector through restructuring ownership and bringing in professional managers; (2) reorganize the financial sector such that banks loan on the basis of creditworthiness rather than the political clout of clients; and (3) create a tax regime to allow Beijing to better control the rich coastal areas and stifle rampant tax evasion. (Periodic executions of tax evaders hasn't ameliorated the problem.)

A milestone among recent reforms in China was the unification of the dual exchange rates of the Renminbi and the foreign exchange certificate (FEC). The function of the official RmB rate had faded as currency swap centers opened. Laws pertaining to foreign banking in China can be expected to be loosened, though foreign participation in the yuan market will continue to be banned. One can also expect that economic and political "policy" will play a decreasing role in loan policy, which will become increasingly based on whether an enterprise has the ability to repay. Financial markets can be expected to open further to foreign participation. Fiscal debt can be expected to be increasingly financed through the issuance of treasury bonds under a standardized system for rating credit. Lastly, the Bank of China can be expected to take command over China's financial system by controlling the money supply and depending on market-based instruments of monetary policy, while conscientiously maintaining the value of the yuan.

### *Will China's state-controlled economy disappear as thousands of foreign-invested and private enterprises are set up in the economy?*

The state-controlled economy and the new foreign-influenced economy will coexist for a decade at least, and longer in many areas. Unlike the shock therapy models applied in the relatively tiny economies of Central Europe, China's socialist economy has been in transition for 15 years and will continue to be into the next century. This coexistence is well illustrated in the insurance industry, in which a deal has been signed between the Shanghai municipality and the American insurance company, AIG. The AIG deal is a major breakthrough in the development of a Western-style capital market in China. The renminbi that AIG earns by selling insurance will be invested in Chinese companies that are promising, which will build real productive growth in the economy. "It won't be just redistributing the wealth like the government does when it bails out the losing enterprises by taking revenues from the winners," says China venture consultant Dean T. W. Ho, President of UBS International. PCCI, China's government-owned insurance company, will continue to be manipulated by government directives from outside organizations, while AIG has been permitted to sell insurance in China and invest its Rmb profits in China in profit-making investments of its choice. AIG will invest wisely in the Chinese economy, seeking out opportunities for gain, while PCCI will continue to operate in the traditional manner of a socialist enterprise pursuing at times a different set of priorities and subject to continuous manipulation from outside governmental entities. In the coming years, we will witness similar developments all across China's economic landscape.

## Economic Conditions in Hong Kong

Hong Kong's economic conditions are closely tied to events unfolding on the Mainland. The treaty signed in 1984 between Great Britain and the People's Republic, handing over Hong Kong to China in 1997, guarantees the future existence of Hong Kong as a capitalist enclave until 2047. "One country, two systems," as the scenario is termed, has also been envisioned for Macau's relationship to the PRC, as embodied in an agreement with the Portuguese that turns over Macau in 1999. Will Hong Kong, or Macau, be able to retain their status as laissez-faire "classrooms for capitalism" under China's Communist regime? That's the $64,000 Yuan question that Hong Kong residents and potential investors alike have been losing sleep over since the Tiananmen Massacre in June, 1989. The U.S. Foreign Commercial Service, for example, "feels that the apprehension about Hong Kong's future has been over-stated... that the People's Republic of China will abide by the Hong Kong Accords, and will do nothing to impede the economic growth and stability of Hong Kong and Macau," because (1) China is a large investor in Hong Kong and its investments are profitable; (2) China depends on Hong Kong's port and trading infrastructure to increase exports; (3) China's leadership, including Deng Xiaoping have used South China and Hong Kong as a model for economic progress for China; and (4) Hong Kong's territorial integrity has never been questioned or threatened militarily before by China, even during the cultural revolution.

Even with an unpredictable giant next door, Hong Kong continues to boom. The Hang Seng stock market has soared after its crash during the aftermath of the Tiananmen uprising. Real estate prices increased by 50 percent in 1992. The only blemish is inflation, which is rising 10 percent a year. In terms of production, much of Hong Kong's manufacturing activities have been moved into South China. The country's manufacturing sector now generates less than one-third of GDP; exports from Hong Kong remain roughly stable while re-exports have skyrocketed.

Hong Kong's center-of-the-Asia-galaxy geographic location, state-of-the-art communications network, immaculate infrastructure, low taxes (16.5 percent corporate tax), congenial commercial environment, skilled labor market, and presence to the "market of one billion" all combine to rank Hong Kong as the location of choice for a corporate headquarters. The principle investor countries in Hong Kong are Japan ($6.9 billion as of 1991), the United States ($6.4 billion), and China ($2.3 billion). Technology marketers should note that Hong Kong's status for importing sensitive technology is higher than China's; it may lose that status in 1997. Should that status be maintained, higher technology sales to China may become possible through Hong Kong, with the added risk that dual-use technologies purchased in Hong Kong end up inside China.

## Economic Conditions in Taiwan

Fantastically productive, Taiwan's 316,712 factories are mostly small and family-run; 85 percent of them employ fewer than 50 workers. Since the end of World War II, the island has experienced an average annual growth rate of almost 9 percent, swiftly moving from an agricultural to an industrial society in the course of the 1950s, and from an industrial society to one based firmly in capital-intensive high-tech manufacturing over the course of the 1960s-1980s. In the 1990s, the island is poised to become an important player in R&D and innovation as well as financial services. Taiwan has more money in reserves than any other country on earth, over $80 billion. Economic growth hums along at 7.3 percent (1991) while unemployment remains below 2 percent.

The economy remains 40 percent dependent on exports, helping it to accrue its $13 billion trade surplus each year, while continuing to merge with that of Mainland China, as the island's offshore plants fuel increasing demand for imports from Taiwan. In fact, this dynamic has played an important role in maintaining the island's export balance while markets in the West have languished due to world-wide recession. Indicative of the island's tenacity in diversifying its trade, the U.S. is now its sixth largest trade partner, well behind first-place Japan, the only country which enjoys a sizable trade surplus with the island. America's share of Taiwan's export market dropped from 44 to 29 percent between 1987 and 1991. Hong Kong's role as entrepôt between the island and the PRC (and as Taiwan's second largest export market) will likely fade after 1997.

### Are Taiwan's firms large state-controlled companies, or smaller and more independent?

While the Taiwan government promotes an "import substitution" industrial strategy for the country's large firms, most of Taiwan's companies are small family-run businesses. Their entrepreneurial super-resourceful and export-driven managers tend to distrust officialdom, and, for that matter anyone that is not a member of their immediate family. In fact, Taiwanese companies are typically limited in size to an extended size of the family, between 5 and 15 employees. As elsewhere in Asia, rising wages and an appreciating currency are forcing Taiwan to shift from labor-intensive production to value-added, more capital intensive production. This shift has fueled Taiwan's heavy investment in cheap-labor areas of Asia like South China, Vietnam, Indonesia, Thailand, and the Philippines, where semi-skilled labor is still inexpensive. For example, over 2,800 Taiwanese enterprises have set up in the PRC as of this writing. Taiwan is expected to achieve 6 percent or greater average annual growth over the next five years, in accordance with its status as a mature economy. Per capita GDP will rise to over $17,000 by 1998, while inflation should remain at about 4 percent. An important development in Taiwan's economy is its increasing integration with the economy of mainland China. Some analysts fear this development will serve to make the Taiwanese economy susceptible to the large fluctuations that have been a feature of China's economic growth in the reform era. Nevertheless, an increasing amount of Taiwanese investment continues to flow to the mainland. Moreover, China is rapidly becoming Taiwan's most important trading partner, and is expected to exceed the U.S. in volume of exports by 1998. Taiwan's influence over the mainland's economy is declining however, as the P.R.C. becomes less dependent on Taiwanese investment and looks to other countries as sources of capital.

### *What are the current goals of Taiwan's government?*

Taiwan's government is making a concentrated effort to improve the country's investment climate. It is taking steps to spur increased foreign investment in the country, particularly in the high-technology sector, and is trying to persuade its citizenry to invest a greater portion of their savings in the domestic economy. The ruling Kuomintang party is in the process of realigning its policy goals to conform to the demands of an increasingly active electorate.

Relations with China continue to dominate Taiwanese foreign affairs. Taiwan is increasingly isolated on the diplomatic front, although this fact seems to have had little effect on the Taiwanese economy. Taiwan's government is continuing to hold out hope of reentering the General Agreement on Tariffs and Trade (GATT) and the International Monetary Fund (IMF). Periodic talks with mainland Chinese government representatives continue, but these discussions are currently bogged down by disputes over fishing rights and the repatriation of airline hijackers from the mainland.

### *What is the business climate like in Taiwan for foreign firms?*

The Taiwan business climate remains generally friendly to outside businesspersons and investors, particularly in the high-tech fields. Taiwan is moving to liberalize its financial sector in anticipation of its re-entry into GATT, and this trend is expected to open new opportunities for foreign investors. There is widespread interest in Taiwan's stock market as a "back door" to profiting on mainland China's dramatic growth. Many foreign investors prefer to invest in Taiwanese companies active in the mainland, rather than subjecting themselves directly to the risks and management responsibilities inherent in foreign direct investment in the P.R.C. Many of the business service fields are also being opened to foreign participation, and opportunities for foreign investment in the service sector are expected to outstrip those in manufacturing. Taiwan is actively seeking to improve its system of protecting intellectual property rights, but abuse remains rampant and infringements of international copyrights is a continuing concern for foreign companies.

The Taiwanese are also making a conscious effort to define the country's role in the booming East Asia macro-region. Fearing its diplomatic isolation may leave it on the sidelines of regional growth, the country is seeking to promote Taipei as an operations center for East Asian or Pan-Asian business units. However, these efforts have thus far met with limited success, and many analysts question the city's ability to emerge as a regional business hub on the order of Hong Kong or Singapore.

Taiwan has cut back its previously announced massive investments in infrastructure and environmental projects. Prospects for huge expenditures for high-speed rail projects, new environmental technologies and wide-scale construction opportunities have declined in recent months. Nevertheless, spending by the state sector on infrastructure remains significant, and foreign companies are often encouraged to bid on construction and clean-up projects.

Taiwan intends to directly target major multinational companies for strategic alliances as a way of cementing its role in the global economy. Major business goals to be pursued with these new allies include raising the level of automation in Taiwan's factories and expanding the value-added portion of Taiwanese manufacturing. New high-tech industrial parks are expected to take the lead in this effort, offering tax incentives and access to superior human capital resources as lures to attract foreign investors. Because Taiwan's companies are generally resistent to buying foreign products which are also made in Taiwan, to sell to them Western suppliers must have representation on the ground in Taiwan. Exhaustive searchers for both buyers and candidate distributors remains an absolute must for foreigners. Even with non-tariff barriers to the market, Taiwan must increase its imports to avoid political problems with its trading partners, and to slake heavy consumer demand for products which have remained unavailable because of import restrictions.

Because the United States does not recognize the Republic of Taiwan as a nation separate from Mainland China, American government representation on the island is coordinated through the American Institute in Taiwan (AIT), a private nonprofit corporation with headquarters in Rosslyn, Virginia (AIT/W) and offices in Taipei (AIT/T) and Kashsiung (AIT/K). Commercial services similar to those provided by the U.S. Foreign Commercial Service can be obtained from AIT's Commercial Section in Taipei and in Kaohsieng.

# INSIDE THE "CHINA TRIANGLE"—REGIONAL ECONOMIC PROFILES

## Guangdong Province

Over the past decade Guangdong Province (see map on page 20) has transformed itself from a largely undeveloped area into China's wealthiest province and the centerpiece of its economic reform policies. Driven by foreign investment and the establishment of export-oriented manufacturing, Guangdong has continually expanded the size and strength of its economy, often posting double-digit annual growth rates while enjoying a sizeable trade surplus.

Guangdong's economy stayed on its high growth path in 1992, with gross domestic product, industrial production, retail sales, capital investment and exports all posting strong double-digit growth. Inflation, officially listed at 9.7 percent, remained under control, while per capita income jumped by 21.1 percent. In response to this unprecedented surge in growth, provincial leaders raised its targeted growth rates in the middle of 1992. Guangdong is now aiming at 13 percent average annual real growth for gross domestic product and 17-18 percent for exports until the year 2000. The province's economic success has been translated into dramatically improved standards of living for its workers. Average per capita wages rose by 20 percent in 1992, helping to boost per capita income by 15 percent to Rmb 3,184 per year. However, rising productivity and devaluation of the Renminbi (Rmb) has blunted the impact of rising labor costs, and thus buoyed export earnings.

Guangdong's growth continues to be led by a rapidly increasing volume of foreign trade and an influx of foreign capital. Actual foreign investment increased by 88.2 percent in 1992 to US$4.9 billion, while new investment contracts leaped 242 percent, foretelling continued rapid expansion of Guangdong's foreign invested sector. At the same time, Guangdong's exports increased by 31.8 percent to US$18 billion. Guangdong's global trade surplus reached US$7.4 billion. Guangdong's external trade continues to expand at a rate far in excess of most other parts of China. Moreover, much of what Guangdong imports is ultimately destined for inland markets. This, together with the province's robust underground commodity markets, makes Guangdong an important trade broker for other parts of China. In the years ahead, the radiation of markets and wealth to the interior will require improved transport and distribution networks between coastal and inland regions.

## Liaoning Province

Once the center of infrastructure development and industrial production under the Japanese, today Liaoning Province is the third largest exporting region in China. With major exports in petroleum products, cement, agriculture, textiles and electronics, Liaoning is making a serious bid as one of China's leading manufacturing centers. The province is also developing ties with Shandong, Shanghai and South Korea in order to take advantage of the emerging growth triangle surrounding the Yellow Sea. Foreign investment in the region is rapidly increasing, driven primarily by investors from Hong Kong, Taiwan, Japan and the United States.

Shenyang, the provincial capital, is a center of investment activity. U.S. investors have received assistance from an active U.S. consulate in Shenyang, and the city's 5 million inhabitants are an emerging market for Western consumer products. Another city of dynamic growth is Dalien. Once occupied by Germany, the city is China's second largest seaport and a popular tourist destination. The eight miles of underground tunnels under the city of Dalien, dug in fear of imperialist invasion, have been converted into the largest underground shopping mall in China, it's corridors lined with state-owned, collective, and privately owned shops. Dalien's port is now the third largest foreign trade port in China, the country's Hong Kong of the north, shipping goods to and from 140 countries. Here, and in other port cities of China, are the ill-effects of opening to the capitalist world—smuggling, heroin trade, venereal disease, gambling, and prostitution. Enter one of the myriad karaoke night clubs and sailor bars and find rich Chinese businessmen paying for the company of Russian hostesses.

## Shanghai Municipality

China's leading commercial center for over 100 years, Shanghai seems posed to dominate business activity in China well into the next century. In fact, the city is fast reclaiming its position as the richest and most cosmopolitan city in the Orient. With population estimates ranging as high as 14 million and a rapidly expanding urban middle class, Shanghai is the center of the consumer boom sweeping China. Investment is another vehicle for Shanghai's growth, and is currently centered around the Pudong Economic Development Zone, a 250-square-km delta area set between the Huangpo and Yangtze rivers. The Shanghai Stock Exchange was set up in 1990 and is located in the ballroom of a hotel built by English traders in the 1800s.

Shanghai is currently home to more than 9,000 industrial enterprises and over 2,000 foreign-invested joint ventures. Total pledged foreign investment in the region exceeded $3 billion in 1993. The city's GNP grew by 22 percent in 1992, the latest year for which figures are available, and is expected to exceed this amount in 1993 and 1994. In a recent survey of U.S. companies with investment projects in Shanghai, over half said that the return on their investments has exceeded their expectations. China's central government has targeted the city as the focal point of its economic development strategy through the year 2000. One reason for its importance to the central leadership is the growing power of Vice-Premier Zhu Rongji. Currently the head of China's People's Bank, Zhu first came to prominence as Shanghai's Mayor in the late 1980s. He was credited with diffusing student protests in the Spring of 1989 without having to resort to violent suppression, in marked contrast to the central leadership's experience in Tiananmen Square. Since then Mr. Zhu has been a leading force behind China's continuing economic reform efforts.

Shanghai's core strength continues to be its role as a port of entry. Over 30 percent of all of the country's imports pass through Shanghai. In order to facilitate import growth, the city recently established the first integrated customs office in the Pudong zone. At this one-stop trade center foreign companies can store goods, pass through customs, establish offices and display their wares in exhibition spaces. Customs officials can facilitate the transshipment of goods to other parts of the country, and goods can be stored without paying duty while being sold to Shanghai's duty-free market.

## Jiangsu Province

While traditionally neglected by central planners during the Maoist era, Jiansu has emerged as an economic powerhouse during the reform period. Benefitting from its proximity to Shanghai and the open-minded, even aggressive attitude of its government towards foreign investment, Jiangsu now ranks as the country's top province in terms of gross industrial output. Since 1992 the province's officials have actively sought to recruit the "three foreigns"—trade, capital, and economic cooperation—to the region. The result has been annual increase in imports to $1.5 billion last year, a 51 percent increase over 1992. Exports have also climbed, reaching $4.67 billion in the same year. Jiangsu may approve more than 10,000 foreign-invested projects by the end of 1994, when foreign ventures will account for more than 35 percent of the province's total exports.

The key to the province's success has been its willingness to abandon the stifling influence of central economic planning. Today, more than 90 percent of the province's economic transactions occur outside of the planned economy, and the prices of over 95 percent of the goods are determined by the market. Even more dramatic has been the province's emphasis on quality and efficiency. Where many provinces still have a large number of enterprises running in the red each year, Jiangsu claims to be making money in 99 percent of its state-run enterprises. Rural enterprises also play an important role in the province's economic success, accounting for more than 50 percent of industrial output and 40 percent of the province's exports.

# CHAPTER 4

# THE POLITICAL

# LANDSCAPE

*"Today's infighting for authority over foreign joint ventures is a modern replay of an ancient Chinese theme: the oft-repeated battles between centralizers and decentralizers—between the emperors and provincial authorities and warlords."*

—**William A. Stoever,** Keating Crawford Professor
of International Business
at Seton Hall University
in *East Asian Executives Reports*

*I*n spite of efforts that began after the death of Mao Zedong in 1976, there has been limited progress in ameliorating many of the country's Maoist legacies. While China's overall production capacity may be large, its lack of a well integrated industrial strategy has created severe inefficiencies. Most state-owned factories still operate at a fraction of capacity, mainly because they lack incentives or pressures to do otherwise. Nearly all Chinese factories still suffer from insufficient capital and access to technology, especially due to foreign exchange limitations. Efforts to break the "iron rice bowl" with employment and wage incentives have achieved only modest success as many workers and managers prefer the security of the past to the uncertainties associated with a market-led system.

## CHINA'S BYZANTINE BUREAUCRATIC SYSTEM

The ongoing repercussions of adopting the Soviet model of central planning in 1949 continue to be felt today, mainly in the form of a gargantuan network of governing bodies, agencies, institutions, and societies. Dense bureaucracy has existed in China for centuries, but reliance on a central planning model accentuated the role of government and gave great impetus to the burgeoning presence of the Chinese Communist Party (CCP) in all spheres of life. Heretofore, our impressions about China were that there existed a "planned economy," organized and monitored at all levels by the government in Beijing. In reality, however, one finds that bureaucratic organizations in the People's Republic tend to compete rather than cooperate. The various elements of the Chinese system actually cooperate in only a handful of isolated cases involving high priority projects, such as in the advanced weapons field, superconductivity, and microelectronics. Historically, there has been only limited collaboration between industries except for critical military projects. Resources are rarely pooled because the system has encouraged self-sufficiency. Centrally organized efforts to create horizontal linkages, while reflecting Beijing's intent to coordinate decision making regarding broad modernization objectives, actually reveal the absence of appropriate structures, channels, and incentives for multifaceted economic intercourse. The great majority of decision makers are motivated more by regional prerogatives than by Central Government objectives. This means that the majority of decisions made within the system tend to be the product of bargaining and negotiation rather than careful orchestration by the center.

### *What form of government administration does China have?*

After decades of Maoist "continual revolution," the Chinese government remains a one-party, centrally planned one that approaches policy choices pragmatically rather than purely ideologically, as in the past. The country's leaders call the system socialism and not communism, though the controlling political force in China remains the Chinese Communist Party.

China's system of administrative hierarchies, or fiefdoms, nearly precludes the possibility of an efficient economic system. As Kenneth Lieberthal and Michael Oksenberg have written: "...Almost every arrangement in China depends on the cooperation of different units that have no power of command over each other. Without sustained interaction among subordinate agencies, new economic initiatives often wither from lack of vital organizational support structures. The "vertical" nature of authority is depicted in the organizational chart on next page.

The National People's Congress is made up of 3,000 seats of administrators who ratify laws, state plans, and formulate the country's budget. The 14th Congress, in place until 1997, has elected a central committee and politburo; the seven men of the politburo's standing committee can be said to be the country's paramount rulers. (Deng Xiaoping holds no official title but will remain China's most powerful decision maker until his death.) The State Council is the highest administrative body, which governs over the country's 59 ministries, a bureaucracy that has been reduced in size by 20 percent in the last few years to a total official staff of 30,000. Related ministries implement directives in the country's 21 provinces, 5 autonomous regions, and 3 municipalities. The State Council occupies the highest level of a four-tiered system of administrative control, responsible for the major decisions of government. Below the State Council are various planning commissions that formulate and oversee the country's industrial and financial policies. The third level of government consists of the ministries—agricultural and industrial—that implement state plans within specific sectors of the economy. The ministries accomplish this through a full complement of similar affiliated bureaus at the provincial and municipal levels—the fourth tier of China's bureaucratic system. The Communist Party, with a membership of over 50 million Chinese, is represented throughout the

China's Four-tiered Bureaucratic Hierachy

NOTES: 1. The CAS reports to the State Council, but its organizationally different from other ministries.

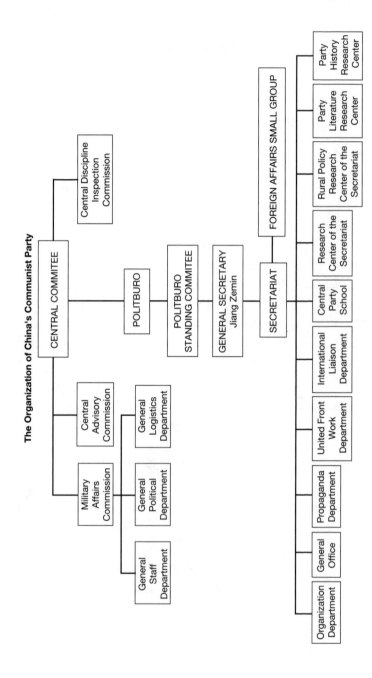

**The Organization of China's Communist Party**

central and local ministries as well as in the enterprises and local production units where people live and work, called the *danwei*.

The State Council also oversees several types of foreign trade entities. The largest entity, Ministry of Foreign Trade and Economic Cooperation (MOFTEC), runs the national trade corporations of China. There also are numerous foreign trade corporations which report directly to the ministries and other high-level bodies such as the Chinese Academy of Sciences. At a third level there exist local foreign trade commissions (e.g., a Shanghai FTC or a Guangzhou FTC). Many of the local branches of the national foreign trade corporations report directly to their local governments rather than to Beijing.

The State Planning Commission and State Economic Commission (merged in 1987), develop import plans which are carried out through a long list of provincial and municipal import/export entities under the oversight of MOFTEC, which is also responsible for approving, monitoring, and supervising the operations of foreign-owned enterprises. In addition, MOFTEC implements and enforces the laws, provisions, and regulations related to technology transfer. Local planning commissions devise annual and long-term economic plans for their respective regions. The State Science and Technology Commission is responsible for formulating and implementing science and technology policy; the State Educational Commission is responsible for administering China's key colleges and universities; the National Defense Science, Technology and Industry Commission is responsible for military science, technology, and industry affairs.

Because of their vertically defined boundaries, many of China's ministries tend to display a distinct unwillingness to share technology, manufacturing capability, or production experience with their counterparts in other related sectors. Most recently, however, Chinese leaders have undertaken a program to transform their existing administrative structure for managing industry. Economic factors are increasingly being used as the criteria to define organizational structures. Nonetheless, a top-down approach to enterprise administration characterizes most sectors of the economy. A number of prevailing irrationalities in the economy, such as shortages of key production inputs and price problems suggest that it will not be easy to fully abandon this general approach.

### *What is the relationship between the central government in Beijing and the outlying provincial governments?*

As control has been decentralized down to the localities, many of China's large industrial ministries have been dispersed and their affiliated enterprises have been either set off on their own or control over them has been decentralized down to the local level. For instance, in the airline industry, direct central control has been relinquished and local carriers have formed independent of the Civil Aviation Administration of China (CAAC). Moreover, cities like Shanghai, which historically had been squeezed by the Central Government for tax revenue, have been brought under the system of *baogan,* a financial contract arrangement between Beijing and certain cities of China designating an amount of each city's revenue to be returned to the central coffers—target commitment that the Central Government desires each city to generate annually. Any additional income accrued by a city can be retained for purposes of upgrading its own infrastructure. This system creates additional incentives for cities to increase production, amass revenue, and invest in their own industrial well-being. The set percentages are designed to decrease, so that cities get to retain a larger proportion of their earnings. Baogan is part of the movement toward making China's localities more responsible for their own welfare and development. Other major cities have developed similar relationships with Beijing.

Provincial protectionism, however, continues to be a major obstacle to greater economic integration. Provincial leaders obviously want to generate profits from production units within their administrative authority and sometimes do so by barring the movement of goods, imposing export duties, or forcing products to move through "turnpikes" collecting tolls on their way from the province to the outside. Unlike some of the inland provinces, China's coastal cities have a long legacy of foreign enclaves and trade entrepôts with more developed transportation systems and communication networks intact. In recent years, the Chinese leadership has recognized this fact and has targeted several of the coastal cities as their country's main link to the outside world. The growing stature of these cities makes the city mayors extremely powerful, in some ways even monarchial. Local policies in these cities often discriminate against not only foreigners but even

Chinese from outside the immediate region. Similar types of obstacles or blockades exist with respect to the diffusion of technology. What becomes clear is that local authorities can successfully resist the will of the Central Government if desired, in ways that foreigners would not believe possible from what has heretofore been their impressions about the authority of the Communist Party in China.

A good example of the conflict between the center and localities is illustrated in the relationship between Shanghai and Beijing in the electronics industry. Coordination and redundancy are critical problems in this relationship. The intense rivalry between the "central" ministries and the localities centers on the desire of each to create and maintain its own capabilities and decision prerogatives. Beginning in mid-1985, the electronics industry underwent a significant decentralization. The MEI relinquished direct managerial control over all but two of its 177 enterprises. But numerous enterprises in the electronics industry are still managed under the principle of "dual leadership," wherein central and local authorities jointly have a voice in enterprise affairs. Factories operating in the electronics industry may have as many as ten different forms of local and central administrative oversight, making it difficult to form clear-cut lines of decision making. Even so, because of their continued reliance on the center for both overhead and project funding, enterprises and their associated bureaus at the provincial and municipal levels cannot totally disregard the wishes of Beijing.

### What system exists in China for the allocation of goods and supplies?

China's traditional system of supply and demand is based on an informal distribution network whereby the movement of goods and services occurs within a web-like series of channels. Agreements are consummated by people in positions of power and influence who are connected through professional, familial, and/or political linkages. Surplus supplies can be bartered as goods in high demand are offered. The business environment epitomizes the adage: "It's not what you know; it's who you know." Although this system has worked for centuries throughout Asia, it constrains many initiatives that cannot progress ahead due to the absence of the appropriate informal relationship.

The trading of goods and services through inside connections spawned an economy that depended on dealing with local government and "unofficial" suppliers in a gray market rather than through official channels. In cities such as Guangzhou, for example, leverage is gained through the vying for influence within the bureaucracy and among distributors by doing favors and offering thinly disguised gifts. The monetary value of goods is, at times, subordinated to the clout one within the distribution network in terms of *guanxi*—backdoor connections and personal ties. Defined as "subtle reciprocity among a network of personal connections," guanxi relationships still form the backbone of decision making, promotions, and resource allocation in China. Guanxi relationships can be described as ingratiating personal relationships that impose multiple obligations on the respective players. Among the Chinese, these guanxi relationships can stem from the town in which one's parents were born, the university one attended, or a direct familial tie. (Later chapters discuss the modernization of China's distribution system.)

### How is Chinese industry being reformed to increase productivity?

China's reform architects have for ten years been trying to break the symbiotic, and at times, parasitic relationship between the Chinese factory and the central or local government agency that has jurisdiction over it. The bottom line about Chinese enterprise is simple: There are 200,000 state-owned, Stalinist-style factories in China and 46 percent of them are in the red, absorbing billions of yuan in state subsidies. Much of what they produce is unsaleable goods, and 63 percent of bank lending to industry is in the form of "working capital loans," which basically cover day-to-day expenses for these firms. These firms simply cannot be left to wither and die like similar state-owned behemoths in East Europe have; too many jobs would be lost and the political cost too high. State firms employ one-third of all Chinese workers—110 million people, which equals the current size of the entire U.S. workforce. With dependents added, the number of Chinese directly affected by the demise of state enterprise in China is 340 million people. Reformers have quite wisely chosen to proceed with restructuring China's state sector haltingly.

The ultimate dilemma for China's leaders is to provide a model for a "reformed" style of factory management to its enterprises. But with new and increasingly entrepreneurial forms of management style being put into action in the country's coastal regions, without government oversight, the notion of Beijing enforcing the implementation of a standardized pseudo-socialist-yet-market-responsive management style grows more far-fetched with each passing upbeat quarter. A number of approaches have been used to restructure ownership of state enterprises and reorganize them to increase efficiency. Selected firms have been permitted to list on China's stock exchanges, while revamping their management to respond to a bottom-line oriented board of directors representing stock holders. Ministries with oversight of state enterprises have hired professional managers on a performance-contract basis to come into a poorly-run firm and turn it around. State firms have been allowed to start up related businesses which operate as self-financed appendages of the parent state firm.

China has also initiated the formation of industrial conglomerates (jituan) in another move against self-contained industrial relations. In the electronics industry, there are now numerous computer conglomerates that have been created, the most significant being the Great Wall Computer Corporation in Beijing. Patterned on an IBM-like model, each of these corporations is endowed with a full complement of services including R&D, production, service, maintenance, and sales. Their fully integrated organizational structure is designed to cut across vertical barriers within the system—i.e., they exist independent of state-run distribution networks, sales agencies, and so on. While the Great Wall Corporation's experience has not been without its problems, the fact is that its creation represents a fundamentally new type of organizational amalgam, that allows a company to obtain approvals for various projects and to do so more rapidly, gain unincumbered access to the domestic market and raw materials, and to be better able to cross provincial distribution lines. They will also have ample foreign exchange to import equipment and license technology. In this way, they may team up with foreign firms more easily in efforts to upgrade component suppliers and set new design standards. In the automobile industry, for example, the country's 120 auto plants are being "rationalized" to create economies of scale and tie together component manufacturers. In the end, 6 or 7 major auto manufacturing groups will emerge, turning out 100,000-300,000 cars per year by 1995. The sector offers huge opportunities for foreign auto and auto parts makers; companies already involved include Audi, Volkswagen, Daihatsu, Chrysler, among several others.

The Chinese have also worked toward the creation of production alliances (lian heti) which help enterprises to cross vertical boundaries within the economy. These have been formed particularly in the textile industry in Northeast China, where, for example, a design institute, a dyeing factory, a cloth printing factory, and a sewing factory will merge together to produce new apparels as part of one operating unit. As lian heti emerge throughout the country, one will witness increased ability of certain industries to more readily traverse the vertically segmented administrative organization of the economy that has traditionally prevented cross-functional cooperation.

## Unforeseen Repercussions of Reform

In the first decade of reform, though China has sustained a high level of industrial growth many unforeseen consequences of the new policies have surfaced that cannot be ignored. Some regions of China are simply not as prepared as others to accept the market-oriented economic levers embodied in the responsibility program. Progress in one area in China is not always duplicated in another area. Some areas naturally are excluded from the decentralization privileges and benefits. Jealousies abound and interprovince turf fighting is exacerbated. Furthermore, local politics have a significant effect on the pace and scope of the reform implementation process. Available knowledge regarding specific reform initiatives suggested by Beijing is extensive in some areas, while in others it is lacking. In general, information concerning the nature, purpose, and methods for adopting specific reforms tends to dissipate the farther it travels from the center, so that by the time local managers and officials receive the information, much of its content and urgency is trivialized. So too, failure to implement certain reforms goes largely unrecognized and unpunished in most cases.

*What will be the effect of the spread of official corruption in China, in conjunction with China's widening income gap?*

The open door to foreign business has generated a significant increase in official crime, a foreboding problem in a country as vast and divided by provincial boundaries as the People's Republic. Corruption is on the rise in China for several reasons: the lack of financial control at the enterprise level, the new doctrine of "rich is glorious," and the decentralization of decision making at the import authorization level. Recently, the number of ministries and commissions that make up China's central bureaucracy were cut in number from 86 to 59. Bureaucratic units are being asked to perform against economic rather than ideological criteria, which is having the effect of reducing the total number of people employed in the state sector, and the movement of these people into the commercial sector. Over 130 million government employees have now started businesses in China. Unfortunately, regional cadres-turned-capitalists (the most senior and powerful of which are called "Monkey Kings" for their sly and clever dealings), grab local taxes for themselves and their personal projects. State officials take money in the form of taxes and use it to pay for their pet projects. Bank loans are often based on guanxi and influence rather than credit worthiness or the potential benefit of a project to the public. Such loans rob the people of resources and waste public funds. In 1993, cadres were permitted to set up their own businesses while keeping their government positions. They were to forego pay and live off these businesses. Ponzi schemes were the outcome with 40 percent returns promised to eager investors who were hard-sold by journalists and dance-hall girls. The sons and daughters of higher-ranking officials use their connections to gain control over scarce resources. Once they control a resource they can move it between the state and factories for a 2 to 3 percent handling fee.

In the eyes of most Chinese, official corruption comes with the territory of transforming China from socialist totalitarianism to market-oriented authoritarianism. Most Chinese are tolerant of graft because it brings along with it prosperity for them; most would choose freedom with corruption than purity with repression. Of course, not all Chinese agree. The bribes necessary to motivate the hospital staff to perform one's surgery—even when one is fully covered by state medical insurance—can amount to many times one's monthly income. Though income first rose in the countryside under China's reforms, now they are falling behind rising incomes in the city. Average annual income in major cities can be as high as $1,200, while in interior rural villages, many Chinese bring home only $50 per year. (More than a few resourceful cab drivers whom the author spoke to recently in Shanghai bring home the equivalent of $1,000 per month, twenty times the average wage.) In the poorer areas, people have begun to blame their plight on corrupt local officials. Rural officials, alas, are no more corrupt than urban ones. The peasants' problems stem from the fact that prices of farm products are still controlled, especially the price of grain, which many farmers depend on for an income. In contrast, farmers in coastal areas can sell numerous cash crops at high profit and start up on nonagricultural private enterprises. How long will inland farmers be placated by Deng's adage about some people getting rich before others is difficult to predict.

In short, reform has its casualties. They line up at construction sites as day laborers. They ride on trains for days to arrive in strange Special Economic Zones along China's coast to seek out assembly jobs in joint venture sweatshops. China's local and central leaders agree on at least one thing—that unemployment causes social instability and must not be allowed to grow uncontrollably; the consequences would be disastrous for China's rulers. China is fast becoming a society of haves and have-nots, like most newly-capitalist economies, and in a country of 1.2 billion, this polarization of people could spell disaster for China's rulers, who only tenuously maintain their grip on the Mandate of Heaven. It's not difficult to see the impact of competitive capitalism on the street in any Chinese city. The newly rich live in pristine apartments, watch Sony Trinitrons and some even drive luxury cars identifiable as privately owned by their "Z" license plates; the less fortunate, like professors, plumbers, and factory managers, live in crumbling apartment blocks and can't afford to eat fast food at McDonald's. As is the case in Central Europe and the former Soviet Union, many Chinese are ill-equipped (perhaps too old or too young) to respond to the opportunities now being touted. On the other side of the coin is the fact that since the open door policies were initiated, literally millions of Chinese people have ascended from a state of life-threatening poverty to a decent standard of living.

### What is the potential for serious social unrest in China in the 1990s?

As if economic problems were not enough, student protests demanding "democratic" reforms broke out in late 1986-87 and again in 1989 which resulted in the Tiananmen uprising. The swiftness of these changes cast some doubt about the future pace and direction of reforms. However, in the early 1990s the Chinese leadership underwent a fundamental change. Much of the centralized government control and discipline is vanishing, though vestiges of it will remain for a long time to come. Social goals are now sought through economic freedoms, private ownership, and greater reward for job performance. Social tensions, however, continue to escalate as income gaps widen, corruption and favoritism grows more blatant, workers and peasants go unpaid as state firms face bankruptcy, and violent crime (often perpetrated by underpaid security personnel) rises with joblessness and vagrancy. The mood on the street in major Chinese cities signals mounting discontentment with high prices and dwindling job opportunities, even as workers organize themselves in hundreds of illegal underground unions; strikes and work stoppages have become commonplace. China's rulers realize there is only one elixir: economic, rather than political, reform. By offering the Chinese people a higher standard of living, Chinese officials hope to maintain social contentment and therefore, social stability.

At the same time, China's political climate continues to depend on one man, Deng Xiaoping. Deng has been grooming a "third tier" of younger leaders while reducing the power of the military and Party bureaucracy. Many influential persons, however, continue to rally in an ongoing public debate over whether China should pursue economic reforms more conservatively and remain more centralized while promoting less autonomy for Chinese trade corporations and enterprises. Moreover, these persons represent a strong and vociferous faction in China that could be a politically influential contingent after Deng's death. They point to official corruption and black marketing as the negative side effects of opening to the West. Unable to wield the political unity to combat Deng openly in the form of a direct challenge, these political dark horses within China resist the reforms by ignoring or obstructing them. The hard-line old guard has dwindled to only three of China's 29 influential leaders "who" are maintaining a traditional Maoist line. The rest agree that reform is due, though 13 of them believe it should come on fast (the extremists, including Deng Xiaoping), and 13 believe in the slow implementation of reforms—a cautious approach.

> *What are the chances that China could return to its Maoist isolationist past?*

The tug-of-war between modernizers and isolationists, centralizers and decentralizeres, hardliners and progressives, has, literally, been going on in China for centuries. The Deng succession will launch the next chapter in China's 40-year shift from an ideologically-based regime espousing social transformation before economic transformation to one run by technocrats whose sole objective is economic modernization with little interest in the ideology of its populous.

Bert Levin runs the Asia Society in Hong Kong, and describes China's inexorable political transmutation in real-life practical terms: "Communism is dead in China. It has been transformed into traditional Chinese authoritarianism, as distinct from a regime committed to an idealogy. People no longer call each other comrade. There is no reference to Marxism in political briefings. There are still people in the leadership with knuckles dragging the ground, but the Chinese people are not suffering under a heavy, repressive hand. There is now materialism, along with Western cultural influences, that offends the leaders, but not because of their ideology. They abhor it because it isn't Chinese." (Quoted in *The New Yorker,* March 15, 1993; page 100.)

# China's Current Attitude Toward Foreign Firms

China welcomes foreign investors in nearly all sectors of the economy, with restrictions in the areas of defense, media (there is only one Sino-American approved joint venture to produce TV shows for broadcast in China), publishing, insurance, and banking. Foreign participation is most sought after in the areas of mineral extraction and refining, telecommunications, aviation, and electronics, though any project involving the transfer of high technology falls on open ears. In fact, the transfer of technology in a project is virtually de rigeur in all sizable projects. At present, the Chinese are cracking down on shell companies, such as in real estate, set up as non-productive fronts for unsanctioned business dealings. With so many foreign companies falling over each other to get into China, the Chinese have become predictably much more selective about who they will deal with, and the terms they will accept. There is increasing government sensitivity about foreign companies buying shares of state enterprises which are restructuring, the fear being that state assets are being pawned off at grossly undervalued prices; (many foreign negotiators who have learned to take Chinese valuations with a large grain of salt get a chuckle out of this). The complaints about foreign companies remaining on the sidelines while China "opened" its economy and even at one time "guaranteed profits to investors" have subsided with the torrent of money that has entered the country since 1991. Gone also is China's sensitivity about allowing multinationals to exploit China's huge labor force in ventures set up purely on "cheap labor, low technology" grounds; over 6 million workers now toil in such ventures. Complaints about foreign firms withholding state-of-the-art technology from their China ventures have also faded as large numbers of firms now are willing to do so in exchange for access to China's market.

# CHAPTER 5

# THE BUSINESS

# SCENE

*"The American way [of business] is, 'Hey, it's costing us $5,000 to $6,000 to send you on this trip; you'd better get the business.' The Oriental idea is, 'We're 2,000 years old, and we want to build a relationship and learn all about you and all about your facilities."*

**—Joseph Dorto**
Chief Executive,
Virginia International Terminals

*"Everything [in Taiwan] is done through relationships. Through give and take. Everyone gets a slice of the pie. Everyone. No one does anything for free. They need tangible incentive to do something for you. Generating this incentive is critical to doing business in Taiwan. Otherwise, nothing is going to happen. Nothing."*

**Domiano Georgino**
General Manager
Dynasty Hotel, Taipei

In 1935, Charles Moser wrote in a Department of Commerce publication that foreign mercantile pioneers in the China market "have learned that vast populations do not necessarily mean vast markets." His reasoning was irrefutable: the Chinese lacked *buying power* to purchase significant quantities of foreign goods since most of the population existed in a state of dire poverty. There were the barriers of language and customs between Chinese and foreigners. Poor communications and transport services (by coolie-back or canal junk), made delivery problematic. The added expense of irregular taxation and "petty exactions" made upon the foreign merchant at every provincial border, and at every customs house led Moser to conclude: "The China merchant who has brought his foreign goods into treaty port with costs, freight, and duty paid, often finds his major problems still ahead of him." More than a few embittered China traders of the present day might claim that the same is true of China trade today! To be sure, many of the earliest stumbling blocks to China trading success are formidable today as they were 50, and even 100, years ago.

## THE UNORTHODOXY OF CHINA TRADE

Ample business opportunities in the Chinese market certainly exist, but there is nothing easy and fast about it. The most vexing of all the obstacles to achieving sustainable sales, as Moser suggested, is the country's long-time lack of buying power relative to the country's huge population, which is still 80 percent rural and very poor. Access to the market remains elusive; the Chinese are prone to guarding their domestic market since access to it is China's major bargaining chip in dealing with multinational firms. China's economy is extremely vulnerable to foreign economic interaction. Chinese officials are also concerned about inflation and the flight of foreign exchange currency out of the country. For these reasons as well, access to China's market is strictly controlled through a system of state-controlled import and export organizations.

Consumers have little, or no, access to foreign exchange to buy imported goods, and Chinese currency (Rmb) is nonconvertible on world markets. Invariably, foreign exchange reserves govern China's buying mood; 80 percent of the foreign exchange earned from export revenue is generated from sales of textiles, lightweight goods, and crude petroleum. The central government, via the State Planning Commission, allocates foreign exchange quotas to certain localities according to the priority it sets in the national economic plan. Allocations can vary from year to year. For example, in the case where foreign exchange reserves become depleted, localities may be restricted from spending their usual allocated amount on imports. Also, the import potential of any locality is linked to its export performance and indigenous foreign exchange earnings.

In their attempts to circumvent China's inability to pay cash for imported goods, foreign firms have tried numerous stratagems, including compensation trade arrangements and barter deals. For some firms, leasing equipment to the Chinese is the answer. China may be an aftermarket for used and/or obsolete equipment, e.g., an idle copper mine. A U.S. company may buy such a set of used equipment and sell it to a leasing company that in turn, leases it to the Chinese. The Chinese, lacking the foreign exchange to purchase the plant outright, arrange to pay with copper on a long-term contract. The U.S. companies involved earn commissions on sourcing the used equipment, leasing the equipment to the Chinese, and selling the copper on the world market.

### What barriers exist to selling to the China market?

High tariffs, which are not always uniformly applied, also restrict access to the China market, and make it difficult for foreigners. Tariff increases are often part of a general tightening over foreign exchange management and spending. The tariff structure is both a tactic to control domestic foreign trade corporations—local and national—and a device to limit domestic sales by foreign companies. Whatever the reason, the tariff system ultimately places the burden of high tariffs on the Chinese end-user. Of course, foreign traders have been hurt as well.

### What are the tariff rates for selling products to China?

China's tariffs are split into two categories: "minimum" tariffs that are applied to Hong Kong, Macao, and other countries that have signed commercial agreements with China; and "general" tariffs that apply to all other countries. Tariffs on machinery and materials that China lacks tend to be low, between 3 to 6 percent. Consumer products are subject to strict import approval and additional surcharges such as the Import Regulatory Tax. For these products, tariffs and surcharges can amount to over 200 percent of the product's original price. Exemptions are made on goods and materials used by companies with foreign capital participation and those used in the manufacturing of products for export. Foreign firms in the SEZs enjoy many exemptions on imported goods, including lower taxes on machinery, equipment, spare parts, raw materials, and an assortment of other goods, depending on the zone. All that said, the savvy trader understands that tariff rates charged often depend on the local whim of customs officials, and the clout and influence of the foreign trade corporation acting as a middle. Numerous traders indicated in interviews for this book that the unpredictable nature of tariff charges—and the fact that their competitors often enjoy rates of 10-40 percent lower than they do on identical products—remains perhaps the most frustrating impediment they face in penetrating the market.

"Nontariff" barriers to the China market include some that are Chinese government inspired and others which are natural limitations of the Chinese market. Import licensing restrictions imposed on Chinese end-users, motivated out of concerns about improvident foreign exchange spending in China, is a serious obstacle to foreign traders attempting to contract China deals, especially in provinces far removed from China's coastal areas where importers enjoy more buying authority. One of the best-known licensing crackdowns came in early 1986, when China curtailed the issuance of import licenses for microcomputers, slamming the door shut on an extremely lucrative market for U.S. computer companies. After selling more microcomputers in 1985 than in all previous years combined, sales of microcomputers to China plummeted to zero.

Government-imposed licensing regulations is a frustrating nontariff barrier because China's industrial priorities in these sectors change quickly and unpredictably, catching many suppliers off guard. By way of example, office copiers would tend to incur a higher tariff and tougher import license restrictions the moment economic planners in China deem to manufacture copiers domestically. The list of goods requiring import licensing therefore could be updated on a monthly basis.

China's morass of industrial bureaucracy has also made it difficult for U.S. suppliers to find appropriate Chinese buyers who are both willing to spend precious foreign exchange on imported products and able to obtain the appropriate import licenses. Without detailed organization charts of central and local government bureaucracy, foreign firms have found it difficult to identify key decision makers in the Chinese bureaucracy, causing time-consuming delays. Indeed, there is a dearth of information available regarding the needs of Chinese consumers and industrial units.

### *Will China's membership in the General Agreement on Tariffs and Trade (GATT) bring down barriers to the China market?*

China participated in the final agreement of GATT in March, 1994, but is not yet an official member. The agreement is expected to double China's share of world GDP from 3 to 6 percent, due to increased purchases of mainly Chinese agricultural goods. In its bid to gain membership in GATT, China is sything down its notoriously high tariff and nontariff barriers. Three tariff cutting initiatives were carried out in 1992, the largest affecting 54 percent of all imported goods. Officials in the PRC have vowed to bring the overall tariff rate to 15 percent by 1995, which is the maximum level allowed by GATT for a developing country. One can expect, however, that China will work to gain GATT membership while keeping strategic tariffs as high as possible to protect its largest companies, which could not compete with foreign suppliers should tariff barriers be removed. The resulting loss of jobs and foreign exchange spent on imports will not be sanctioned by Beijing.

### *How does a company gain leverage in the China Market?*

To gauge the marketing leverage points that U.S. corporations have found effective in the People's Republic of China, a questionnaire was sent to 150 U.S. Fortune 500 corporations currently selling goods to China. The results clearly indicated the fact that the China market is a particularly hard sell, and an unorthodox place to conduct direct sales. The following analysis of the responses seems the most practical method to discuss some of the unique features of the market and how U.S. firms has sought to gain leverage in their dealings with the People's Republic.

*What does your firm consider crucial in order to succeed at selling products in the People's Republic?*

| | Not Important | Important | Crucial |
|---|---|---|---|
| "State-of-the-art technology and superior quality" | 0% | 64% | 36% |
| "Knowledge of specific needs of the end user" | 4% | 64% | 32% |
| "Old friend status among Chinese in a position to influence decision to purchase" | 14% | 59% | 27% |
| "Firm/brand name recognition among Chinese industrial managers and officials" | 23% | 59% | 18% |
| "Low-bid price" | 22% | 69% | 9% |
| "Flexibility in payment terms/financing" | 28% | 72% | 0% |

**TECHNOLOGY AS A BARGAINING CHIP.** First and foremost, the respondents indicated that offering China state-of-the-art technology was key to success in selling to the Chinese. China clearly needs to attract foreign investment to achieve its modernization goals. In order to meet those goals, the Chinese are willing to trade their market for high technology and management expertise. China has begun to target world markets for its export goods through a program which develops export-oriented manufacturing based on technology, equipment, and managerial expertise imported from abroad. Those foreign firms willing to transfer key technology that solves salient problems in Chinese industry have been assured of heightened access to all or part of the domestic market. Firms with an open attitude to transferring technology that helps China increase its export earnings, renovate old factories, or develop emerging industries, have found greater market leverage than those companies without such an attitude. In many cases—especially joint ventures in special economic zones, factories built specifically to replace imports, and joint venture firms that transfer high technology into China—foreign firms have been allowed to sell directly to the domestic market.

**UNDERSTANDING END-USER NEEDS.** Pertinent information about end-user needs and preferences is especially difficult to find without spending time and energy scouting opportunities in person, in China. The advantages to gaining this knowledge, say companies working in China, provides a supplier a clear advantage. Numerous firms conduct costly marketing assaults on China including direct introduction of products to end-users and import officials, trade fair participation, and sponsoring technical seminars for potential customers. Promotional activities certainly help, but "getting down under the machinery with the Chinese end-user and solving problems" is clearly the best sales activity.

**INSIDE CONNECTION.** Questionnaire respondents also indicated that the market is a "who you know" market, and those with old friend status among acquisition decision makers tend to sign contracts. The China market differs from other East Asian markets in terms of the level of bureaucratic involvement in the marketing and distribution process. Entrenched producer-distributor relationships based on *guanxi* (backdoor) connections represent a formidable obstacle to marketing foreign products in China. New products may be held off the market by these strong relationships. Even though a new product may be better, cheaper, and more available, closed distribution channels can make sales impossible. Foreign sellers must fit into what has been called the "iron triangle," which involves a government oversight entity, an end-user, and an import/export agency. Selling to the Chinese market involves much more than locating the trading arm of the relevant ministry in Beijing. Foreign firms must obtain key provincial, municipal, and factory-level official approval of all sales as well.

**COMPANY REPUTATION.** The Chinese buy from those foreign firms that they recognize, often from pre-revolutionary days, and/or those that have a renowned brand name reputation. Thus, the old pioneer firms in China such as General Electric, Mobil Oil, and Siemens of West Germany enjoy an advantage in their marketing efforts over newcomers with less name recognition among Chinese industrial end users.

**LOW PRICE.** Strangely, offering low prices was rated as "crucial" by only 9 percent of the firms responding to the questionnaire. A common perception of Chinese buying priorities is that low price is key to selling in China; this is not necessarily the case in an environment where just assembling and influencing the appropriate players on the Chinese side is a monumental task. (In any case, foreign traders of all nationalities have indicated repeatedly that the Chinese will not buy unless the price is rock bottom.)

**PREFERENTIAL FINANCING/TERMS.** Although concessionary financing was ranked behind all the other selling criteria tested, to questionnaire respondents, it definitely plays a central role in obtaining contracts for large infrastructural development projects in China. To win large contracts in China it is imperative for foreign firms to offer creative packaging of credit and loan guarantees.

### *What has been the general approach to gaining a share of the China market?*

Corporate America has discovered that obtaining inside information on Chinese buying patterns and specific needs is a Sisyphean task. Secondly, they find it problematic selling technology to China since the Chinese cannot adequately pay for it outright, and often Chinese enterprises lack the necessary capabilities to assimilate advanced technology, requiring assistance on the part of the foreign firm that China cannot reasonably afford to procure. Thirdly, U.S. companies have found the whole process of networking among procurement decision makers while building a sound corporate reputation in China, expensive and sometimes impossible unless they take their China involvement a step further. In rapidly expanding numbers, U.S. corporations have found it necessary to set up collaborative or solely owned ventures on Chinese soil in order to gain the above mentioned leverage strengths in the China market. Whether a venture in manufacturing, distribution, or a service, these corporations have decided that the problems of market access can best be surmounted by deepening their relationship with the Chinese through a China venture. Unable to offer large-scale government-backed financing, or compete with Japan's soga sosha in terms of price, corporate America has come to realize that its most direct and sustainable avenue into the China market is one of equity investment in China-based enterprises to which it must transfer technology, share management expertise, and jointly own. As such, many U.S. firms have discovered that selling to the China market requires *investing* in the China market.

## RELATIONSHIPS FIRST, BUSINESS LATER

Most North American business people think of building a "business relationship" abroad as a rather straightforward task in which any cultural differences can be easily overcome through informality, "eye-to-eye" talk, and having a few drinks together. In Greater China the meaning of the word "relationship" is much deeper.

The government of ancient China depended upon a system of client-patron relationships to maintain stability throughout the vast provinces of the country. Client-patron relationships were called *kan-ch'ing*. In the village level, to have "good *kan-ch'ing*" was to have a sense of well-being, a feeling of being at ease, in a relationship, say, with your landlord. Those who had good kan-ch'ing would help each other rather than compete. For example, the landlord was dependent on the goodwill of the tenant if he was to get his rent. The tenant normally paid his rent but if he could not pay the entire amount he would open negotiations with the landlord. If there had been a drought, a flood, or rain that came at the wrong time of the year, or insects plagued the crops, the landlords obligation to the tenant demanded that rent be postponed as a necessity for the tenant to survive. If good *kan-ch'ing* existed the landlord would not press for the rent and the tenant would pay up in bountiful years. Relationships and "good *kan-ch'ing*" remain vital in China business cultures today.

Chinese maintain their business relationships through reciprocal exchange of gifts, favors, and promotions. *Guanxi* relationships among Chinese business people wherever they are located, can be described as ingratiating personal relationships that impose multiple obligations on the respective players. These relationships can stem from the town in which one's parents were born, the university one attended, or a direct familial tie. *Guanxi* is the reason why managerial positions in China are filled with family members, friends, and co-workers rather than those who are simply well qualified. It also explains why many Chinese university students studying abroad are usually the offspring of high officials. Nonetheless, *guanxi* relations, like their equivalent throughout Asia, can make things happen when and where they otherwise might not.

### On what basis are Chinese relationships formed and maintained?

Business relationships among Chinese everywhere are clearly based on trust, dependency and obligation—but reciprocity is their lifeblood. The Chinese carry around a ledger in their heads. A person knows exactly what debts he owes and what debts are owed to him by others at any given time. The balancing of reciprocal debt never really occurs, nor should it occur. The point is for the relationships to remain in a dynamic state; one person or the other is at all times wanting for a favor to be reciprocated at some time in the future.

Now for the dependency part. When a reciprocal relationship includes a dependent and a benefactor, it becomes one based on the dependence of a subordinate upon a superior. These paternalistic relationships, however, are sought after rather than avoided. For now, suffice it to say that buyers and sellers in China tend to enter these ongoing dependent-benefactor relationships. Sellers look after their buyers' every wish, and in return they receive loyal business from the buyer.

Lingering personal or business debt like that I've described above is distasteful to Westerners who consider such ongoing commitments to reciprocity an invasion of privacy and an infringement upon their personal liberty. In our ethos of social equality, no person should be overly indebted to another. Because ongoing indebtedness of any kind is a cause for anxiety in the West, we tend to be "instant reciprocators" in our business dealings that involve trade offs. In China repayment of a favor is always delayed, especially if the acquaintance or business relationship is new. To pay back a favor quickly is actually an antagonistic gesture because it connotes reticence or unwillingness to become attached or involved with the other party and forge an ongoing obligatory relationship. Balanced reciprocity implies that the relationship has ended, that one person or the other has opted to discontinue the association. By delaying the balancing of debt in a relationship, the Chinese sustain their friendships and business partnerships.

One more thing about business relationships in China. The Chinese perceive business relationships, and business contracts, *holistically*. You can't look for equanimity in one dimension of the relationship to the exclusion of all others. In business relationships with the Chinese you may find that your Chinese counterparts feel the relationship is equitable while you feel he hasn't lived up to the letter of your contract. The important thing is to view the total collaboration with a macro lens when trying to solve micro problems.

### *How do I turn business relationships with Chinese into profit?*

Without relationships, connections, and the right friends and allies in the right places, a foreign firm has little chance of comprehensive China business success. Foreign firms and their representatives are expected to build business relationships and networks, just as Chinese must. With a hit-and-run approach, a foreign firm won't succeed in entering into these ongoing relationships—you won't be able to foster a long and trustful relationship. You have to invest in people and in relationships with them. Go to Asia and build relationships first. Don't try to close deals and do things fast. Build relationships. Be helpful. Establish expertise. Take your time and you invest in people.

Once you've invested in people then there will be a trial test. As Sun Tze writes in *The Art of War,* "Test them to find out where they are sufficient and where they are lacking." Do more than you promise on the test trial. The trial test might be as small as a $5,000 order but that $5,000 may become, over the years, hundreds of thousands of dollars in annual orders if you perform well.

### *How do I effectively and appropriately reciprocate favors, gifts etc. with Chinese?*

Reciprocity is the key to relationship-building in Asia. Perform favors for potential Asian business partners to generate connectedness and indebtedness. No favor is forgotten. Modern Asians don't consciously think about reciprocity in Confucian terms, but reciprocity and obligation is behind most of their actions. Their response to you and their loyalty to serving your needs is conditioned by whether you respond to them in a proprietary and civilized manner, that is, reciprocally. You might have to have coffee with a stuffy old bureaucrat every time you visit a ministry before getting your meeting. And you may have to thank him profusely and bring a small gift every time you see him. You'd rather just walk by him and have your meeting, but don't. You will almost certainly need him at some point in the future.

Take your time in reciprocating favors. You don't need to "tie things up" immediately. You can leave things hanging, in a state of unequal or imbalanced reciprocity. The future will bring balance through another exchange.

While we're on the subject of favor, we should talk about influence-peddling and corruption in Greater China, and how it touches on commercial dealings.

### Do Chinese local bureaucrats participate directly in commercial dealings?

You bet they do. Increasingly their incomes depend on yearly bonuses that are tied to the profit performance of scores of local firms operated by town council under their auspices. The typical local bureaucrat typically earned $500-1000 per year. Now the commercially involved official can take home over $3,000 (in RmB) per year—more than the official wage of the head of the Communist Party in Beijing. Freedom to carry forward economic experiments in their towns and villages have made many mayors wealthy and extremely powerful, even though it is technically illegal for cadres to double as business executives. As one such small town mayor gleefully told a *Wall Street Journal* reporter recently, "It's against the rules if the mayor heads my company and deals in a day-to-day business, but it's all right for him to head the administrative holding company for those businesses." However, not every official has been so successful in setting up profitable businesses. In early 1994, the central government had to order local authorities to stop spending their town's education funds on business schemes. Local cadres had been withholding teacher's pay in order to start up speculative businesses, buy luxury cars, and build hotels, often in areas that clearly cannot support tourism. Thus, while Deng has encouraged local officials to experiment with market forces by setting up businesses, there remains an absence of the regulatory institutions to ensure that those impacted are protected. In some cases, peasants have become rich by leasing their land for commercial purposes, but in other cases, locals have had to accept IOUs from a local state entity that has squandered the people's money.

### Are large PRC corporations controlled by relatives of Chinese leaders?

Often, they are. Especially those large companies that have listed stock in China and abroad have members of their boards who are the sons, daughters, or relatives of high-ranking Chinese officials, known as the "princelings" in China. CITIC, for example, is led by Wan Jun, the eldest son of China's late President Wang Zhen. The Vice President of China Venturetech Investment Corporation, another mainland heavyweight which has listed in Hong Kong, is Chen Weili, the third daughter of the former chairman of the Central Advisory commission of the Communist Party of China. The list is long.

### How corrupt is business in Taiwan?

The commercial system in Taiwan functions by way of commissions, kick backs, and "grease." Everyone is on the take, because this is how people make ends meet. Nobody works for free, nor is expected to, and nobody provides a decision or even gets out of the way without being paid. Is this corrupt? Yes, in the eyes of Americans who refuse to deal in this manner, and find themselves on the outside of most deals. In most deals in Taiwan, you will eventually learn who is the so called "godfather" who controls its approval or interminable delay. Influencing this person is a critical and delicate matter best left to an adept go-between. You have to look no further than Taipei's ill-fated rapid transit system to see evidence of high-level commercial corruption in Taiwan. Numerous foreign consulting companies were paid to design and build the huge new system of elevated train tracks and stations. The budget for the project vaulted to more than ten times the estimated cost, due to bad decisions motivated by payoffs.

Moreover, as an ethic in Taiwan it is believed that it's bad business not to double or triple one's money by playing both sides of a deal. (That is, by double crossing you.) Never expect your Taiwanese intermediary or advisor not to "double agent" for both you and entities with whom you are negotiating. This seemingly unethical behavior takes place all the time in Taiwan, often at the expense of naive foreigners. Such behavior is not considered morally wrong, though it is legally wrong. In the West, what is immoral is associated strongly with that which is illegal. The distinction is not made too clearly in all of Asia.

### How does organized crime operate in Taiwan?

Working in organized crime in Taiwan is a job for its members. Each syndicate is a multileveled organization with its own management and operational headaches, system of promotions, and daily legal problems. Each "brother" works to rise in the hierarchy, collecting debt, obtaining protection money, running a casino, and so on. The term *Bamboo* refers to organized crime in general in Taiwan. In doing business in Taiwan you will almost certainly have to confront and assuage Bamboo elements with a cut, a kick back, or a favor. Don't try to buck the system; you will quickly learn how pervasive the Bamboo is—you won't be able to get an electrician sent out, your retail outlet will be closed down by building inspectors—eventually you will learn or leave Taiwan in disgust. A friend of mine worked six months to get the Bamboo out of the operation of a major U.S. food company with franchises in Taiwan. Sixty Bamboo gangsters had to be convinced, somehow, that they should return control of the operation to the American company. After endless haggling in a tea house, an arrangement was made for the U.S. company to pay off a key Bamboo leader. "It was solved as a business deal," says my security expert friend.

# PART TWO

## Trading with China

# CHAPTER 6

# CHINA'S

# FIVE-PART MARKET

$T$here are three types of international markets: (1) existing markets, in which customer needs are currently being served; (2) latent markets, in which customer needs are present but not being adequately served; and (3) incipient markets, in which customer needs have not yet emerged. The China market weighs heavily toward the later two types; for companies which enter early and build a presence, the potential for long-term sales growth—as opposed to immediate sales—is clearly enormous in numerous market sectors.

*What are the key opportunities for U.S. firms in the China market?*

A company that is intent upon entering China and prospering must have a broad, sector-specific knowledge of the opportunities the China market offers. Obviously, to cover the entire market in detail would require another volume, but the following

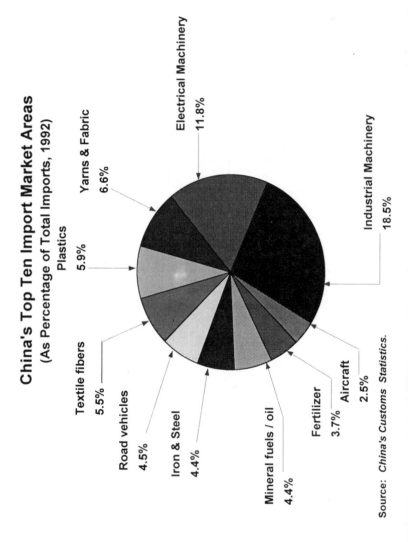

## China's Top Ten Import Market Areas
### (As Percentage of Total Imports, 1992)

Electrical Machinery
11.8%

Yarns & Fabric
6.6%

Plastics
5.9%

Textile fibers
5.5%

Road vehicles
4.5%

Iron & Steel
4.4%

Mineral fuels / oil
4.4%

Fertilizer
3.7%

Aircraft
2.5%

Industrial Machinery
18.5%

Source: *China's Customs Statistics.*

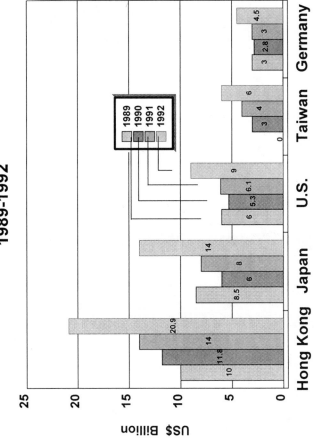

PRC Imports From Major Supplying Countries 1989-1992

Legend:
- 1989
- 1990
- 1991
- 1992

Germany: 4.5, 3, 2.8, 3
Taiwan: 6, 4, 3, 0
U.S.: 9, 6.1, 5.3, 6
Japan: 14, 8, 6, 8.5
Hong Kong: 20.9, 14, 11.8, 10

US$ Billion (axis: 0, 5, 10, 15, 20, 25)

Source: *China's Customs Statistics.*

overview should acquaint the reader with what is perceived as the five market segments of the China market. End-users in China are currently under increasing pressure to upgrade production and quality in the Chinese enterprise and thus, will become buyers of a spectrum of products in response to an array of new requisites being imposed upon Chinese industry by government policy makers. As the Chinese consumer becomes increasingly exposed to Western culture and fashion, the Western marketer can expect to see increased sales of consumer products in response to new Chinese consumer desires. As China's exports continue to diversify, China's need for primary goods and manufactured goods will diversify as well.

# CHINA'S FIVE-PART MARKET

## 1. China as a Market for Foreign Technology

To reach the plan's goals, China is importing advanced technologies and capital goods under an open-door economic policy. Priority is given to acquiring know-how and assistance in developing domestic manufacturing capability rather than importing final product. Though foreign capital—loans and investment—will finance part of this development effort, the Chinese hope to pay for imported technology by increasing export earnings. The emphasis on development of the export sector will further shift the Chinese's import priorities toward technologies that will enable them to diversify to production of new, more sophisticated export commodities and improve their manufacture of export goods.

Technology is transferred to China under license or through outright purchase. However, to minimize the foreign exchange costs of importing technology, the Chinese favor such arrangements as processing and assembly of imported parts; barter trade and offset purchases of Chinese products by the foreign technology supplier or a third party; and compensation trade—paying for imported equipment, technology, and materials with resulting product. The Chinese also encourage technology transfer in conjunction with investment, the technology being considered part of the foreign investor's contribution to the venture, to defer foreign exchange costs, and to involve the supplier in the success of the transfer.

A key component of China's modernization program is the renovation of over 400,000 state- and collectively-owned industrial factories. These projects are valued at between US$500,000 and US$2 million each. The emphasis is on computer manufacturing, construction materials, food processing, and other projects likely to reduce energy consumption. In almost all cases these projects involve the licensing of foreign technology. Recently, transportation and communications have been added to the list of renovation priorities. Five foreign companies have been chosen, including AT&T, to participate in joint ventures producing switching systems for China's lucrative telecommunications market; the country's fast expanding automobile market will allow for the participation of scores of foreign component manufacturers willing to share technology. Already a $160 million fund has been set up in the U.S. to invest in PRC auto component alliances. In light of China's continuing attempts to control foreign exchange spending, foreign firms should select projects in provinces and areas directly related to the central government, and negotiate with Chinese partners who offer the government connections to get projects approved and foreign exchange allocated. Officially discouraged areas include consumer electronics and light industries. One exception in light industries may be in areas where import substitution might be achieved and foreign technology is utilized. The list of opportunities in licensing technology in China grows daily, but competition for such projects is keen, both in price and in packaging attractive financing.

**CIVIL AVIATION.** No section of China's transportation infrastructure has undergone a more radical transformation in the last decade than the country's airline industry. The pace of economic development in China, in combination with the rapid growth in tourism, has caused demand for airline seats to reach all-time highs. The response of the Chinese government has been to break up the old state-run airline into regionally-based airlines that compete for passenger and freight customers. Over the past five years airline traffic in China has doubled, reaching 29 million passengers last year. The growth in passengers has been matched by a 33 percent annual increase in airline revenues. Most domestic routes achieve an average of 90 percent of seating capacity, and many flights are booked to the last seat. Typically a Chinese air traveler will book their seat weeks in advance.

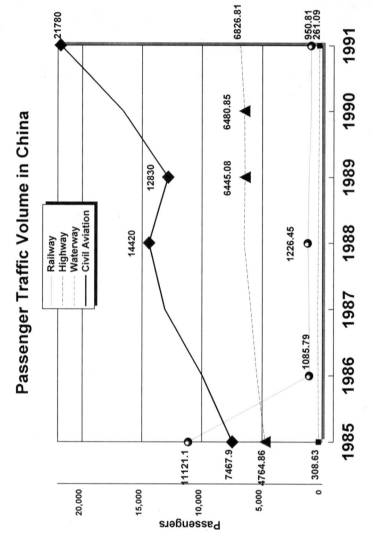

Passenger Traffic Volume in China

Source: *Statistical Yearbook of China.*

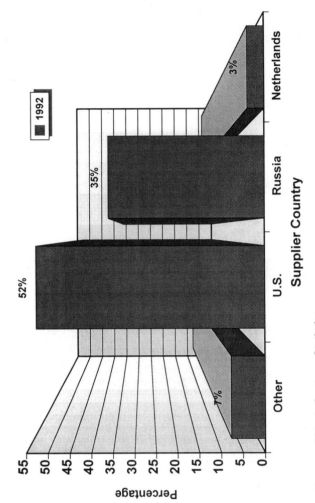

Source:   *China's Customs Statistics.*

Commercial aviation has received a high priority position in the Chinese government's economic planning apparatus. The Government's Eighth Five-Year Plan (1991-1995) calls for an extensive upgrading of China's transportation infrastructure, including the acquisition of more aircraft, the development of new flight routes, building new airports, expansion of maintenance facilities, and a modern system of air traffic control. (Seventy-three people were killed in 3 air crashes in China in 1993; nearly a dozen planes were hijacked in that year.) Yet even these efforts are not expected to keep pace with exploding demand. Air traffic increases have already exceeded levels predicted for 1996 and no abatement is expected in the near future. In fact, the head of the Planning Department of China's Central Aviation Administration (CAAC) predicts capacity shortfalls will continue for at least the next ten years. It is likely that Chinese airlines in the future will be allowed to privatize in order to attract foreign capital and engage in joint ventures with foreign companies. Already many of the regional airlines are employing foreign firms to assist in the upgrading of service on their flights. Opportunities for foreign involvement also exist in the areas of systems engineering, traffic control systems development, and parts and maintenance training agreements.

Of course, the overwhelming role of foreign companies in China's airline industry is as a source of import for modern jet aircraft. China's large carriers are all expanding their fleets while new, smaller airlines are appearing in selected regions of the country. All of these airlines are in need of modern aircraft. The current Chinese air fleet totals just over 300 aircraft, to serve a population of 1.2 billion. This contrasts with a U.S. air fleet of 5,000 commercial aircraft serving a population a quarter of China's. The annual market for imported aircraft in China is now estimated at over $2 billion.

The growth of China's air industry is being strongly influenced by patterns of regional economic development and the increasingly important roles of Hong Kong and Taiwan. Hong Kong's Kai Tak airport will soon reach a saturation point with the dramatic increase of goods and travellers moving through South China. While Hong Kong's new airport remains mired in bureaucratic wrangling, four other airports have sprung up in the Pearl Delta region. The new focal point of air traffic in South China may bypass Hong Kong and instead be centered around Guangzhou's new $1.77 billion airport, which will be the largest in China.

**COMPUTER TECHNOLOGY.** Computerization is emphasized in every applicable Chinese industry in the hope of developing a domestic computer base. Therefore, there will continue to be a high dependence on foreign manufacturing joint ventures to initiate domestic computer production. The import of microcomputers from foreign countries has been virtually brought to a standstill through import restrictions and tariff barriers. In addition, many of the ventures set up in China by foreign firms to sell computers to the Chinese, rather than indigenize production of computer parts in China, are now experiencing very difficult times. Even so, opportunities are growing in the field of microelectronics. China lacks production facilities to produce large-scale integrated circuits to meet the demands of its fledgling computer industry.

China has acquired a wide range of computer equipment over the last several years, much of it purchased from U.S. firms. However, China's computer capabilities lag far behind its current equipment acquisitions. Computers are desperately needed for application in Chinese industry and R&D sectors. United States companies have sold thousands of computers to China, many of which are under-utilized or simply stored in warehouses. These U.S. firms could have undertaken to assist China in developing its computer knowledge and applications as part of the sales. The end result of the oversaturation of microcomputers in China has been periodic halts to microcomputer imports since 1985. In the computer field, China will continue to seek mainframes, peripherals, software, and semiconductors.

China's computer industry has undergone rapid changes during the reform era. Until the 1980s, China attempted to develop a full line of indigenously produced computer hardware and software. However, since the advent of economic reform, the country's computer industry has shifted towards the development and production of internationally competitive information technology products. Production of computer hardware grew by an average of 31 percent annually between 1989 and 1992. With its market potential, engineers, computer scientists, and a pool of low-cost, semi-skilled labor, China is likely to emerge as a global producer of low-end computer hardware and software applications. While China's skilled labor force is relatively small as a percentage of the total population, the overwhelming size of the country offers significant human capital resources. For example, China currently has nearly four times as many computer engineers as South Korea.

The process of developing China's computer industry has been paralleled by a systematic incorporation of computer technology in many of China's largest government agencies and state-owned companies. Computer use, as measured by the annual investments of government enterprises and agencies, has grown about 20 percent annually since 1980. The total size of the Chinese computer market is now estimated at $1000 million, and estimated average annual growth for the next three years is projected at 42 percent. Imports represent a significant share of the Chinese computer market. American companies such as AST and Compaq dominate the import market, offering IBM-compatible personal computers, as well as workstations and minicomputers. Imports are expected to jump in 1995, as all quotas and licenses are due to be phased out as of December 31, 1994 and tariffs have officially dropped from 40 to 20 percent. Some analysts predict the tariff rates will drop further to nine percent by the end of this year.

The development of China's computer industry will largely be dependent on the course of China's total reform plan. Complementary industries such as electronics and telecommunications will play an important role in the "informatization" of Chinese society. Moreover, advances in China's indigenous computer technology will be a function of the government's financial commitment to research and development. China's technology policy currently calls for the development of over 50 technology development zones, and actively encourages multinational firms operating in China to make commitments to local sourcing, training, and technology transfer. An additional variable in the development of China's computer industry is the separation of enterprises from government policy-making and regulatory bodies. The Ministry of Electronics currently owns 216 computer factories, 36 of which manufacture personal computers. Only five of these state-owned enterprises are responsible for over 80 percent of China's computer output. The government is actively seeking to spin off these companies and is seeking joint venture partners to bring foreign technology and management expertise to these firms.

**FOOD PROCESSING.** China spent over $1 billion in 1993 on imported food processing equipment and technology. The country is buying foreign machinery and equipment in order to produce food for its growing population as well as for export markets in the future. Foreign firms capable of providing small-scale machinery and product lines that are easy to assimilate into existing Chinese food processing factories will find receptive Chinese partners. Opportunities exist in the following product lines: canning, bakery equipment, dairy processing equipment, brewery equipment, soy texturization, corn processing, condiment processing, frozen foods, and food preservation. The outlook for the food processing sector is good for foreign firms because of rising wages in China. As working hours have changed, fast food has become more important in the Chinese working environment. The United States has achieved a high degree of expertise in this field and the opportunities are promising, especially in light of the successes of Kentucky Fried Chicken and McDonald's in the PRC already.

**ELECTRONICS.** One of the most conspicuous items on China's import list is electrical home appliances, such as television sets, audio-cassette players, radios, refrigerators, calculators, and videocassette recorders. With China's constant foreign exchange shortages, China's leaders have moved to localize the production of consumer electronic goods to offset the financial strain of importing them. Foreign firms offering processing and technologies in the electronic sector will find the Chinese very receptive. Specifically, areas worth investigating include semiconductors and integrated circuits. China has been an importer of the full range of equipment to produce semiconductors and integrated circuits. Equipment is also needed to process the raw materials, such as silicon, that make up finished electronics products. Opportunities exist for sales and equipment to produce capacitors and resistors as well as technological know-how relating to advanced components. Opportunities still exist in printing and etching equipment. Other areas of opportunity include switch products, boxing products, packaging, and assembling process.

During the reform era, China's government has consistently increased funding for the modernization of its electronics industry. China views the development of its electronic research and manufacturing capabilities as a cornerstone of its industrial development. It realizes that if it is to achieve a strong, competitive position in the global economy, it will have to create a foundation in a wide range of information technologies. China's electronics sector grew at an annual rate of 16 percent in 1992, reaching a production record of 18.5 billion U.S. dollars. In 1993, the industry is expected to grow by more than 20 percent, hitting a record high of 125 billion yuan ($20 billion according to current exchange rates). China's government has identified the electronics industry as a key sector in its Eighth Five-Year plan, indicating it would be the recipient of channeled state investment and foreign loans through 1995. In addition, China's microelectronics industry should continue to accelerate next year, as the country enters the third year of the Eighth Five-Year Plan. Reports have circulated that the Chinese government may spend up to U.S. $2 billion in the microelectronics industry by the end of the five-year plan in 1995.

Because China's electronic manufacturing concerns have grown faster than its microelectronic industry, the country remains a large and growing market for electronic components. China used approximately 400 million integrated circuits in 1989, though it produced only 110 million. By 1995 consumption is estimated to be 1.2 billion ICs, with 600 million produced domestically. By that time it is estimated that China will be able to produce 400,000 microcomputers, 15 million telephones and 12 million color televisions annually.

**MEDICAL EQUIPMENT.** China's health care system represents a major industry for producers and exporters of medical technology. Currently the health care system includes over 2 million beds in more than 60,000 hospitals. In recent years, China has spent an average of $278 million per year on Western medical supplies and equipment. The size of China's health care system has meant significant market segments co-exist for several types of health care equipment. Since the Chinese began large-scale purchases of foreign medical equipment in the early 1980s, Japan, Germany, and the United States have dominated the market, comprising approximately 80 percent of all sales. Other sources, such as South Korea and Taiwan are marketing their products aggressively, but are generally regarded as lower-end suppliers.

In recent years, United States suppliers have made significant advances into the Chinese market. In 1985, the United States had a 17.5 percent share of the China market, with gross sales of $42 million. By 1991, U.S. market share had expanded to 31.9 percent, with $107 million in sales. During the course of China's reform era (1980-present), the country has developed a consistent pattern of spending in its acquisition of Western medical technology. Typically, the Chinese will purchase large amounts of medical equipment in the first two years of a five-year plan, with a drop in the third and fourth years before a surge in imports in the fifth year. Current spending seem to be adhering to this pattern, with increases in 1990 and 1991 being followed by a slower rate of growth during the first quarter of 1993.

Over the past ten years, purchasing decision-making has been increasingly decentralized. Chinese hospitals are now empowered to acquire their own equipment using their own earned income. In addition, health care systems at the provincial and local levels have greater flexibility in importing equipment and medical supplies. Most Chinese hospitals buy foreign equipment with retained earnings from patient and insurance payments, or through bank financing "backed" by local or provincial authorities. Hospitals may now exchange their own renminbi earnings for hard currency using local swap centers. While bank financing is often a critical component of a hospital's acquisition of large-scale foreign technology, many Chinese banks are willing to provide financing with only the hospital's projected earnings as a guarantee of repayment. In practice, high-end products China cannot manufacture itself tend to be imported, while lower end products are acquired from domestic producers. Obtaining official approval to import products valued at under $20,000 is relatively straightforward, particularly for mid-level diagnostic and therapeutic equipment with no domestic equivalents. Licenses are required for importers of equipment costing more than $20,000, though there is generally no fixed limit on the number of units that can be imported each year.

## 2. China as a Market for Capital Goods

Chinese officials have announced plans to increase investments in energy, transportation, and the development of raw materials. The volume of passenger traffic in China doubles every four to five years. This means that infrastructural improvements in highways, railways, and airport facilities will expand commensurately, boosting sales of trucks, diesel engines for locomotives, railway technology, airplanes, and airport equipment. Foreign suppliers of advanced capital goods in the priority areas that have been mentioned throughout this chapter should find better prospects, even with China's shortages of foreign exchange. The most serious barriers to the market are the high tariffs placed on certain items (microcomputers, for example).

**ELECTRIC POWER.** The power sector in China is the fastest growing in the world. The demands of China's rapid economic development have placed enormous pressures on the country's already overtaxed power system. Due to the country's inexperience in advanced power generation processes, imports of technology and equipment are being actively sought by national and provincial authorities. China's power industry has grown at an annual rate of 10 percent over the last several years, yet lack of available power continues to frustrate the modernization of other sectors of the Chinese economy. By some estimates, power shortages have held back industrial production by 20 to 40 percent since the late 1980s. Brownouts remain common and up to 120 million Chinese continue to live virtually without electricity across the country. The total size of China's power market is currently estimated at $12.4 billion, with projected annual market growth of 10 percent over the next three years. Chinese planning authorities are trying to add 15,000 MW of new capacity to total installed capacity each year. Imports account for nearly half of this market. Estimated imports of plants and equipment for 1993 totaled $695 million. China's hydroelectric power needs are enormous.

One key project under consideration is the Three Gorges Hydroelectric project, for which a number of studies are underway that address the technical, environmental, and financial feasibility of the project. Although the United States possesses the world's most advanced nuclear power technology, U.S. firms have been left out of China's nuclear power projects because of delays by the U.S. government in approving the transfer of nuclear technology to China's delays caused by China's lack of nuclear waste disposal legislation.

Foreign-made coal processing and technologies are also greatly needed for China's energy development. China is the sec-

# China's Electric Power Sector

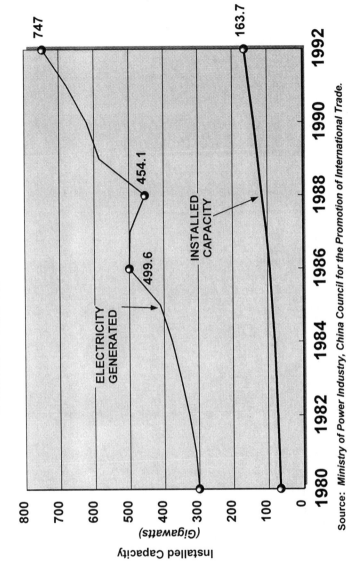

- 747
- 163.7
- 454.1
- 499.6

INSTALLED
CAPACITY

ELECTRICITY
GENERATED

Installed Capacity
*(Gigawatts)*

1980   1982   1984   1986   1988   1990   1992

800   700   600   500   400   300   200   100   0

Source: *Ministry of Power Industry, China Council for the Promotion of International Trade.*

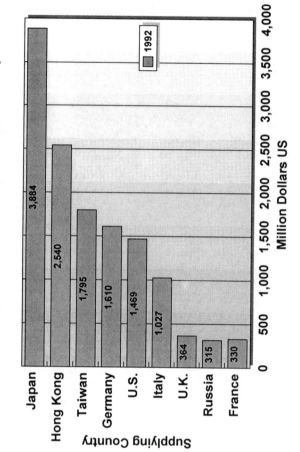

PRC Purchases of Power
Generating & Industrial Machinery

Supplying Country: Japan 3,884; Hong Kong 2,540; Taiwan 1,795; Germany 1,610; U.S. 1,469; Italy 1,027; U.K. 364; Russia 315; France 330

Million Dollars US

1992

Source: *The Economist Intelligence Unit.*

ond largest coal producer in the world, behind the United States. Coal accounts for 70 percent of China's energy production. The United States is in a strong position to work with China in open strip mine development, especially in project management services, engineering, and specialized equipment sales. China's coal-related projects include slurry pipelines, downstream coal utilization projects involving coal gasification, coal liquefaction, and coal chemical technology. Because China's modernization stresses upgrading existing plants, opportunities are emerging for cooperation in technologies for the manufacture of coal mining equipment, including tunneling machines, monitoring devices, and safety equipment. Significant sales of used equipment may also be possible in this sector.

Financing for the upgrade of China's power system is largely derived from loans and grants offered by international development agencies. The Asian Development Bank is expected to take the lead in financing the modernization of China's electric power system, with additional support coming from the World Bank and U.S. agencies. Private lenders will also contribute to the modernization effort, although their activities are more likely to be concentrated in the thriving coastal provinces rather than inland. The most promising markets for foreign exporters are in steam and gas turbine generators, boilers, and control equipment. Foreign companies are also likely to find opportunities in producer-gas and water-gas generators. Foreign participation in the construction and management of entire power plants is now possible due to deregulation and the official approval of two methods of direct investment in China's power sector. Foreign companies may participate in build-operate-transfer (BOT) arrangements in which turnkey power plants are imported, assembled and activated by a joint venture between Chinese and foreign entities. The foreign company then trains Chinese personnel in the operation of the plant and transfers control to the Chinese partner. As an alternative, foreign companies also participate in build-own-operate (BOO) arrangements in which a power plant is constructed and then operated with foreign involvement. While legally permissible, no BOO plants have yet been built in the PRC. American firms are in a solid position because the Chinese are very interested in utilizing their technology and management expertise. However, the success of these firms will depend on a competitive mix of price,

financing, and attractive technology transfer arrangements. The
Chinese bargaining position is currently to demand 100 percent
countertrade arrangements on equipment purchases. Competition
from European countries and Japan is intense, particularly in the
concessionary financing these countries offer China.

**TELECOMMUNICATIONS.** China's phone density nationwide stands at 1
phone per 100 persons, one of the lowest rates in the world. Rural
telephone service in China features manual switchboards and
open wires for long distance communications. There is an increasing emphasis in China's modernization program to upgrade its
telephone system and telephone services. At this time, those firms
willing to transfer technology and offer concessionary financing in
this sector are being given preferential treatment. There is fierce
competition among the industrialized countries—the United States,
European nations, and Japan—for China's telecommunications
projects. Other related telecommunication areas include defense-
related telecommunication equipment, satellite receiving stations,
direct broadcast satellite systems, ship communication equipment,
VHF-UHF equipment, and portable airborne receivers.

Today telecommunications is one of the fastest growing sectors of the Chinese economy. Unlike areas such as real estate
development, telecommunications development shows little sign
of 'overheating,' as efforts to expand capacity continue to lag far
behind surging demand. Instead, the Chinese government has
adopted a set of goals for telecommunications development that
should continue market growth in this sector well into the next
century. The Chinese government, under the auspices of the
Ministry of Post and Telecommunications (MPT) spent nearly $2
billion on modernizing the nation's telecommunications infrastructure in the Seventh Five-Year Plan (1987-1991), and consistently
exceeded spending projections. During that same period, China
imported over $460 million worth of U.S. telecommunications
equipment. The government has been aggressively expanding the
number of telephone lines in service in China, adding nearly 3 million new telephone lines in 1992, a 44 percent increase over 1991.
Total fixed investment for 1992 reached RMB 14.72 billion, a 70
percent increase over 1991. In the future the M.P.T. expects to
achieve even faster rates of telecommunications development.
Using targets set for the Eighth and Ninth Five-Year Plans, it is

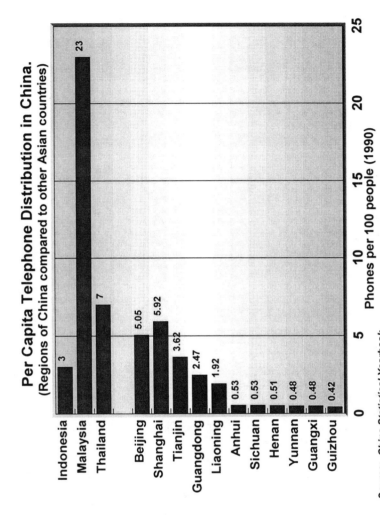

**Per Capita Telephone Distribution in China.**
(Regions of China compared to other Asian countries)

| Region | Phones per 100 people (1990) |
|---|---|
| Indonesia | 3 |
| Malaysia | 23 |
| Thailand | 7 |
| Beijing | 5.05 |
| Shanghai | 5.92 |
| Tianjin | 3.62 |
| Guangdong | 2.47 |
| Liaoning | 1.92 |
| Anhui | 0.53 |
| Sichuan | 0.53 |
| Henan | 0.51 |
| Yunnan | 0.48 |
| Guangxi | 0.48 |
| Guizhou | 0.42 |

Source: *China Statistical Yearbook.*

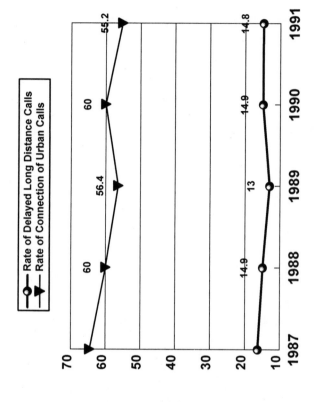

# Telephone Service in the P.R.C.

**Rate of Delayed Long Distance Calls**
**Rate of Connection of Urban Calls**

Rate (% of Calls)

Source: *Chinese Statistical Yearbook.*

clear that China now wishes to reach its year 2000 goals by 1995. The M.P.T. wishes to expand the country's total switching capacity to 26.5 million lines by 1995, about five times the total number of lines available in 1991. In addition, the country is in the process of developing a national data transmission network, integrated cellular systems and new fiber optic capabilities. In total, investment in telecommunications could reach $13 billion in the Eighth Five-Year Plan.

### *How developed is the phone system in China, especially for business use?*

Almost all business hotels already have International direct dial services and many offer advanced fax and other telecommunications services in their business centers. The ability to contact one's company while in China should never be a problem. In contrast, the ability to contact a Chinese entity is often hampered by a system that is still overwhelmed by call traffic. Even with current government expansion plans, it is unlikely China will achieve more than 6 telephones per 100 persons before the end of the century.

**BUILDING MATERIALS.** While the real estate development of new property in China has abated over the last nine months, the country continues to be a burgeoning market for building materials. Products used in high-rise buildings, low-rise complexes, interior decoration and joint venture manufacturing facilities are all in demand. Major urban centers in China are in the process of upgrading buildings to attract foreign clients and well-to-do Chinese. The total size of the building industry was valued at $2.175 billion in 1993, while the market for imports hit $450 million. In the next five years, it is estimated that Shanghai alone will import over $200 million worth of building materials to renovate the city's hotels and office buildings. Housing construction will be an additional source of demand for imported materials, as single family homes and large apartments become realistic options for the highest stratum of Chinese society. Sino-foreign joint ventures are also important end-users of imported building materials. Targeting marketing efforts to Chinese development zones can help to identify foreign joint ventures as potential customers.

Most Chinese developers and builders delegate the purchase of imported building materials to Hong Kong-based trading agencies. Foreign manufacturers must target their marketing efforts to these Hong Kong trading companies, as well as their mainland Chinese counterparts.

## 3. China as a Market for Consumer Goods/Health Products

Chinese consumers have rabid desire for the "four essentials"—a television, washing machine, refrigerator, and videocassette recorder. However, sales of consumer goods have been periodically curtailed by China's crackdown on foreign exchange spending. Much of the foreign exchange problem was caused by rampant, uncontrolled spending by the importing of mainly Japanese consumer products by local foreign trade corporations (FTCs). The great demand for products such as videocassette recorders, radios, and color television sets has been the cause of one form of corruption in China, involving resale of goods, illegal sale of goods, and illegal price increases. Tariffs were put in place to protect the economy from further foreign exchange drain back in the late 1980s. Average import tariffs are nearly impossible to calculate because they vary from region to region, seemingly governed by the whim of individual customs officials. Yet import tariffs on consumer products are extremely high, which slows the import of such products to China, and increases the number of ventures producing them inside China. The Japanese firms in the consumer market are extremely competitive in China, mainly because of their close proximity and strong presence in remote provinces through their large *soga sosha* trading firms.

### What is the profile of the typical Chinese urban and rural consumer?

The typical Chinese urban consumer is drawing a paycheck whose level has increased dramatically over the last five to seven years, but many of those gains have been eliminated by inflation. They live in a small but relatively new apartment, are married and typically have one child. Rent, medical care, and day care/education are all heavily subsidized, and a large portion of their income

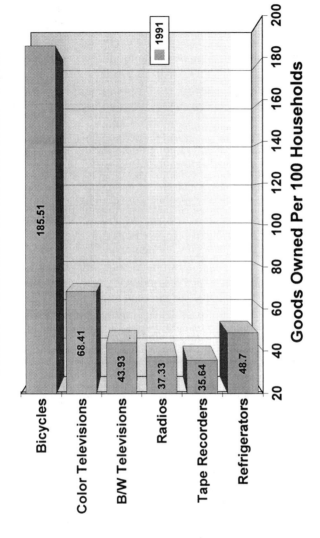

## What Chinese Households Own

| | |
|---|---|
| Bicycles | 185.51 |
| Color Televisions | 68.41 |
| B/W Televisions | 43.93 |
| Radios | 37.33 |
| Tape Recorders | 35.64 |
| Refrigerators | 48.7 |

☐ 1991

Goods Owned Per 100 Households

20  40  60  80  100  120  140  160  180  200

**Source:** *Statistical Yearbook of China.*

goes into food and other consumable goods. An extraordinary amount of attention is placed on the needs and wants of their child, but they have also made conscious efforts to improve their own lifestyle. In 1994, the typical household already possesses most of the trapping of modern, urban life we associate with the middle class in the West. They have a washing machine, refrigerator, color television, and stereo. Many are looking to expand or upgrade their consumer goods by buying VCRs, larger televisions, and even computers. A large percentage of households are still without a phone, though phone service is assessed through collective lines. The householder may work two or more jobs, in an effort to prosper from the highly segmented growth of China's economy.

The rural consumer has also seen their standard of living increase dramatically over the last ten years. Many are now in a situation similar to the urban household a decade ago. However, they will often forego many "necessities," as defined by Western standards, in order to access additional consumer goods. They will have access to electricity, own a radio and probably a television.

### What is the average income of the Chinese citizen?

Average urban income in China is officially only 150 RmB per month, about $15. However, the figure is perhaps twice this amount when one factors in unrecorded income from second jobs. Personal savings are high as well, and may raise the figure even higher.

### How much money does the Chinese consumer have to spend?

The Chinese people have $250 billion in domestic savings and an estimated additional $250 billion socked away and not held in low-interest bearing bank accounts. These savings, however, are in the form of non-convertible Chinese currency; the Chinese currently possess about $10 billion in foreign exchange disposable income.

Estimates of Chinese disposable income vary dramatically based on the region surveyed and the methods employed. Reliable data now places about 16 million Chinese in the category of "affluent," that is, with monthly incomes of at least Yuan 800 (or $1,655 a year). While still extremely poor by Western standards, one needs to take into account that this population is overwhelmingly urban and enjoys a large subsidization of many of their basic needs. One estimate suggests that the average Chinese urban household spends only 13 percent of its income on rent, education, medical and welfare payments. Therefore, a large proportion of a typical urban consumer's income is disposable income.

McKinsey and Co. make even more optimistic projections. By their estimates, over 60 million Chinese currently have annual per capita incomes of $1,000 or more, at the going exchange rate. The firm forecasts that this number could rise to compose a consumer market of 200 million by the year 2000.

### Who are the "big spenders" in new China?

China's "consumer aristocracy" is made up of growing numbers of private business people (mainly men), their shopping-crazed wives (and mistresses), officials on the take or abusing a state expense account, newlyweds on a one-time splurge, and gangsters. These people, who frequent the dark karaoke clubs by night and gleaming new department stores by day, have been dubbed "da kuan," or "big money."

### Does China have a middle class?

Yes. It's growing fast and driving up sales of consumer goods in urban areas. In 1992, sales in China's 35 largest department stores soared by 31 percent, indicated by an Economic Information Daily survey. Sales of indoor exercise equipment and air conditioners weren't the only products coveted by emerging consumers. Imported cameras jumped 43 percent; jewelry 44 percent; cosmetics 34 percent; home appliances 39 percent; and western suits 110 percent.

An office clerk at a city telephone company earns 1,500 yuan per month; a transfer agent at a bank earns 400 yuan per month. More and more, however, you meet people who have done well for themselves and are becoming capable entrepreneurs. A friend of mine who worked at Shenda Telephone company in Shenzhen, saved her money until she could open two stores to sell telephones. With the profits from the stores she invested in real estate and now wants to invest in stocks. She is not alone in Shenzhen. She earns enough to buy luxuries such as stereos and television equipment, a motorcycle, and high fashion. Literally thousands of people like her now live and do business in South China and fuel a fast-expanding consumer market. China's new middle (capitalist) class will play an increasingly important role in the growth of Asia's consumer market overall. Currently, Japan is home to the largest middle class in Asia, and Indonesia is second. Soon China will be third.

### Is China's retail market ready for upscale, brand name, consumer goods?

In "pockets of affluence," the luxury consumer market has proven a rich vein, namely in Guangzhou, Shanghai, Beijing, and Shenzhen. In these cities foreign retailers can effectively increase brand awareness among status-conscious Chinese, and could see sales soar. Consider the lead recently taken by Dickson Concepts (International), whose Dickson's stores are well-known in Singapore, Hong Kong, Taiwan, and Europe. Led by its retail maven, Dickson Poon, the company launched its international watch and jewelry brand names (which it distributes) with major exhibitors in four cities of China, $65 million to be invested in retail outlets, property, and a business consulting service, and the opening of two department stores, one in Shanghai and the other in Shenzhen. A year before the company's Innovions Holdings subsidiary started a handful of manufacturing plants to facilitate low-cost production of its luxury product line, to be sold inside and outside China. Bold is the only way to describe Dickson Poon, yet the approach may be appropriate in building brand name dominance among China's elite class before the competition. The residual product profile could last for years.

### Does the Chinese consumer have the buying power to support retail business?

In the first half of 1993 China's 10 million retail enterprises secured sales of $96.3 billion, up 24 percent over 1992. The total retail market is estimated at $200 billion annually, and is expected to triple by the year 2000. Individual household income has skyrocketed in recent years, particularly in urban areas and the developing coastal region.

*Do Chinese buy consumer gifts at certain times of the year, for example at New Year's?*

The Chinese are not obliged to exchange store-bought gifts to one another during Chinese Lunar New Year in early February, though some companies do exchange them. Nor do many Chinese celebrate Christmas. However, gift sales do increase during collage exams as parents purchase gifts for their graduating children. Consumer buying patterns in China remain somewhat of a mystery behind the fact that they are strongly affected by promotional activities.

## 4. China as a Site for Service Industries

As in other developing nations, Chinese trade officials have imposed strict regulations on service ventures operating in the People's Republic. China's market remains restricted or closed to most foreign service industries: banking, insurance, legal services, accountancy, shipping, retailing, and provision of after-sales service. Foreign lawyers, accountants, banks and financial institutions must largely limit their activities to servicing foreign firms or to addressing business matters outside China, such as Chinese firms' investing in the United States. Only one insurance company from the United States is known to have successfully entered the China market, while government-owned companies maintain a monopoly in the sector. American bankers have flocked into China following their corporate customers, yet they cannot perform many of their normal functions, including lending funds and guaranteeing loans. Foreign firms are also not allowed to engage in shipment inspection services.

Changes are being made, however. U.S. shipping companies have established ventures in China and can solicit cargo directly. China has also opened the market further to airlines with the approval for two U.S. carriers to add flights from China to the U.S. and the addition of an all-cargo route for an American carrier. Retailing is opening to foreign investment on a selective basis. Selective bank branches have been approved, but are restricted from dealing in the local currency (the renminbi). Joint ventures in accounting and commodity inspection services have been established. And there are indications that the insurance industry will open selectively to foreign participation.

Advertising agencies from around the world are now producing promotional angles to sell the Chinese. Since 1979, the advertising industry has grown at an average annual rate of 50 percent. The country's 680 domestic agencies pulled in $163 million (in RMB currency) in 1985 and over five times that figure 1993. Advertising by American firms on Chinese television was initiated when the Central Chinese Television purchased 64 hours of American programming from CBS. During these hours, U.S. firms such as Boeing, Kodak, Proctor & Gamble, and IBM advertised on Chinese television for the first time. In 1986, Walt Disney Company traded 104 episodes of "Mickey Mouse and Donald Duck" animated cartoons, to be aired in China over the course of two years, in exchange for two minutes of commercial time per program, worth about $20,000 a minute. (See the figures for more about advertising in China.)

**OIL AND GAS FIELD MACHINERY AND SERVICES.** China's move towards developing its national petroleum resources is driven by the realization that the country is incapable of driving a modern industrial economy on its current primary energy resource, coal. Today, energy is among China's highest development priorities, and a large portion of its activities are focused on exploiting its petroleum resources. Offshore discoveries and fruitful explorations in the Tarim Basin are expected to bring future investments in production and pipeline facilities, as well as refinery construction. Furthermore, the opening of the East China Sea and new onshore areas to foreign exploration and production represents an expanding market for foreign oil and gas companies.

The total market size of China's petroleum industry was estimated at $5.5 billion in 1993. Analysts expect the market will continue to grow at an average of 10 percent annually for the next several years, as the country expands production and links interior petroleum facilities to the oil-consuming regions of Eastern China. The growth in the market for imports is expected to outpace the development of the entire industry, as import levels rise at an average of 20 percent annually for the next few years. Major opportunities for foreign involvement in the petroleum field are divided between onshore platform equipment and services ($1 billion), offshore production equipment and services ($1 billion) and major pipeline projects ($1 billion). Geophysical instruments and secondary recovery equipment represents an additional $200 million market for foreign imports.

## 5. China as a Site for Tourist Ventures

With the rapid increase of visiting tourists and international business people to the People's Republic since 1978, foreign firms have undertaken scores of tourist ventures, such as hotels and other services for foreigners, often as a strategy to balance the foreign exchange accounts of separate joint ventures operated by these same firms, or other foreign firms, in China. Some of these hotels have proved quite profitable, both in revenue as well as benefits to their international image; however, since many major Chinese cities now experience hotel glut, some of these ventures are in trouble. China now discourages small tertiary-sector ventures such as taxi services, photo processing labs, and other quick-return investments designed to serve foreigners.

After the dramatic drop in tourism following the Tiananmen crisis of 1989, the Chinese tourist industry has recently surged to new heights. Today the number of foreign visitors to the PRC is nearly twice the annual rate prior to 1989. Taiwan is largely responsible for the recovery of the Chinese tourist industry. As restrictions on Taiwanese travel in mainland China have been lifted, record numbers of Taiwan's citizens are visiting the PRC. China's tourist industry has also benefitted from an influx of tourists from the former Soviet Union. With the lifting of travel restrictions following the breakup of the U.S.S.R., tourist visits by C.I.S. citizens to China has jumped 90 percent in less than three years. The tourist boom is helping China's battled hotel industry recover and is permitting many foreign-invested hotels to show a profit for the first time. Hotels in China's major urban areas are expected to enjoy occupancy rates of 75-80 percent through 1994. The boom has led to a recent spurt of new hotel deals, many of which are concentrated in nationally-designated 'tourist zones.' China believes its international tourism receipts will reach $5.1 billion by 1995, and could climb to $11 billion by the year 2000.

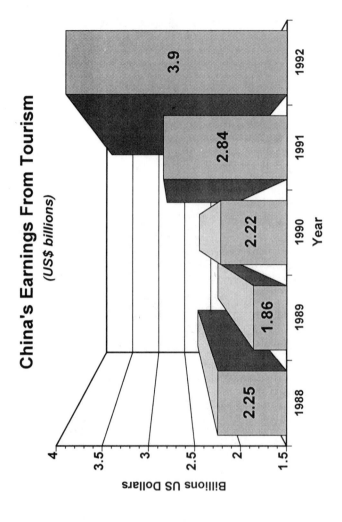

China's Earnings From Tourism
*(US$ billions)*

3.9   2.84   2.22   1.86   2.25

Year

1992   1991   1990   1989   1988

Billions US Dollars

4   3.5   3   2.5   2   1.5

**Source:** *China's National Tourism Authority.*

Fueling this trend will be the emergence of a new tourism triangle linking Hong Kong, China, and Taiwan in a network of transportation alternatives catering to business and recreational travellers. With the return of Hong Kong to Chinese sovereignty and the re-establishment of direct flights between Taiwan and the mainland, the desire of Chinese to travel within Greater China will create increasing demand for foreign travel service management, skills, and technology.

## RESEARCHING CHINA'S CHANGING MARKETPLACE

In appraising the China market, a firm should begin by recognizing a few broad trends in China's recent buying patterns. First, there has been a continuing shift from the importing of primary goods, including food and live animals, to that of manufactured goods. In 1984, China's imports of manufactured goods amounted to 81 percent of all imports; in 1994, the figure had risen over 90 percent, and the trend will continue. Secondly, China's $43.2 billion annual imports originate from many more sources than in the past; Italy and France can now claim almost $1 billion each per year, and this implies that the market is becoming much less a "vast, untapped market," and much more a "niche" market, where intelligent marketing strategists can sell sophisticated and specialized products that make up only one element in a complex set of equipment. Thirdly, the market is rapidly diversifying into a multitude of small, but expanding, new markets that include areas of high tech manufactured products.

The infrastructural demands of the China market remain lasting areas of opportunity for the foreign supplier: $2.5 billion per year for crude materials excluding fuels; $7.1 billion per year for iron and steel; and 4.5 billion per year for chemical products. But smaller markets are emerging alongside the traditional sectors: $1.3 billion per year for power machinery; $2.5 billion per year for telecommunications; $3.1 billion per year for land vehicles; $2 billion per year for specialized industrial machinery; and $8 billion per year for machinery and transport equipment. American companies should be able to significantly increase their $7.1 billion sales to China (1993) in these emerging market niches.

*Is it difficult to obtain market information about these market niches?*

Up-to-date information concerning the supply and demand of specific products in various areas of China remains difficult to obtain. The scarcity of market information makes it largely impossible to measure the size of the market for specific products, ascertain customer tastes and preferences, and compare various avenues for product distribution. Thus, as with other developing markets, China's should be analyzed by personnel at ground level, inside China, as well as through written reports. In such reports, especially those produced by Chinese sources, large population numbers are often mistaken for large numbers of potential buyers. Even with the help of a Chinese partner, ascertaining how big the China market actually is for a certain foreign product can be a time-consuming and costly process. Thus, any preinvestment activity in the China market should be directed toward feasibility studies and product-usage surveys rather than initiating a corporate presence in China, which can be much more expensive and will likely produce only negligible returns. Preinvestment in China might also include the strategic cultivation of contacts among China's trade officials and participation in trade seminars, technical seminars, and trade fairs by company representatives destined to be expatriated to China.

*How does a foreign company best approach the China market? Who are the buyers of foreign products?*

The China market is currently being fragmented into four or five distinct market sectors, based not so much on the type of product, but type of Chinese buyer. The largest market segment in dollar value continues to be the *Chinese government* and its related purchasing agents. These entities purchase the large, capital-intensive products such as airplanes and turnkey power plants that represent the greatest percentage of Chinese imports in dollar terms. In addition, large *state-owned Chinese companies* and their trading arms represent a separate market segment for U.S. exporters. These groups concentrate their purchases on large industrial equipment, manufacturing processes and technology licensing agreements. A third category is Chinese *light industry*. These companies, often collectives or privately owned, are also interested in importing manufacturing technology. A new category of *service markets* has also arisen in China. While many service fields continue to be blocked to foreign participation, loosening regulations are allowing entry by new market players. Finally, China's *expanding urban consumer class* yields a new market of direct endusers for foreign products. This schematic offers a variety of approaches to the China market for foreign firms. Small companies who have developed an expertise in a particular market niche can explore that niche in China. Large multinational companies may have the capability to market to all of the above segments. Consider the possible strategy mix for a large U.S. telecommunications company atttempting to address all of these market segments:

| | |
|---|---|
| *Chinese Government:* | Network planning and integration |
| *State-owned Companies:* | Switching Systems<br>Private-Branch Exchanges (PBX) |
| *Light Industry:* | Licensing agreement to manufacture telephones |
| *Services:* | Network management training and periodic software upgrades |
| *Consumers:* | Direct retail of cellular phones and pagers |

Such a marketing mix will not appear overnight. U.S. companies should target their strengths and try to gain a lever into the China market by offering a superior product or service. The nature of the Chinese economy will encourage expansion and further market penetration, and over the long term, this company should have the opportunity to radiate into most or all of the above market segments.

### What are the selling opportunities in Taiwan?

Taiwan's Six Year National Development Plan (1991-1996) includes plans for numerous and, for U.S. firms, potentially lucrative infrastructural projects. The projects are divided into four sectors—transportation, telecommunications, power generation, and environmental protection. Projects in these areas make up two-thirds of the total plan and amount to $192 billion in total investment.

The breakdown of investment is as follow:

| | |
|---|---|
| *Transportation* | $121.9 billion |
| *Power Generation* | $ 38.9 billion |
| *Telecommunications* | $ 16.3 billion |
| *Environmental Protection* | $ 15.1 billion |

The consulting companies of William Reinfeld & Associates, Productivity Asia, Ltd., Arthur D. Little Asia Pacific, Inc., with The American Institute in Taiwan, estimate the dollar value for participating U.S. firms could be as significant as follows:

| | |
|---|---|
| *Transportation* | $97.6 billion |
| *Power Generation* | $30.0 billion |
| *Telecommunications* | $14.5 billion |
| *Environmental Protection* | $12.4 billion |

Of course, foreign engineering and consulting companies from around the world have descended upon the island wanting to win a piece of this huge pie. Unfortunately, the Plan lays out plans for projects which are already underway and already mired in problems resulting from Taiwan's opaque, often corrupt, and certainly not in line with international standards, bidding process for these large projects. American Bechtal, Inc. is one of the foreign engineering firms participating in the constructions of Taipei's new subway system, a project that has come to epitomize the problems foreign companies encounter in dealing with Taiwan's decision making bureaucracy.

### *Can you expect selling to cash-rich Taiwan to be relatively quick and easy, at least compared to China?*

Taiwanese customers come to the negotiating table armed with a great deal of knowledge about their industry and the product you are trying to sell. You won't find any suckers in Taiwan prone to sign a quick-kill cash deal. In fact, unless you really have something they want, and can't get anywhere else, do not think selling to Taiwan will be easy just because you have heard or read that "the Taiwanese are loaded with money." The typical

Taiwanese businessperson really doesn't want to deal with a foreigner unless they absolutely must to obtain what they need. First, the foreigner doesn't normally speak their language, which makes them uneasy because they can't speak perfect English. Second, all communication such as faxes, would have to be done in English, presumably, and they do not feel that they can accommodate that. In other words, dealing directly with a foreign supplier is a hassle best avoided. Because of this, the use of a local Taiwanese agent is essential in building customer relations in Taiwan.

# ENTERING

# THE MARKET

*"Every time we get a piece of information, it changes by the next time we talk."*

**—An American marketer working in China**

## CHINA IS A "MARKET OF ONE BILLION"...NOT!

China's market of one billion consumers is really a set of seven densely populated areas of economic resurgences. Each contains growing numbers of consumers who have the disposable income to buy foreign imports, enterprises which are attempting to upgrade by purchasing new production technology, and localities where foreign investment has been concentrated. However, the China market as a whole is not yet thoroughly tied together across these regions in terms of communications, team sport links, or distribution channels. Each region also has built up its own synergies with outside economies. Guangdong and Fujian have become linked economically to Hong Kong and Taiwan. Korean and Japanese investment has been concentrated in Liaoning Province, specifically in the cities of Dalian and Shenyang. Parts of China's northern border area is becoming linked to Russia while additional ties can be expected to grow between the Southern Provinces and Vietnam. Thus, investigating specific economic regions of Greater China is the first step for the company interested in getting involved in the so-called market of one billion.

### *How do I launch a product line in a country as large as China?*

China's trading landscape is comprised of seven distinct economic regions. Historically, virtually impenetrable barriers exist between regions to cross-province trade, movement of goods, as well as labor. Now, regionalism is dissolving though it remains a key factor to consider carefully in a business plan. Only a handful of products can be distributed on a truly national basis; most enter regional markets selectively. The task of supplying a venture, or financing one, from outside its regional location is still impossible in the majority of cases.. For some years the lack of geographic integration of economic areas in the PRC will remain a significant barrier to foreign traders, not to mention Chinese companies which desire to sell nationwide.

Only large companies have the financial wherewithal to set up an office in Beijing and all large cities in China to begin the process of setting up a distribution network. Smaller companies and those getting their feet wet in the market need to concentrate on only one of China's 30 provinces at first, and expand from there. The first choice for most companies is Guangdong Province in which there are now 25,000 enterprises and 3 million workers involved in import/export manufacturing. During 1993 imports grew enormously in many other Chinese provinces as well: Fujian (38 percent), Hobei (45 percent), Hunan (178 percent), Jiangshu (32 percent), Jiangxi (37 percent) Liaoning (37 percent), Ningxia Hui Autonomous Region (55 percent), Shaanxi (49 percent), Yunnan (31 percent), and Zhejian (62 percent). Each of these provinces presents a unique business climate and set of import priorities. For the company just entering the market, think about skipping Beijing alltogether and setting up a representative office in a less traveled area where your competition might be lagging. Should you decide on Guangdong or Fujian, you may be able to service customers there from an office in comfortable Hong Kong.

### How do I begin the task of researching the potential of my product or service in the China market?

Start with finding out about the needs of your Chinese customer. You might consider hiring one of the scores of companies now conducting market research in China. The information provided by private companies is generally more accurate than anything that the Chinese government can offer through its Statistical Bureau. This information, however, is often outdated and always of questionable accuracy. Market information companies normally specialize in a single industrial sector. Don't go with a generalist. Find someone who has experience in your industry in China and is currently tightly focused on that sector. Your Chinese enterprise partner may be willing to supply you with market research, but the quality is usually exceedingly low and unqualified; moreover, figures can be skewed for the purpose of attracting you as a joint venture partner.

### What kind of market research companies exist in China?

The days are gone of having to rely on MOFTEC or the State Statistical Bureau for data on the China market. More than a dozen market research firms in the form of foreign joint ventures now have offices in Guangzhou, Shanghai, and Beijing. All concentrate on codifying and monitoring Chinese consumer tastes and trends. Local Chinese-run firms have started up as well. A local choice is best because each province varies widely in terms of tastes, preferences, buying power, and exposure to foreign products.

After the 14th Party Congress committed China to shift from a planned economy to one moved by the market in 1992, the service sector was flagged for high growth and a source of new jobs for unneeded state administrators. Market research companies began to come into existence, run by former bureaucrats. The largest is China Market Research Organization in Beijing started by ten former state officials in 1986, with a staff of 70 and a foreign joint venture partner. More partnerships in this area are in the pipeline. The proliferation is fueled as much by indigenous firms as it is by foreign companies. Approximately 20,000 new products are now launched in the PRC each year, and increasingly Chinese manufacturer's are paying to have ample market research conducted on the market. Hundreds of surveys have now been compiled, most based on street or home interviews of consumers since only one in 100 Chinese own a telephone. (The Chinese actually enjoy being quizzed on their opinions about products and this has greatly facilitated the research process.)

### How do I find out which entities I need to deal with in order to sell my product in China?

Distribution channels in the PRC vary by industry and product line. However, more than one distribution channel can be pursued simultaneously. Start with the country desk officer at the Department of Commerce, as well as the U.S. and Foreign Commercial Service in Beijing, in order to determine the level of demand for your product. Then turn to relevant ministry that controls your product's industrial classification. Use the Chinese consulates in the United States to put you in touch with the foreign trade arm of that ministry. At the same time, contact MOFTEC and CITIC to check for further trade leads. Investigate trading companies in your city that specialize in the PRC, and see if they have any experience in your industry. Check to see if your city has a sister-city relationship with a city in China, and then follow-up with their regional economic development corporation. Target dynamic market centers in China such as Shanghai, Guangdong, and Liaoning, and interface with their local trade and investment corporations. Or try regionally based trade and investment agencies, such as the entities governing the Yangzte River or the areas bordering the Sea of Japan. You should also pursue trade agents based in Hong Kong, but don't put them on retainer and ensure that they can offer coverage of more than simply South China. Finally, check for private regional or industrial groups that now have a presence in China. For example, the American Soybean Association now has an office representing U.S. growers in Beijing. The California Chamber of Commerce represents California businesses in China through its Hong Kong office. And the city of San Diego has a sister-city trade relationship with Yantai.

### What's the best, and most cost-effective way to introduce a product in the China market?

Attempt first to sell directly to the Chinese end-user. Local bureaus and FTCs have influence over the Chinese end-user, making it difficult, though not impossible, to approach them directly. All parties—the end-user, FTC, and local ministry or bureau—must agree on import sales after lengthy negotiations. The process puts foreigners in a weak position because they must locate not only the end-user interested in purchasing their goods, but an FTC with the needed foreign exchange and the governmental authority to approve the sale. One good sign is that the end-user plays an increasingly important role in the acquisition of foreign goods. A number of avenues lead to direct contact with customers in China that you need to consider in your marketing strategy. The first is to locate a foreign trade corporation in your industry which buys and sells on behalf of end-users. FTCs maintain lists of client firms and their specific needs; there are 3,000 of them spread all across the country. As enterprises try to circumvent the hassle and cost of being forced to deal with foreign suppliers through an FTC, they are fighting for and often obtaining the right to register as new foreign trade enterprises. When they do this, they immediately enter the business of import and export trade, not just for their own needs, but on behalf of other companies that they are connected with. Thus, the list of FTCs will continue to grow in the short run as China moves toward a state of complete decentralization of trade in which all Chinese enterprises will be able to buy and sell with complete autonomy.

Another means by which you can locate appropriate foreign trade corporations is to solicit the services of one of the many business information services springing up in every Chinese city. (See list in the appendix.) Chinese city telephone books are another source as are Chinese government offices, which can provide lists of FTCs that work in a specific industry. For example, the Ministry of Electronics would be a good place to seek a list of FTCs that import electronic components. Remember, however, that information gathered by this route will be less accurate and timely than that obtained through a private nongovernmental source. Yet another method is to utilize an agent, of which there are three types. The first is the Hong Kong-based agent, who can provide direct connections to FTCs inside China in specific industries. The key is to link up with a Hong Kong agent which truly possesses industry-specific links in China. Inquire as to whether the company maintains offices inside China, and in which cities. An agent in Hong Kong that claims to sell electronics goods in China but that has no office in Shanghai, where China's electronic industry is focused, may not be your best choice. Additionally, both public and private agencies have popped up inside China, which you should interview as a potential representative. Again, the agents that have emerged out of public entities will not be as efficient as those that are privately owned. A Chinese agent must prove to you that it offers multiple and long running relationships with clients that you want to sell to. Find a proficient Chinese company in your business that is NOT government owned.

Perhaps the best way to get into contact with FTCs and with Chinese end-users is to cooperate with a Chinese-owned entity located inside China. Because of the cultural barriers between foreign and Chinese business people, there are drawbacks inherent in both dealing through a solely Chinese-controlled entity or through a solely foreign-owned entity. The former may have the connections and guanxi but lack the marketing know-how, while the later may provide the efficiency and marketing know-how but lack the government connections that win deals, and the necessary knowledge of China's administrative trade system. Remember that even if you do business directly with an FTC, you will need an agent to represent you inside China; in other words, it is not recommended that you deal directly with a Chinese FTC. Your Chinese agent (partner) actively promotes your product line to the FTC, and negotiates on your behalf with the FTC. In short you will need a Chinese agent to maintain the relationship between you and the FTC.

Consider forming a combination of the two by teaming up with a Chinese agency that has the guanxi connections in place. Such a Chinese partner would offer an information channel with all of the relevant FTCs and their affiliated companies in your industry. The Chinese believe that American companies offer the best price for the highest quality equipment, but they also will tell you that the Americans in China often lack the guanxi to make deals work. Consider seriously this advice from prominent Hong Kong trader Li Wo Hing: "American companies need to work with a joint venture trading partner in order to market their goods in the PRC."

One of the best marketing strategies, and certainly the most challenging to U.S. firms, is educating end-users. This strategy allows firms to enter the market through the end-user, placing the products directly into the workplace where quality and performance can be seen. Name recognition grows from here.

Also watch for companies which are in the process of listing on a stock market inside or outside China, or have just listed. They will likely have fresh cash to spend on equipment renovation. After they purchase an initial package of imported equipment, they normally cannot afford large purchases again, unless their foreign exchange revenues suddenly skyrocket. Take advantage of their stock issue windfall when the opportunity to sell is at its peak.

### How important are references from other Chinese buyers?

A real estate consultant with the largest real estate firm in Canada, came up to me after a seminar and asked for advice in dealing with a number of Hong Kong real estate companies that had remained reticent to hire him as a marketing consultant. He explained to me his frustration at getting hired by the Hong Kong Chinese that he had dealt with at these companies. I asked if he knew any of these people from past business endeavors or social ties. He said no. He has met with the Hong Kong representatives periodically, they inquire about his services, he makes a sales presentation, and tells them his price. He was at a loss as to why he was not being hired. My advice was simply: "Do a freebie for one of these Hong Kong guys in order to get a reference." Without an introductory reference that he could use in pitching his services in Hong Kong's tight-knit real estate community, he was never going to be hired. He was still an outsider.

The same advice generalizes for all industries throughout Greater China. You need personal introductions and references *from other Chinese* in the business community to be successful. Your business just won't get very far without them.

*Are "networking" and "cold calling" appropriate ways of introducing a product in Greater China?*

The only way to expand your China business network and social milieu is via formal introduction by a Chinese counterpart who sees a clear purpose in making the introduction. The yuppie phenomenon of business networking, in which you attend cocktail parties and meet business partners, is only nascent in most of Asia. Business connection-making happens at the initiation of a Chinese associate (who is also your friend), who can trust you. He or she will introduce you to opportunities that they feel are appropriate and compatible with your interests; they also will help themselves and their friends to those they introduce to you. Introductions are not made lightly, they are made for a reason. The more reasons you can offer your Chinese colleagues to introduce you to others, the better off you'll be. Cold-calling potential customers is a strictly Western business practice.

**INTRODUCING IS A GRAVE RESPONSIBILITY.** When you are introduced to a Chinese business person, the person who introduced you instantly becomes *responsible* for the quality of the business relationship you form with the new associate. This explains why Chinese take any introduction very seriously. The business relationship generated by a formal introduction reflects on the personal integrity of the introducer.

Sometimes your close Chinese friend will warn you before he introduces someone to you. He may state that he can't guarantee the credibility of the other party and won't be taking responsibility for the relationship that might be forged. Remember too, that sometimes you will not be introduced to a stranger by your Chinese friend because your friend may not see any reason why the two of you should be introduced. This might feel awkward for you, but it's part of introduction protocol in China.

**CONSULTANTS AS MATCHMAKERS.** A consultant can be a good liaison, but don't fall into the "Chopstick Syndrome," the tendency to hire a Chinese person to represent your company because "he has a cousin in Taipei" or "a well-connected uncle in Chongqing." Hire a consultant based on his verifiable potential to introduce your company to the highest echelon of potential customers and relevant government officials. Don't measure a consultant's value on how much he or she will cost you, but on the amount of money, time, and resources he or she can save you in gaining fast entry into a desired China market.

Here's an example, based on my own experience, of how much of an asset a trained consultant/introducer can be to your company. As a manufacturer's agent for a large American company, I decided to attend a "Purchasing Mission" from China for the purpose of introducing the high technology products that I represented to potential Chinese customers. I solicited the assistance of a consultant (also an old friend) who was raised in the country from where the mission came from. He had connections with the country's consulate, which was involved in sponsoring the mission. Before the arrival of the mission, he set up a formal meeting with the visiting delegation to be held after an opening VIP reception, in private. The conference started the next day and it soon became apparent that the most important Chinese were suspiciously absent. "Plane delayed," was the excuse. The American executives who had paid to attend were irate. Later, our meeting was held as preplanned, the delegation finally arriving late in the afternoon. We made great strides in setting up a major purchase of products, all because of the prior arrangements made by my well-connected consultant. Incidentally, the delegation hadn't been delayed at all. They had made a stop in Las Vegas enroute to the conference!

### *What questions should be answered in a China market feasibility study?*

— Does the marketing study profile potential customers? What do Chinese customers need in terms of new products? Can customers afford to pay more for improved and/or newer products?

— Does the marketing study include an analysis of products made by existing Chinese factories? How could these products be improved? Are similar products on the Chinese market?

— Does the marketing study profile domestic and foreign competition, taking into account the possible appearance of a competing joint venture? Does it calculate the time and resources required to break into new channels of distribution?

— Does the marketing plan outline methods for breaking into new markets in China, taking into account the difficulties and expenses involved? Will sales be regional only? How long will it take to expand market base?

### *What institutions have the most experience with the China trade?*

The U.S.-China Business Council is the oldest private organization of businesses dealing with China in the United States. The Council is based in Washington D.C. and frequently lobbies Congress and U.S. government agencies on behalf of U.S. firms. The Council also publishes the widely read China Business Review, a monthly profile of business activity in the P.R.C. Contact information for the Council is given at the end of this book. Other relevant organizations with extensive business experience in China include the U.S. Chamber of Commerce, with offices in Beijing and Shanghai, and the China Association of Enterprises with Foreign Investment, based in Beijing. Contact information for these agencies may also be found in the appendix.

## OBTAINING MARKET INFORMATION

The following lists federal and nonprofit agencies capable of providing additional, more detailed information regarding trading and investing in the People's Republic of China. For the most part, the information held by these agencies is provided free-of-charge or for a nominal fee to U.S. businesses. The section concludes with selected contact information for Chinese commercial agencies.

### Market Research

The U.S. Department of Commerce/International Trade Administration's Office of the PRC and Hong Kong supplies basic information to U.S. firms interested in developing commercial relations with China and directs business people to additional sources of information. The office also publishes reports on economic and business conditions in China. Their address is:

> U.S. Department of Commerce
> International Trade Administration
> Office of the PRC and Hong Kong
> Room H2317
> Washington, D.C. 20230
> Tel.: (202) 377-3583

**Foreign Commercial Service Officers** are posted at the United States Embassy in Beijing and at the United States Consulates in Guangzhou, Shanghai, Shenyang, and Hong Kong. The Commercial Officers are able to provide American business people with up-to-date information on local business opportunities and conditions and on the current economic and political situation in China. The commercial sections of the Embassy and Consulates have limited quantities of office and audio-visual equipment available for use by American business people. Correspondence to the Embassy and Consulates should be sent to the following addresses.

> U.S. Embassy
> 3 Xiushui Bei Jie
> Jianguomenwai
> Beijing, People's Republic of China
> Tel.: 532-3831
> Tlx.: 22701 AMEMB CN    Fax: (011-86-1) 532-3297

> U.S. Consulate General
> China Hotel Office Tower
> Room 1262-64
> Liu Hua Lu
> Guangzhou, People's Republic of China
> Tel.: 677842, or 663388, ext. 1293/4
> Tlx.: 44888 GZDFH CN
> (Attn.: U.S. Consulate)    Fax: (011-86-20) 66-6409

U.S. Consulate General
1469 Huaihai Zhong Lu
Shanghai, People's Republic of China
Tel.: 379-880
Tlx.: 33383 USCG CN    Fax: (011-86-21) 33-4122

U.S. Consulate General
No. 40, Lane 4, Section 5
Sanjing Street, Heping District
Shenyang, People's Republic of China
Tel.: 290038
Tlx.: 80011 AMCS CN    Fax: (011-86-24) 29-0074

U.S. Consulate General
26 Garden Road
Hong Kong
Tel.: 5-211467
Tlx.: 63141 USDOC HX    Fax: (011-852-5) 845-0943

U.S. Commercial Service Officers in the **International Trade Administration's district offices** throughout the United States can furnish business people interested in China with basic information.

The Marketing Publications and Services Division of the U.S. and Foreign Commercial Service's **Export Promotion Services (EPS)** commissions market research on China and publishes the results. The **Event Promotions Division (EPD)** of EPS certifies trade shows and exhibitions in China that meet the criteria of the Trade Fair Certification Program. The addresses for EPC and EPD are:

U.S. Department of Commerce
U.S. & Foreign Commercial Service
Marketing Programs Division
Room H2116
Washington, D.C. 20230

U.S. Department of Commerce
U.S. & Foreign Commercial Service
Trade Events Division
Room H1510
Washington, D.C. 20230

## Export Financing

The U.S. Trade and Development Program (TDP) is part of the International Development Cooperation Agency. It finances feasibility studies and other planning services for major public sector projects in developing countries that are potential export markets for U.S. goods and services. TDP also co-finances, on a reimbursable grant basis, planning services for projects in which a private U.S. investor potentially has equity participation.

About 25 percent of TDP's $20 million budget is directed to projects in China. Since 1983, MOFTEC has served as TDP's principal point of contact in China and now compiles a list of projects for TDP's consideration. TDP chooses the projects that appear to meet its criteria and, in most cases, sends a technical team or definitional mission to investigate the project on site. Upon the mission's recommendation, TDP agrees to fund a full-scale feasibility study.

TDP grants to China are used to pay for the services of U.S. firms chosen by the grantee on the basis of federal competitive procurement procedures. For additional information on TDP's grants to China, write to:

U.S. Trade and Development Program
Director for Asia
Room 309, SA-16
Washington, D.C. 20523
Tel.: (703) 875-4357

**Export-Import Bank of the United States.** Eximbank lends or guarantees credits to a foreign borrower or to an intermediary to finance U.S. exports. Its current policy is to offer direct loans only when a U.S. company is competing against a foreign bidder who is assisted by a government-subsidized export credit. Eximbank offers China the most favorable interest rates and repayment terms allowed under the Arrangement on Official Export Credits of the Organization for Economic Development (OECD). China has made limited use of the long-term credits offered it by Eximbank and has not used Eximbank's medium- and short-term facilities, preferring instead the concessional, aid-type financing available from other countries and the World Bank. Concessionary or "mixed" credits are offered by Eximbank only on a selective, case-by-case basis to combat predatory export financing by other countries. For additional information on Eximbank's China program, write to:

> Export-Import Bank of the United States
> Vice President for Asia
> 811 Vermont Avenue, NW
> Washington, D.C. 20571
> Tel.: (202) 566-2117

**Overseas Private Investment Corporation.** OPIC offers loans and loan guarantees to ventures in China (and elsewhere) involving substantial equity or risk exposure and management participation by U.S. companies. OPIC project financing is based on the economic, technical, marketing, and financial soundness of the project, with repayment anticipated from the project itself. Under this direct loan program, OPIC offers up to $5 million at commercial rates to small- and medium-size U.S. businesses investing in China. It also guarantees loans for China investments up to $50 million made by U.S. financial institutions to companies of any size.

OPIC provides political risk insurance to U.S. investors overseas. In China, OPIC provides insurance against the risks of expropriation and war/revolution/insurrection/civil strife. Coverage against the risk of inconvertibility of currency is not available because Chinese law affords no legal right to convert Chinese currency. In the case of disputes between the investor and his Chinese partner, OPIC insures against government frustration of the arbitration process outlined in the project agreement between the partners. There is no difference in the war coverage OPIC offers in China from that which it offers elsewhere. For further information about OPIC, write to:

Overseas Private Investment Corporation
1615 M Street, NW
Washington, D.C.
Tel.: (202) 457-7010

## Export Licensing

U.S. firms are encouraged to contact the Exporter Services Staff of the **Office of Export Licensing (OEL)** to obtain detailed information on licensing requirements for exports to China. No official determination on licensing can be made before a formal application is filed, but OEL can often provide an advisory opinion on the prospects for approval. OEL's address is:

U.S. Department of Commerce
Bureau of Export Administration
Office of Export Licensing
Exporter Services Staff
Room H1099
Washington, D.C. 20230
Tel.: (202) 377-4811

*What nonprofit organizations provide Chinese market information?*

**The U.S.-China Business Council,** formerly known as the National Council for U.S.-China Trade, is a private, nonprofit organization which assists its member firms in their business dealings with the People's Republic of China in a variety of ways. The Council also publishes the bimonthly China Business Review. Its address is:

U.S.-China Business Council
1818 N Street, NW
Suite 500
Washington, D.C. 20036
Tel.: (202) 429-0340

**The American Chamber of Commerce** maintains an office in Beijing and can provide information services to visiting American executives attending business meetings in the PRC.

American Chamber of Commerce (AMCHAM)
Great Wall Sheraton Hotel
Beijing 100026
Tel.: 500-5566 x2271
Fax: (001 86 1) 501-8273

*Can information be obtained from the Chinese embassy
in the U.S.? What about the Chinese government?*

The **Chinese Embassy** in Washington maintains a commercial section that can provide marketing information of a general nature, including lists of potential business partners such as agents and distributors. The address is:

Embassy of the People's Republic of China
2300 Connecticut Avenue, NW
Washington, D.C. 20008
Tel.: (202) 328-2520 or 2527

# CHAPTER 8

# CHANNELS OF

# DISTRIBUTION

*B*usiness people in America tend to take their country's distribution system for granted. Not only is the U.S. system of distribution extraordinarily efficient, terms and conditions of transport are typically fixed. China sits on the other extreme of international distribution systems. Hampered by an inadequate and overcrowded infrastructure, China's distribution system can tax the patience of the most savvy marketers. Companies cannot enter the China market expecting fixed terms and conditions; instead they should be prepared to negotiate and compromise at every stage until their goods finally reach the end-user.

## CHINA'S DISTRIBUTION REVOLUTION

Prior to 1985, large enterprises would deliver their output to one of three types of state-controlled wholesalers. The first type—

"number one wholesale stations"—provided both national and regional coverage, and were located in large cities only, including Beijing, Guangzhou, and Shanghai. All goods were shipped to these sites before being directed to a second and third tier of distribution. The second type of distributor covered only one province, and the third type covered only selected cities and counties. Some wholesale stations specialized in a certain product line but in general, products moved from type one, to two, down to the third. Delays were endemic and the red tape horrific. The system was deaf to consumer preference or current demand; in China's economy of scarcity everything would sell anyway. The majority of retail and commodity prices were controlled by the state. Now, in addition to using the old system, an enterprise can contact department stores and smaller customers directly. And department stores want to buy direct from the supplier because it cuts their costs by cutting out the commissioned state-run domestic trading corporation. Eighty percent of all retail sales are now made at decontrolled market prices. Only roughly 30 percent of commodity prices are set by the government. However, the older wholesalers have not vanished. Especially in South China, many of the old wholesalers have, in fact, resuscitated themselves and survived in the face of newly formed marketing outfits all over the country. They remain extremely well connected with, and knowledgeable of, the enterprises they have worked with in the past. Many are registered to handle product lines which newly formed distributors are not, at least as of yet.

Thus, as a foreign company, you want to locate as close to your market as possible since the customers want to contact your factory direct. Beyond local efforts to distribute products directly to customers, foreign companies have not yet been able to set up their own distribution networks that span provinces. Beyond the markets that you can serve directly, you will have to utilize the existing wholesale system.

### *What distribution and sales channels are available to the foreign firm in the PRC?*

Until several years ago, foreign suppliers were not concerned with marketing and distribution in China; they sold only to the government's import-export corporations, often without even knowing the identity of the end-user. Today, however, foreign companies use a variety of distribution channels to market their products in Chinese customers.

In the past 10 years, several hundred U.S. companies have established representative offices in China, the majority of which are located in Beijing and Shanghai. In the past, representative offices were viewed solely as 'liaison offices' that were forbidden by Chinese law from participating in direct sales or service relationships with clients. Companies seeking these relationships were forced to incorporate a subsidiary company within China, making the company liable for Chinese corporate taxes. However, this year China announced a major revision of its Company Law, the effect of which is to allow foreign companies to establish full branch offices in the P.R.C. These entities can provide full sales and service support to customers while continuing to pay corporate income taxes in their home company.

The relatively high cost of maintaining office facilities and supporting expatriate staff in China has led some companies to use Hong Kong as their base of operations for China. It is interesting to note that certain U.S. companies, in apparent recognition of the emerging Greater China macro-region, have established separate business units, based in the P.R.C., with full responsibility for the company's complete business activities in the P.R.C., Hong Kong and Taiwan.

Other companies have chosen trading companies, banks, and various consultants—American, Hong Kong, Chinese, and other—to represent their interests on a day-to-day basis, sending company personnel to China when business activity warrants. Some companies have also formed joint ventures with Chinese partners to handle distribution of their products and provide after-sales service.

### *Can foreign companies now control their own distribution in China?*

Yes. Coca-Cola, for example, has attempted to localize the bottling, advertising, and distribution of its soft drink products in China. Its 10 bottling plants control distribution of product, which makes it possible for it to quickly react to consumer needs.

### The Process of Selling to a Chinese Enterprise

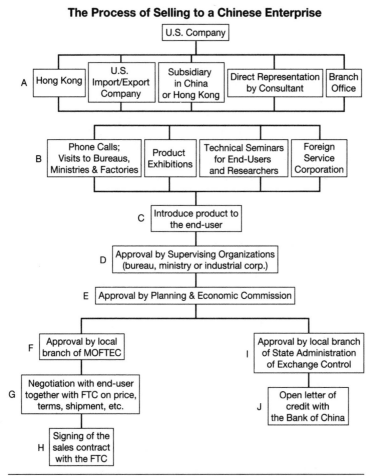

Successfully selling a product in China – whether produced in China or imported – depends on introducing the product directly to the end-user. Half of the respondents to one of the author's questionnaires discovered that the end-users they dealt with had the power to authorize or veto the purchase. Sixty-five percent of respondents said they hold technical seminars (at an average cost of $20,450) to gain introduction to end-users. Once an end-user desires to buy, selling to China then becomes a task of gaining purchase approvals. If an FTC is the purchaser, MOFTEC approval will be necessary (F, G, H); if a bureau, ministry, or industrial corporation is the purchaser, the sale can be made once the foreign exchange is released by the State Administration of Exchange Control (I, J).

Source: Adapted from: *Intertrade*, February 1987. p 35.

Let's look more closely at one distribution deal that illustrates a forthright foreign approach to setting up a selling network in China, as well as the changes taking place inside Chinese enterprises to set up distribution networks to serve foreign suppliers. The supplier is a Taiwanese consumer electronics company called Inventa. One of the company's products is a pocket electronic Chinese-English dictionary that can vocalize word pronunciations. (You might have noticed the billboards in airports in South China advertising the product.) Inventa approached China by signing up six selling agents to handle separate regions of China. The agents have the exclusive right to market is Beijing, Shanghai, Shenzhen, Xinjiang, Chengdu, and Southwest China. To handle Southwest China, Inventa hired a company called V.I.P. in Chongqing, a fledgling company that has been formed within a large state-owned enterprise called the Institute of Science & Technology Information Corporation (CB-ISTIC). The parent company is in the throes of transition to the market, as are most state-run Chinese enterprises. In short, it needs to make ends meet without as much state support as in the past.

With a huge database of Chinese companies to call on, CB-ISTIC is in a mode of experimentation with market-oriented commercial endeavors that promise to generate revenue. So, the vice director of the institute formed a marketing company within the enterprise to represent foreign supplies of personal electronic products. Lacking in-house talent to run the operation, the vice director hired a marketer from outside, and put him under contract. The marketer was to sell 1,000 Inventa units in the course of the first year, and would earn a salary of 840 Yuan per month, plus commissions.

VIP must buy foreign goods through an FTC since it is not yet an authorized FTC itself. It pays for product using Renminbi at exchange rate used for such purchases (for which the Chinese currency is pegged below the official value by about 30 percent), plus a 10 percent commission. VIP sells the product to Chinese consumers for Renminbi. After six months, VIP was selling 200 Inventa units per month. Their story is being repeated all over China as a new web of distribution widens atop the state-controlled wholesale distribution system of the past.

VIP pursued a three-pronged strategy to sell foreign products in Southwest China: (1) it set up retail stores in the Chongqing area; (2) it initiated direct mail order sales through advertisements in newspapers and magazines; and (3) it hired another Chinese trading company to move product in cities where Inventa had not hired exclusive agents—twenty cities in all. Fifty percent of sales are generated by the subcontracted trading company, 30 percent is generated by the two VIP stores, and the remaining 20 percent come from direct sales to customers by mail, fax, or phone. Primarily, VIP utilizes CB-ISTIC's massive list of 20,000 Chinese companies to solicit direct sales and leads to trading companies which might be interested in handling the Inventa product. A prime market, Chinese officials, are contacted directly by phone. If the official is interested in seeing the product and is located near Chungking, VIP provides a sample of the product. With sales growing, VIP had to hire more salespeople. Again, they sought people from outside CB-ISTIC through advertisements and personal introductions. Now the company employs seven full-time sales people earning 300 Yuan per month plus 2-3 commission on each US$200 sales of the Inventa unit. A good salesperson makes more on commissions than salary.

### *What is the current role and function of China's foreign trade corporations (FTCs)?*

The middle man role of the foreign trade corporation is guaranteed by law. Only joint ventures, 100 percent foreign-owned factories, and large state-owned firms can do a deal directly with a foreign buyer or seller. The FTC is the exclusive representative of the factories under its auspices. The financial arrangements vary in percentage of the total deal, but the FTC can receive as high as 10 percent of the dollar. However, each department of an FTC has little control over its total take, as FTCs are large government-owned companies that pay for workers' housing, food, and education—as any danwei does.

During the 1950s, China's foreign trade was controlled by the state ministries. In the 1970s, as Chinese firms began to produce goods for export, twenty or so foreign trade corporations were (FTCs) formed to facilitate the trading of goods with foreign buyers and sellers. In the late 1970s only a handful of FTCs existed; by the mid-1980s, there were almost 6,000 FTCs spread all over the country. The number contracted to 3,000 with recentralization of trade in 1986-1987. FTCs range in character from those specializing in a single product line and representing very few companies, to those—like Japan's soga sosha trading companies—which handle hundreds of product lines and act as an agent for hundreds of Chinese firms. Generalized FTCs have the authority to import virtually any product while an industry specific one—say a medical supplies FTC—will often be restricted from importing any product not related to its industry.

FTCs remain in the middle of 80-90 percent of trade deals with China, though their role is clearly on a slow decline. Most deals still include that role of a foreign trade corporation, or FTC. The situation is changing, however, as buyers gain more autonomy to purchase the goods that they want to buy. Not long ago, the FTC would decide what, and when, the enterprise would buy! Nowadays, an enterprise that cannot convince an FTC to purchase the equipment that it wants can dump the FTC and hire another one in its place that will purchase the goods that it wants. Thus, in order to sell to China, you must reach the end-users. This was not the case a few short years ago when FTCs had a pervasive influence over the import purchasing decision (if not the last word). In fact, your first question for an end-user in China is whether the enterprise is authorized to trade independent of an FTC.

Many enterprises and state-owned corporations which produce goods or provide services are currently trying to find ways to become authorized foreign trade corporations. Why? To save the cost of commissions. This tactic is especially important to enterprises that have set up their own domestic distribution systems to sell their goods inside China. Using this system they often desire to move foreign-made products as well, (since in many cases foreign products simply sell better). By forming a joint venture with a foreign company, a Chinese company automatically gains the status of a foreign trade corporation, allowing it to save 10-14 percent on all of its import purchases, not to mention a lot of time dealing with bureaucratic red tape dealing with the FTC. A chief motivation on the part of the Chinese partner in forming a joint venture is often to achieve this status—something you should be aware of before investing the necessary capital in a venture.

### *What is the process by which a foreign company sells through an FTC to an end-user?*

The process of a foreign seller working a deal through an FTC would typically go like this: First, the Chinese customer decides that he wants to purchase a certain product from a foreign company, say, after looking through a catalog or seeing an advertisement. The factory may also contact a municipal-level ministry or office of MOFERT to request to import the product. The factory pays in Rmb to the FTC, which then purchases the product with foreign currency. The FTC uses its Rmb inputs to pay its workers and other in-China expenses. The FTC will charge the Chinese factory import duties for purchases of products that are not exempt. The FTC must obtain approval for the purchases from a government entity to carry out the import of the equipment. If the goods are to be used exclusively for assembly into final products for reexport, there will be no import duty levied. If the import is only to be sold domestically, import duties range from 10-60 percent, with duties on consumer goods and automobiles especially high.

### *Is it important to meet with the end-user directly to facilitate a sale to China?*

China specialist Roy F. Grow, in extensive surveys of American and Japanese companies involved in China, has provided clear evidence of how our two approaches to the market differ. In terms of the information which company executives find useful in selling to China, the Japanese place a significantly higher priority on learning about "the specific end-users of their products," the enterprises internal "decision-making," and the "unit's ability to buy from abroad." The Americans are more interested than the Japanese in learning about China's overall need for their product to technology and the U.S. laws and regulations that apply to trading with China. Other recent surveys have indicated the competitive advantage of getting close to, and knowledgeable about, the specific needs, priorities, personnel, clout, and finance position of the Chinese end-user. Specific information about Chinese enterprises is increasingly available and the proven method to gather it is through on-site visits by company representatives. The personal interview facilitates the process of relationship building, hands-on problem identifications, and selling through "solution-finding" as opposed to merely making the offer.

### *Which Chinese entity ultimately makes the buying decision?*

Traditionally, the ultimate choice of vendor and approval would come from someone not directly involved in the implementation of the equipment being imported. Often, this entity was an FTC; in other cases it was a related ministry. Either way, the person or persons who approved the deal often lacked the technical or managerial knowledge to make such a decision. China is rife with technology duplication and under utilization of imported technology due to this tendency. Now, decisions to import often fall squarely on the shoulders of factory managers and directors. The foreign seller deals only with the buyer or end user and does not have to negotiate with the FTC at all. The initiative to buy comes from the actual buying enterprise and not the FTC. However, government players will be involved on most large purchases because the enterprise will not be funding the purchase itself. Thus, final decisions are often made by interested officials. This is where American companies need to concentrate more energy, at least as much as the Japanese do—in influencing the real decision maker. That is, finding out what he wants and obtaining it for him. Answering his questions. Solving his problems with the purchase. Without *guanxi* with this person you won't be as influential in a buying decision as you could be.

### *How does a foreign company set up a retail outlet in China?*

Participating in China's booming retail sector is an unusual challenge for foreign companies. Eager to access the Chinese consumer dollar, many foreign companies have rushed into cooperative arrangements without realistically analyzing the risks associated with investment in China's retail sector. Investment in a retail operation is limited to cooperative or equity-based joint ventures; wholly-foreign-owned enterprises in the retail sector are not permitted.

Regulations governing the establishment of a foreign-invested enterprise (FIE) in the retail sector are similar to those concerning manufacturing FIEs, with some important exceptions. Most importantly, retail-oriented FIEs may not serve as wholesalers or import-export corporations, but must sell their goods in their own retail establishments. Except for retail FIEs located in the Special Economic Zones, FIEs in the retail sector are not eligible for the national tax holidays extended to manufacturing joint ventures. However, local authorities can extend tax holidays on local income taxes.

Typically, a retail FIE comes about because a Chinese property owner approaches a foreign company to open a retail outlet on their property. The Chinese partner will then contribute land, buildings and materials/furniture as registered capital, while the foreign partner imports products for sale and also contributes management expertise. The foreign company may wish to extend management of the enterprise under a separate contract for the first few years of the venture. Retail FIEs are responsible for securing their own hard currency for the repatriation of profits out of the country.

### Will transportation of product inside China be a problem?

The most effective approach to hurdling the physical distribution challenge is to explore several modes of transport simultaneously. Close ties to Chinese customs officials and employing South China-based trading companies are two ways to overcome the initial challenge of customs. While no foreign companies yet provide distribution-related services, many groups are apparently in the discussion stages with potential Chinese partners. Joint venture production can offer another way to reduce distribution headaches, by providing a ready Chinese partner to reserve space on rails and trucks, cover intermodal transport and smooth government relationships along the way. Many of the most successful joint ventures producing items for domestic consumption have allowed the foreign company to take the lead in strategic marketing, while the Chinese partner addresses the tactical challenges of moving goods through the country.

*Do Chinese companies typically have representatives in the United States?*

It is rare to find an individual Chinese company with a representative office in the U.S. Many regional and national trading companies now have foreign offices abroad, and a large number of Chinese ministries have commercial offices in foreign countries. You will also find a wide network of agencies offering quasi-representative services through China's embassy and consulates. Even more common is a private U.S. company run by Chinese with family ties to the PRC. Many of these companies have a regional focus in China, and may have one or more offices staffed by relatives in the PRC. While they can offer excellent contacts in China and can often smooth over road bumps, foreign businesspersons should treat such companies with caution. Assess the size of their operation and the depth of their experience. Avoid putting "China consultants" on retainer, but instead offer them a commission upon the signing of a sales contract.

*Should you engage with a subsidiary of a Chinese company, or only deal with the parent company?*

Subsidiaries in China are often independent business entities with their own network of contacts and investment opportunities. Parent companies may provide high-level contacts in the Chinese bureaucracy or access to critical hard currency, but one should assume that a subsidiary in China has a fair degree of operational autonomy. Assess a subsidiary the way you would examine any Chinese company. What are their strengths? Who do they know in the bureaucracy? What are their ties to banks and regional development corporations? Often subsidiaries are created by Chinese companies as investment vehicles to allow them to invest capital in areas of the economy outside of their primary line of business.

*How do I choose a distributor in China?*

The best source of judgment about a potential distributor in China is the method of referral to the foreign company. A distributor should be referred by a reliable source and have a proven track record in China. Nevertheless, a foreign company may be faced with distributor candidates that need further evaluation before an agreement is signed. The following are meant to be some basic guidelines for evaluating a potential distributor.

- What written goals for the market will the distributor agree to? Goals may be expressed in the dollar value of sales or market share.

- Measure the distributor's ability to cover the market, in geographic terms and in market segments. Who are the distributor's existing customers? How big is the distributor's sales force?

- What is the going markup or commission in China for your product? How does this compare to the distributor's quotation?

- Is the distributor willing to assume responsibility for the physical distribution of the product? What will be the penalties for late delivery? How can you measure the quality of service the distributor is providing to the end-user?

- What other types of support (eg. warehousing, promotion, after-sales service) can the distributor provide?

- What are the hidden costs of selecting this distributor for the foreign company? Consider the cost of support and motivation, communication, travel, promotion, and training.

- Evaluate the distributor's backing and support. It is almost impossible in China to evaluate the financial standing of a Chinese company. However, one can gain a good sense of the company's position by examining its origins, ties to the local and national bureaucracy and its Chinese clients.

- What are the local laws of termination? How will the foreign company judge when it is time to terminate this distribution arrangement?

- Match this distributor against your profile of an 'ideal' distributor. How does this distributor compare?

*What information can, and should, be requested from a Chinese distributor in order to thoroughly evaluate it?*

After initial contact, a foreign company should have certain expectations regarding information to be provided by the Chinese entity. A potential Chinese distributor may object to the volume or level of detail of the information requested. The foreign company should stress that it is seeking a long-term relationship and is deeply committed to expanding into the Chinese market. The distributor may attempt to delay releasing some of the information requested. While the foreign company may accept the delays, it should also stress that is currently evaluating other distributors and will be making a decision soon. A suggested checklist for information to be requested includes the following:

1. Contact information regarding suppliers, Chinese bank representatives and customers willing to recommend the distributor.

2. List of past and present product lines handled by the distributor.

3. Evidence of experience with product lines similar to the product of the foreign company.

4. Evidence of the size of the sales force and sales productivity.

5. Evidence of sales volume and record of sales growth.

6. Current and past geographical areas covered by the distributor.

7. Annotated breakdown of the distributor's costs.

8. Description of the distributor's physical facilities.

9. Evidence of experience with after-sales service.

10. Knowledge of revised Chinese and international accounting and measurement standards.

11. Knowledge of Chinese customs regulations.

12. Written evidence of the distributor's knowledge of English

# CHAPTER 9

# ADVERTISING

# AND PROMOTION

*L*abeled as a capitalist tool, advertising was totally banned for more than three decades prior to 1978. These restrictions were partially lifted under the government of Deng Xiaoping as a means of promoting product knowledge and economic growth. In 1978, China's only ad agency, the Shanghai Advertising Company, was reopened. The Chinese government began permitting substantial increases of foreign advertising on Chinese television, radio, billboards, and in printed publications.

## FROM CAPITALIST TOOL TO SALES TOOL

There is still a certain novelty value to advertising in China and the Chinese react to it with more enthusiasm than their more saturated Western counterparts. One clever recent advertisement was for

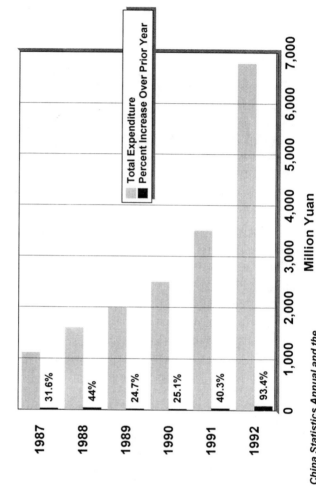

**Advertising Expenditures In China**

| Year | Percent Increase Over Prior Year |
|------|----------------------------------|
| 1987 | 31.6% |
| 1988 | 44% |
| 1989 | 24.7% |
| 1990 | 25.1% |
| 1991 | 40.3% |
| 1992 | 93.4% |

Total Expenditure
Percent Increase Over Prior Year

Million Yuan

Source: *China Statistics Annual and the Chinese Advertising Association.*

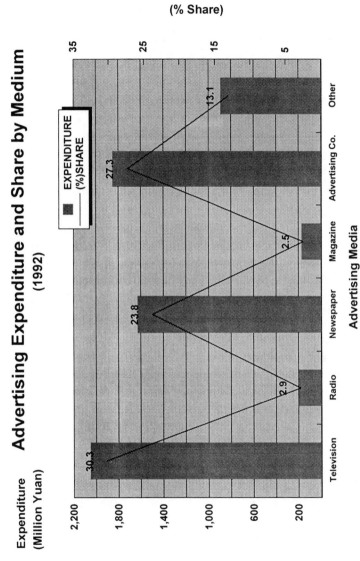

Advertising Expenditure and Share by Medium
(1992)

(% Share)

Expenditure
(Million Yuan)

EXPENDITURE
(%)SHARE

30.3　2.9　23.8　2.5　27.3　13.1

Television　Radio　Newspaper　Magazine　Advertising Co.　Other

Advertising Media

Source: JETRO Chinese Newsletter.

Macintosh Computers. The company runs Chinese characters that read "The Four Modernizations." The "four" is crossed out and replaced with a "five," referring to the Apple computer depicted just above the phrase. "Very clever," admitted a Chinese Shanghai Star reporter who was with me when I visited the company's representative in Shanghai. Then there's "Big Dog Big," the advertising slogan for a Taiwanese mobile phone company. The phrase refers to another well known slogan for a corn dog, which incidentally looks similar to a mobile phone. The corn dog is called Big Brother Big, so the advertisement rings familiar for the Shanghaiese. Coca-cola's 1993 commercial campaign in China was the first produced completely inside the PRC.

In the industrial sector, product advertising is less effective. The Chinese are extremely loyal to their established suppliers; only a handful of American firms can claim customer loyalty in the industrial field. Mobil Oil introduced its logo in China 40 years ago. Based on Mobil's experience in China, advertising is not helpful to oil firms without long-term recognition. Mobil relates its rising sales in China directly to the recognition of its Pegasus logo by Chinese users. General Electric is another company well known in China because of its logo recognition. Decades ago, GE sold fans to China which displayed the common "GE" symbol. In the mid-1980s, GE decided to advertise using a billboard in Beijing. Despite the recognition it had built up over the years, only two calls were received in response. Hewlett-Packard has taken an even lower profile than GE in its advertising, catering to industrial end-users with technical advertisement on television and in magazines.

One should recognize the importance of stationing marketing representatives in China who can attend trade fairs, introduce product lines, company history, and personnel to Chinese end-users and officials directly. Factory visits are effective as well. Telexing and mail communications should illustrate committed presence and be geared to the personalization of the business relationship.

### *What are the various modes of advertising in China? How do they work?*

The economic growth that has characterized the reform era in China has led to an explosion in advertising there. (See table.)

Traditional media such as state-run television and newspapers now accept advertisements from both Chinese and foreign companies, while new advertising mediums ranging from bus kiosks to door-to-door salespeople are emerging across the country. The variety of advertising formats include 210 TV stations, 500 local radio stations, 5,000 newspapers and magazines, as well as billboards, sponsorship, and direct mail. Foreign companies advertise in China mostly on television, which is estimated to reach 90 percent of China's urban population. An advertisement on television during the evening news in China will typically reach an astounding 600 million viewers. At least at the outset of a product launch, television is the most cost-effective method for building brand awareness, though actual sales may not be generated overnight. It should be noted that regional television advertisements can be more cost-effective than national spots; local stations often preempt national broadcasts while running a locally produced ad over and over to fill air time. Advertisements are normally grouped according to use for the consumer, such that you will watch a string of pharmaceutical advertisements about products for stomach problems followed by those for say, industrial quality control.

### *How do the Chinese regulate advertising in China?*

Advertising in the PRC is still tightly regulated by the Chinese government. Entities offering advertising must secure a permit from the State Administration for Industry and Commerce (SAIC), and are then termed "advertising business entities" or *Guanggao Jingying Danwei*. This generic term covers the media, advertising companies and other related agencies. By the end of 1992 there were over 16,000 such entities in the PRC. Chinese regulations cover the sanctioning of advertising entities and the permissibility of individual advertisements. For example, the Chinese do not permit cigarette advertising in any medium.

### *Are Chinese companies increasingly advertising their products?*

Yes, and at a surprisingly high level of sophistication and inventiveness. One example is the story of Caotian Cosmetic Company started up in 1993 in Jilin Province and launching its age-defying cosmetics in Shanghai. Coatian plans to start with the

PRC market and then expand into East Asia, taking advantage of "an old Chinese tradition of taking powders internally [to cure ailments and slow the aging process]." The company raises bears on a farm in the North where it extracts the bear bile which is the active ingredient in its products.

Caotian designed its promotion effort to establish Caotian as a household name in China within two months, starting with name recognition ads followed by information spots touting the effectiveness of the Caotian formula. It held a 350-Yuan giveaway contest on local radio in which contestants were challenged with tongue twisters that naturally emphasized the Caotian name. Finally, questionaires were used to solicit customer opinions about the prices they would pay for Caotian products.

### What are the rates for advertising in the PRC?

The cost of advertising in China has increased ten-fold during the past 24 months. Rates are based on a three-tiered system in which foreign companies get bilked relative to Chinese firms (see chart of advertising rates). Joint ventures enjoyed a slight discount while Chinese firms enjoy the lowest rates. Advertisements in China follow a set rate established by the entities and the relevant Chinese regulatory agencies. While some discounts may be available for frequent use, in general advertisers have little to no flexibility to negotiate rates with end-users. However, rates do differ based on whether the advertiser is a purely Chinese enterprise, a foreign-invested joint venture or a foreign company. Wholly foreign-owned companies are charged rates denominated in U.S. dollars that are significantly higher than rates charged to Chinese enterprises. Joint ventures also pay higher prices, but can use renminbi for their placed advertising.

### How important is packaging of the product in selling to the PRC?

Invest in packaging and in designing your marketing strategy long before breaking ground building a joint venture factory. Put a great deal of effort into choosing a proper name for your offering and having it translated into Chinese. Have the name analyzed by people who speak each of the main Chinese language dialects, including Mandarin, Cantonese, Sichuanese, and

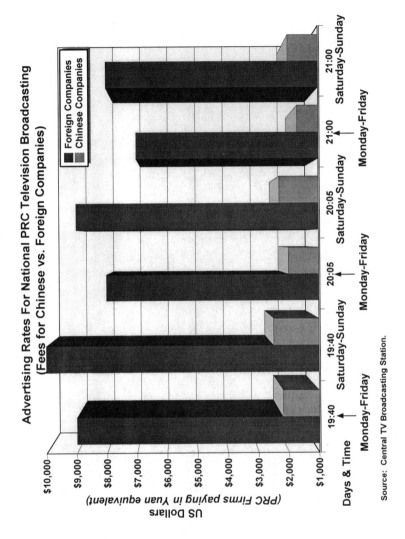

Advertising Rates For National PRC Television Broadcasting
(Fees for Chinese vs. Foreign Companies)

Source: Central TV Broadcasting Station.

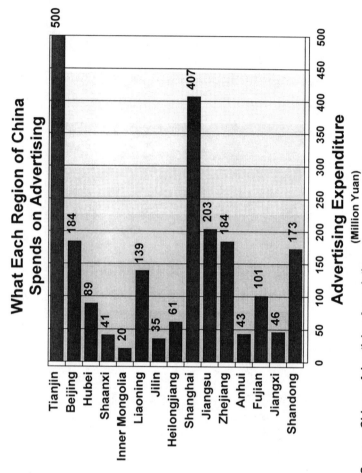

## What Each Region of China Spends on Advertising

Tianjin: 500
Beijing: 184
Hubei: 89
Shaanxi: 41
Inner Mongolia: 20
Liaoning: 139
Jilin: 35
Heilongjiang: 61
Shanghai: 407
Jiangsu: 203
Zhejiang: 184
Anhui: 43
Fujian: 101
Jiangxi: 46
Shandong: 173

### Advertising Expenditure
(Million Yuan)

Source: *Chinese Advertising Association.*

Shanghaiese to ensure that the pronunciation in each is free of unwanted connotations. Spend time choosing the right characters to express your product and company name, not to mention your own name.

## Advertising Guidelines

- Rely on the precise presentation of a product's technical specifications to attract Chinese buyers rather than glossy graphics and alluring photographs.

- Advertise in the Chinese language translated from English by qualified professionals experienced in translating promotional literature.

- Avoid political and sexual innuendo and the use of cultural stereotypes.

- Highlight durability rather than innovation, performance rather than trendiness.

- Collect, collate, and follow-up on all direct consumer responses.

- Promote brand and company loyalty by emphasizing quality and dependability.

## A NOTE ON BROCHURES AND THEIR TRANSLATION

The golden rule of communicating in writing with Chinese is to do it in English *unless* you have a native-speaking in-house translator that can translate your English documents perfectly. Better to say it in English than send a badly translated business correspondence. Just ask KFC, whose slogan, "finger-lickin' good" was first translated in China as "eat your fingers off." The Library of Congress once hired someone to translate documents from Chinese into English. It was discovered later that the translation read like a children's book in Chinese. In the document, "People got off the big boat...," rather than the "ship"! If the Library of Congress can't get it right, your company may not either unless you subject all of your translations to stringent quality control. Most firms find it too expensive to hire an in house native speaker to review marketing materials and advertising slogans. The best alternative is to find someone to do a sample translation and then send it to a perspective translator who has a recognized respectability in the field to have it checked over. Finally, have a *native speaker of the local dialect* read and review the materials and suggest changes. Often problems with unattractive homonyms occur in a dialect other than Mandarin. Solicit the person's gut feelings about the letter, brochure, or advertisement—whether it's funny, somber, ridiculous, too lofty, conceited, lacking in humility, and the like.

# CHAPTER 10

# SHIPPING AND

# DOCUMENTATION

*E*xporters to the PRC need to be concerned with three logistical problems of trading right at the outset: Customs and duties, getting paid, and shipping product to China. Attention to detail in dealing with these key aspects will save you much time and numerous headaches.

## DEALING WITH CHINA'S CUSTOMS SYSTEM

While China has currently set up over 110 customs posts to oversee the flow of goods in and out of the country, many critics continue to charge that China's customs system is incapable of managing the country's flow of foreign trade. China trade is governed by the 1987 Customs Law of the People's Republic of China. The law is supplemented by additional rules and regulations, which are updated on a periodic basis.

## _What are China's customs regulations, and what exemptions exist?_

China Customs Administration (CCA) initiated a new set of regulations in October of 1992 to manage the exchange of goods through the country's trade ports. It defines the scope of goods that can be taken in and out of China without having to pay the customs duty. Key business items on this list include cameras, minicassette recorders, portable video equipment, and portable computers.

In addition, the CCA adopted a comprehensive set of customs regulations in July of the same year. The new set of regulations described the types of items that qualify for duty exemption and is designed to offer a uniform set of regulations that apply to all foreign-invested ventures in the PRC. The law refers to foreign-invested ventures (FIVs) as an inclusive term that encompasses equity joint ventures, contractual joint ventures and wholly foreign-owned enterprises. Among its different regulations, the new law offers the following highlights of interest to foreign investors.

- The law shortens the time required by all FIVs to pass through customs procedures.

- The law allows FIVs to build and staff bonded warehouses where local customs staff can handle all customs procedures locally.

- The law permits FIVs to import a "reasonable" number of personal items for the FIV's use, without having to report those items to customs officials

- Duty-exemption certificates offered on duty-free goods brought into the country can now be extended for an additional three months, after the initial three-month period has expired.

- FIVs can continue to import duty-free components, parts, and raw materials necessary for the production of export products.

The new law also clarifies the difference between duty exemptions offered for equity joint ventures (EJVs) and contractual joint ventures (CJVs).

For equity joint ventures, duty-free importation is offered for:

1. machinery and equipment, as well as building materials, components, and other related materials, imported as part of the foreign investment for the foreign-invested enterprise.

2. machinery, equipment, and components imported by the FIV with foreign cash investment.

3. machinery, equipment, and components unavailable from Chinese domestic sources.

4. production management systems.

For contractual joint ventures, duty-free imports are limited to those CJVs related to the development of China's natural resources or infrastructure. Potential CJV areas that can benefit from duty-free imports of machinery, equipment or components include: offshore oil and gas resources; energy projects (hydropower, turnkey power plants); railroad, highway, and port construction; agriculture and forestry; education; medical equipment and health care.

Additional exemptions are available on vehicles, office equipment and other administrative resources required by the FIV. However, the value of the imported products may not exceed the total value of the investment project.

### By locating in a duty-free zone, will I gain additional exemptions?

In recent years a number of bonded, duty-free import areas have developed along China's coast, including within the country's Special Economic Zones, Shanghai's Pudong Development Zone, and Tianjin's Economic-Technological Development Area. While such areas often have higher land-use costs, development or factory construction within these areas offer significant benefits in terms of duties and customs, including duty-free importation of all related machinery, equipment, components, and related materials, access to rapid customs clearance, access to frequently used sea routes, and avoidance of inland transportation costs. Note, however, that the majority of these benefits will apply only to *export-oriented ventures that intend to re-export* a large percentage of the

## Chinese Import Tariff Rates on Selected Consumer Goods

| | | | | |
|---|---|---|---|---|
| Coffee | 20% | Gems, rough | 20% |
| Substitutes with coffee | 60 | Gems polished | 50 |
| Bean oil, peanut oil | 6 | Jewelry, metal & imitation | 100 |
| Sesame oil, prepared | 9 | Aluminum home product | 70 |
| Confectionery with no cocoa | 40 | Stand-alone air conditioners | 100 |
| Chocolate, etc, with cocoa | 40 | Refrigerators, freeze equip. | 100 |
| Beverage concentrate | 80 | Home washing machines | 100 |
| Beer brewed with malt | 120 | Electric calculators | 60 |
| Tobacco products | 150 | Home electric fans | 100 |
| Soap and other detergents | 60 | TV receivers, video recorders | 80 |
| Color films | 70 | Cameras | 80 |
| Travel equip., briefcases, etc. | 80 | Electronic watches | 80 |
| Leather art, leather clothes | 80 | Other watches | 60 |
| Wooden household goods | 80 | Tape recorders | 60 |
| Cotton, linen clothes | 70 | Furniture | 80 |
| Other clothing | 80-100 | Toys, sports equipment | 60-80 |
| Footwear | 80 | Electronic games | 60-80 |

value of the imported goods. These goods are often not permitted to enter the domestic market, and the foreign-invested enterprise may have to make specific export commitments in order to gain access to these areas.

### What are China's import and export duty rates?

China's import tariffs are divided into 21 categories with two applicable tariff rates: the minimum tariff rate and the general tariff rate. The minimum tariff rate, which varies from 0 to 150 percent, normally applies to countries which have signed trade pacts with the PRC. The general tariff rate, which varies from 0 to 180 percent, is applicable to countries where no such agreements exist. Duties on imported goods are assessed on a *cif* basis. In order to encourage exports, few goods are subject to export duties in the PRC. The current duty rates on imports of key products are to be found in the table above.

*Do foreign representatives have to pay duty on the personal effects which they bring into the PRC?*

A representative of a foreign company may bring into the PRC one shipment of personal effects duty-free after they have obtained a permanent residence permit. If the total number of articles exceeds the quantitative limit set by customs authorities they may still be admitted duty-free with special approval from the customs office. Motor vehicles may be imported by the representative (one per person) on payment of the customs duty. However, foreign personnel should be aware that the tariff is likely to be at least 100 percent of the value of the vehicle. Personal effects approved for import by the customs office should be imported within six months of the date of approval.

## The Purchase Contract

*What does the typical PRC contract look like for an import purchase?*

China's foreign trade corporations will normally insist that the foreign supplier or partner use a "standard" contract form as the basis for negotiating purchase and sale transactions, technology transfers, and even joint ventures. In general, the foreigner is advised to negotiate a contract suited to the needs of the partners rather than accept what the Chinese claim to be a standard contract.

*How do the Chinese quote price in a purchase contract?*

Price is usually quoted in a readily convertible, relatively stable currency; for U.S. trade partners, the quote is usually in U.S. dollars. The negotiated price is usually firm, with no provision for inflation. Terms are generally *fob* at a United States port in a purchase contract, though *cif* or *c.&f.* may be accepted when the goods are to be shipped by air. Export sales by China are usually designated *cif*. These terms allow shipping and insurance to be handled by Chinese companies, thus reducing the Chinese trade partner's foreign exchange expenditure.

### *How will the Chinese pay for a foreign import?*

A Chinese importer may pay the full value of a purchase in a single lump sum or payment may be made in installments, particularly for such large purchases as turnkey plant and complete production lines, or as royalty payments in technology licensing agreements. Chinese foreign trade corporations pay for imports by irrevocable unconfirmed letters of credit issued by the Bank of China. Alternatively, established suppliers may be asked to make sales on an open account or documentary collection basis supported by a People's Bank of China (PBOC) letter of guarantee. PBOC letters of credit are usually payable only by the branch which opened the credit, thus requiring the seller's bank to forward the necessary documents to that branch for review. Payment is generally made in 10 to 14 days, if the letter of credit specifies payment by telegraphic transfer. PBOC may permit the importer to review documents before paying.

Chinese buyers may accept the standard practice of paying all banking charges, including those outside China, though PBOC does not permit this to be explicitly stated in the letter of credit. Sales drafts drawn under PBOC letters of credit are permitted. The People's Bank of China's documentation requirements for letters of credit will typically include:

- Commercial invoice

- Ocean bill of lading or air waybill

- Packing list/weight memo

- Manufacturer's certificate of quality

- Copy of exporter's notification of shipment

- Statement that carrying vessel is chartered by a Chinese shipping corporation

- Insurance certificate covering at least 100 percent of the invoice value

- U.S. export license, if required

- Certificate of origin

Some purchase contracts require the supplier to post a bond as protection for the buyer against failure to deliver. PBOC will open a bid bond or a performance letter of credit (advance payment bond) in a Chinese buyer's favor against an irrevocable or standby letter of credit issued by the foreign supplier's bank in favor of the People's Bank of China.

## Shipping to the PRC

It is recommended that foreign companies signing trade or technology transfer agreements with Chinese entities specify in the contract that shipping from U.S. ports to Chinese destinations is the responsibility of the Chinese party. Chinese companies will be more adept at arranging cost-effective and efficient transhipment of goods and can navigate the intricacies of the Chinese bureaucracy more easily than their foreign counterparts. If the U.S. firm does accept responsibility for shipping, it should use an international freight forwarder with joint venture arrangements in the PRC.

### How do I arrange my product to be shipped to China?

By importing on an *fob* basis and exporting *cif,* Chinese foreign trade corporations are able to book transport in both directions through the state freight forwarder, China National Foreign Trade Transportation Corporation (SINOTRANS). A wholly owned subsidiary of SINOTRANS, China Inter-ocean Transport, Inc., provides freight-forwarding services out of New York. An *fob* purchase contract will often require the seller to notify the buyer in advance when the goods are to arrive at the U.S. port to allow SINOTRANS to book cargo space through the China National Chartering Corporation, SINOCHART.

China Ocean Shipping Company runs the only direct surface shipping service between China and the United States. Two U.S. companies, American President Lines and Sea-Land Service, transship cargo to China through Hong Kong or Kobe, mostly via Chinese and Japanese feeder lines.

China has over 20 ports open for direct handling of foreign trade. However, congestion at most ports and inadequate facilities add to shipping delays stemming from frequently inefficient cargo-handling procedures and inaccurate preparation of shipping documents. Partly as a consequence, the volume of commercial shipments moved by air freight between China and the United States has been increasing. In addition to the Chinese airline, CAAC, United and Northwest airlines fly scheduled services directly between the United States and China. Flying Tiger Line and CAAC have formed a joint venture to carry air freight, and EAS-Sino Pacific Inc. offers project cargo and courier services between the two countries. Courier service is also provided by DHL, Airborne Express, and United Parcel Service, who have formed joint ventures with SINOTRANS and China Courier Service.

SINOTRANS handles delivery of freight from the Chinese port to final inland destination. Foreign companies are not allowed to engage in freight-forwarding within China, although one U.S. company, Schenkers, has a joint venture with SINOTRANS for land transportation and offers internodal service for U.S. exports.

### What are the primary modes of physical distribution of product inside the PRC?

Railroad provides the primary mode of transport of products in China, and the rail system is 20-30 years old. Shipping by air using the MD82, a small cargo plane, is too costly unless the product is small and lightweight. A new Shanghai-Chicago air cargo route has been extremely helpful to traders. Shipping by barge is the cheapest mode. Container trains are safer than using regular train lines. Shipping by truck presents nightmare delays and the potential for theft. One of the key areas of needed improvement is in transportation standardization, such that containers, trailer hitches, cargo equipment handling devices can all be uniform and compatible, which is not the case in China. Transportation infrastructure improvements are sorely needed, and expected. Forty-two airports are to be built throughout China, new port facilities to serve Shanghai, and a freeway connecting Hong Kong and Southern China.

# CHAPTER 11

# BANKING AND

# INSURANCE

*C*hina lacks a central bank equivalent to the Federal Reserve in the United States, although the People's Bank of China often nominally fills this role. Decisions regarding the monetary system are made by central economic planners in Beijing, particularly by the Economic Planning Leading Group, a Communist party entity whose recommendations are implemented by the State Council. Monetary issues relating to foreign exchange are typically governed by the Bank of China.

## CHINA'S BANKING SYSTEM

The People's Bank of China (PBOC) serves as a central bank in name only, and actually competes with other banks in China throughout its vast network of branches throughout the country.

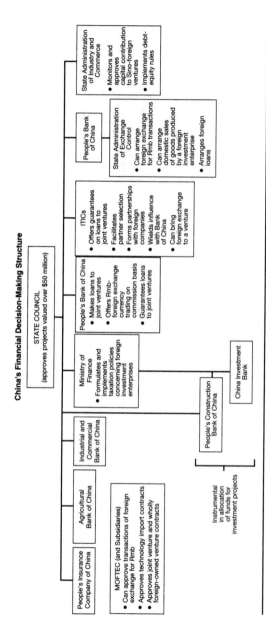

**China's Financial Decision-Making Structure**

STATE COUNCIL
(approves projects valued over $50 million)

**People's Insurance Company of China**

**Agricultural Bank of China**

**Industrial and Commercial Bank of China**

**MOFTEC (and Subsidiaries)**
- Can approve transactions of foreign exchange for Rmb
- Approves technology import contracts
- Approves joint venture and wholly foreign-owned venture contracts

**Ministry of Finance**
- Formulates and implements taxation policies concerning foreign investment enterprises

**People's Bank of China**
- Makes loans to joint ventures
- Offers Rmb-foreign exchange currency trading on commission basis
- Guarantees loans to joint ventures

**ITICs**
- Offers guarantees on loans to joint ventures
- Facilitates partner selection
- Forms partnerships with foreign companies
- Wields influence with Bank of China
- Can bring foreign exchange to a venture

**People's Bank of China**

**State Administration of Exchange Control**
- Can arrange foreign exchange for Rmb transactions
- Can arrange domestic sales of goods produced by a foreign investment enterprise
- Arranges foreign loans

**State Administration of Industry and Commerce**
- Monitors and approves capital contribution to Sino-foreign ventures
- Implements debt-equity rules

**People's Construction Bank of China**

**China Investment Bank**

Instrumental in allocation of funds for investment projects

China's soon-to-be reformed financial structure promotes a tightly knit, "old boy" solidarity when collaborating with foreigners on financial matters. Two general elements of project financing frustrate the investor: (1) obtaining loans for initial start-up, and (2) balancing foreign exchange after start-up. Foreign investors seek loans from the People's Bank of China (PBOC) often in conjunction with foreign banks. However, through an exclusionary system of loan syndication, the PBOC has made it difficult for foreign banks to participate in loans to foreign investment enterprises. (International trade and investment corporations [called ITICs], offer the necessary leverage to get loan guarantees.) Balancing foreign exchange accounts can be accomplished by swapping Rmb earned from domestic sales through organizations such as MOFTEC, the State Administration of Exchange Control, or the PBOC.

SOURCES: China International Consultants, Inc., *The China Investment Guide*, and the table compiled by John Frisbie in *China Business Review* (March–April, 1988, 34,35).

The PBOC has responsibility for foreign exchange transactions and international payments. It implements reforms in China's foreign exchange system and manages the country's foreign exchange swap centers. The People's Construction Bank of China oversees the country's capital investments and serves as a vehicle to disperse money from the state budget into Chinese state and quasi-state enterprises. It also supervises the Chinese Investment Bank, which appropriates World Bank loans inside the PRC.

The Industrial and Commercial Bank of China covers commercial transactions within the PRC, although it is also involved in foreign enterprise financing and invests Chinese capital abroad. The China International Trust and Investment Corporation (CITIC) also serves a financing role by investing in various foreign enterprises and handling international foreign exchange transactions.

CITIC and its counterparts throughout China are China's de facto investment banks. Every major Chinese city and province has an "ITIC": the most powerful are, besides CITIC, the Dalian International Trust & Investment Corporation, the Shanghai International Trust & Investment Corporation, and the Guangdong International Trust & Investment Corporation. These organizations finance equity investment, make loans to joint ventures, and are external Chinese borrowing groups authorized by the PRC government. CITIC has the status of ministry and reports to the State Council. Newly approved financing vehicles include the Export-Import Bank and the Long-Term Credit Bank. While not currently in operation, these vehicles are expected to participate in foreign enterprise financing and trade guarantees for strategically-important segments of the Chinese economy.

### *Can foreign invested enterprises or traders utilize the services of a Chinese bank?*

Most foreign ventures in the PRC rely on internal resources, parent company backing, or foreign government financing to support the financial needs of their enterprise. Local banks may offer renminbi denominated loans or lines of credit to support operating expenses or provide working capital. However, foreign-invested enterprises usually look elsewhere for sources of foreign currency financing. Private venture capital firms and foreign commercial banks operating in China's special economic zones and other developing coastal regions can offer foreign currency financing. In addition, the World Bank's International Finance Corporation and other international development agencies also make loans to the private sector.

### How does foreign exchange work in China?

China's convoluted foreign exchange system has been simplified with the elimination of the foreign exchange certificate (FEC) and the unification of the official and swap exchange rates. The Chinese currency is now convertible on current account and its set rate has been replaced with a managed floating rate. With the elimination of the FEC the renminbi depreciated by 30 percent against the dollar. However, the rate has now stabilized and is expected to depreciate gently in the future as China continues to run diminishing trade and current-account deficits.

On January 1, 1994, the Chinese government abolished the official exchange rate for China's currency, the Renminbi (RMB), thus ending more than four decades of government-imposed exchange rates. In its place Chinese officials have instituted a managed floating exchange rate that currently values the currency at approximately 8.7 RMB to the dollar. This level is roughly equivalent to the rate that the currency was trading at on China's official swap centers up to the end of 1993. Future fluctuations in the exchange rate will reflect changes in demand for currency as measured at the swap centers. Authorities will continue to intervene to keep the rate within a set (though unpublicized) range in order to ensure stability.

The current exchange rate is approximately 30 percent lower than the official 5.8 RMB to $1 rate that existed on December 31, 1993. Although many analysts have expressed concern about the radical devaluation of the Renminbi, the fact is that only 20 percent of all foreign exchange transactions in China prior to the elimination of the set rate were conducted at the official amount. Most foreign transactions occurred (and continue to occur) on the swap centers or the black market.

Under the managed floating rate system the government has abolished the institution of the Foreign Exchange Certificate (FEC). These special notes are no longer being printed by the Chinese government, although it is unclear how long existing notes will continue to hold value. On the day the change was announced, Chinese holding FEC currency began a panic buying spree of luxury items such as gold and golf club memberships. On New Year's Day, FEC prices in hotels, restaurants, and high-end stores were marked up 40 to 70 percent.

### *Why was the dual-currency system abolished?*

To help foreign investors in China. The official rate was artificially strong, effectively granting a subsidy to Chinese companies who could obtain cheap foreign currency to buy imported components and raw materials. The move was also made to eliminate the booming black market for hard currency and to improve China's chances for reentering the General Agreement on Tariffs and Trade (GATT). China is expected to re-enter the international trade system by the beginning of 1995.

### *How will the change effect foreign investors?*

The changes eliminate the costly and complicated currency transactions that serve to penalize foreign companies doing business in the PRC, while encouraging new investors considering investment in China by effectively increasing the value of their contributed capital by approximately 50 percent. The changes also substantially depreciate the U.S.-listed value of existing assets in foreign invested enterprises. Many international economists now believe that the foreign exchange rate will stabilize and remain at around 9 renminbi to the dollar through the year 2000.

### *How will foreign firms get joint venture or wholly owned venture profits out of China now, and in the future?*

While the Renminbi is considered fully convertible under the managed floating rate system, actual profit repatriation continues to be problematic for U.S. companies. A foreign company may use various methods to remove profits in hard currency from the country. Whatever mix of methods is employed, issues of profit repatriation should be clearly spelled out in the joint venture contract.

- **Export of manufactured components.** Firms may elect to manufacture components for other company assembly plants located outside of the PRC.

- **Production of import-substitutes.** If a venture produces products that the Chinese government would otherwise have to import, the government or other Chinese end-users should be willing to pay hard currency for the products.

- **Use of swap centers.** Companies can employ the government-sponsored swap markets in Guangzhou and Shanghai to exchange their renminbi for foreign currency. Additional swap markets are slated to be opened in the future.

- **Purchase of local products for export.** Joint ventures may produce foreign exchange by purchasing local products for renminbi and selling the products abroad for foreign exchange.

- **Tax-free reinvestment.** In addition to reinvestment in one's own enterprise, with MOFTEC approval venture partners may invest other joint ventures capable of generating foreign exchange. This will entitle the investor to a refund on the Chinese income tax paid on the invested amount.

FORECASTED EXCHANGE RATES

|                        | 1995 | 1996 | 1997 | 1998 | 1999 |
|------------------------|------|------|------|------|------|
| Exchange Rate (RMB/$)  | 8.9  | 8.9  | 9.0  | 9.1  | 9.2  |

*Source:* Economist Intelligence Unit

*Where can my Chinese customers obtain hard currency to purchase imports?*

There are now more sources of financing for imports into China than ever before. These options present ways around the limited quantities of hard currency available to Chinese purchasers. Financing options for exports to China include the following.

CENTRAL GOVERNMENT RESERVES. China's official foreign exchange reserves at the end of 1992 stood at $19.4 billion. The country's debt service ratio is well below the 20 percent benchmark set by most banks as the threshold between healthy and unhealthy international financial accounts. As such, the Chinese government can authorize hard currency allocations for major purchases from foreign companies. It also delegates foreign currency allocations to individual Chinese enterprises for the purchase of required imports.

**THE WORLD BANK.** The World Bank maintains a large loan program in China, primarily in key infrastructure industries such as transportation, power, energy, and agriculture. The World Bank conducts its procurement by international competitive bids using the China National Technical Import Corporation or China National Instruments Import and Export Corporation. Project opportunities are published in the English-language China Daily.

**THE ASIAN DEVELOPMENT BANK.** The Asian Development Bank, based in the Philippines, conducts its procurement through international competitive bidding. Opportunities are managed by the same Chinese companies discussed above. The emphasis of Asian Development Bank projects are also on major infrastructure projects. Future Asian Development Bank projects are published in the ADB's own English-language publications and are also listed with the U.S. Department of Commerce.

**THE OVERSEAS ECONOMIC COOPERATION FUND (OECF) OF JAPAN.** The OECF is a Japanese government organization that extends development assistance to developing countries. China is the second largest recipient of such assistance, after Indonesia. Japan's loan agreements with China usually coincide with the five-year economic plans. China is now drawing on the third yen loan, of about US$5 billion, which was designed to cover the eighth five-year plan (1990-1995). Project tenders are conducted under rules of international competitive bidding, which differ in some important ways from those of the World Bank. Tenders are announced in the Chinese press and are conducted, in most cases, by China National Technical Import Corporation.

**EXPORT CREDITS.** The Export-Import Bank of the United States offers a full range of export loans and loan guarantees for companies exporting products with at least 51 percent U.S. content. The bank works regularly with Bank of China and People's Construction Bank of China, and will occasionally work with other financial entities, including China International Trust and Investment Corporation and the China Industrial and Commercial Bank. Contact information at the U.S. Export-Import Bank is provided in the last section of this publication.

### What type of payment arrangements are most common in China trade deals?

General import payment practices are, for the most part, the same in China as in most other countries. Regardless of the source of financing there are usually two common payment mechanisms: **letter of credit** and **documents against payment.**

**LETTER OF CREDIT.** Although the Bank of China (BOC) dominates China's trade finance business, several banks, both Chinese and foreign, have the authority to issue letters of credit for Chinese imports. Other major Chinese banks operating trade finance businesses are People's Construction Bank of China, Industrial and Commercial Bank of China, Agricultural Bank of China and CITIC Industrial Bank. *Foreign banks with branch or representative offices in China can also issue letters of credit.*

There are a few peculiarities about letters of credit issued by Chinese banks. First, China will not allow letters of credit issued by its banks to be confirmed by other banks, Chinese or foreign. Second, China is not a member of the International Chamber of Commerce and, therefore, is not subject to the Unified Customs and Practices (UCP) 400 code regarding international trade payments. Some Chinese practices may diverge from the practices established under the UCP regime. For example, Chinese banks usually release funds, not at sight, but only after the headquarters office in China receives and examines all of the trade documents. UCP rules require at sight payments from the branch office overseas upon receipt of the full set of required trade documents.

Although there are still standard letter of credit forms, terms and conditions are generally negotiable, and are now set on a transaction-by-transaction basis.

The Bank of China's documentation requirements for letters of credit can include:

- Commercial invoice

- Ocean bill of lading or air waybill

- Packing list/weight memo

- Manufacturer's certificate of quality

- Copy of exporter's notification of shipment

- Statement that carrying vessel is chartered by a Chinese shipping corporation

- Insurance certificate covering at least 100 percent of the invoice value

- U.S. export license, if required

- Certificate of origin

Foreign companies should confirm in writing the document requirements of the BOC branch issuing a LC prior to signing the contract.

Some purchase contracts require the supplier to post a bond as protection for the buyer against failure to deliver. BOC will open a bid bond or a performance letter of credit (advance payment bond) in a Chinese buyer's favor against an irrevocable or standby letter of credit issued by the foreign supplier's bank in favor of the Bank of China.

DOCUMENTS AGAINST PAYMENT. This method of payment is similar to a letter of credit, but less formal and more flexible. Just as with letters of credit, the exporter submits a full set of trade documents for payments collection to the bank designated in the contract. The Chinese bank will send the documents to the home office, which examines them and, in some cases, passes them to the buyer for further examination. Payment is made after the documents have met the approval of all parties. This method of payment provides rather thin coverage against default. It can be considerably less expensive than a letter of credit, but should be used with some degree of caution.

Alternative payment practices include Letters of Guarantee and Open Accounts.

**Letters of Guarantee** (LGs) from Chinese banks to back up importer obligations are fairly common. However, they are considered much weaker than LCs for a number of reasons: LG text/undertakings vary considerably, and often include ambiguous references to underlying contract terms or penalties and deductions; LGs are not usually governed by UPC/ICC or other international guidelines; LGs are understood to be secondary obligations of the issuer under Chinese law. In addition, Chinese banks do not always require collateral of importers for LGs. LGs are commonly offered for transactions involving payment extending over one year or more, or by importers who do not wish to encumber their cash or credit lines by issuing LCs.

**Open Account** terms are also used for shipments to China, usually by companies with longstanding relationships with Chinese entities. Both Western and Chinese banks lack the power to enforce prompt importer payment for open account transactions.

### *How do the nese normally structure the payment schedule?*

Most People's Bank of China LCs are sight LCs. Payment is made only after the headquarters of the Chinese bank which issued the LC has received the export documents. This means a minimum 10 to 20 day wait before the U.S. exporter can collect payment for goods delivered. (For example, a U.S. exporter would arrange for all export documents to be shipped to PBOC, and then would have to wait for PBOC and the importer to review the documents before being paid.)

Another Chinese payment practice affects large equipment sales and technology exports to China. For such sales, Chinese buyers typically make a 10 to 25 percent down payment, then pay 70 to 75 percent on delivery and the remaining 10 to 15 percent on installation. However, at the time of the initial down payment, Chinese buyers often require a Standby Letter of Credit from the seller's bank, guaranteeing the return of the down payment if sales terms are not met. A problem arises when a smaller U.S. exporter does not have a credit line sufficient to issue the required Standby

LC. (*Note:* this special provision does not usually apply to sales of commodities or to sales of simple goods.)

### *What role can a foreign bank play in a trade transaction in China?*

China's banking market remains tightly regulated and strictly limits the involvement of foreign banks in the Chinese economy. However, recent actions by the government have served to expand the range of services now offered by foreign financial institutions in the PRC. Foreign bank involvement traditionally takes the form of representative offices or foreign joint venture. The lion's share of foreign banks in China retain only representative offices that are barred from undertaking income-generating activities (e.g. trade discounts, foreign exchange loans, loans to Chinese enterprises). However, recent reforms now allow foreign banks to issue letters of credit to foreign companies.

The exception to this rule is the role of foreign banks in China's special economic zones (SEZs) and designated developing coastal cities. Currently foreign banks are authorized to open branches or head offices in Shenzhen, Shekou, Zhuhai, Shantou, Xiamen and Hainan, as well as Shanghai and a number of other coastal cities. These offices can issue letters of credit, offer overdrafts and short-term loans, provide bank guarantees and trade discounting and open current accounts and time deposits for foreign-currency-denominated company and personal accounts.

A select group of Asian banks maintain branch offices in several regions of the PRC, including Hong Kong and Shanghai Banking Corporation, Bank of East Asia, and Standard Chartered Bank. These institutions have long-standing ties to the Chinese government and have maintained a presence in China that predates the 1949 revolution.

Many foreign financial institutions in China are evolving into investment consultants and investment partners. Foreign banks have intervened to settle trade transactions, offered assistance in the preparation of feasibility studies for joint ventures and assisted in the development of China's fledgling capital markets.

*Should countertrade be considered as a method of reducing the foreign exchange burden on a Chinese buyer?*

There are no formal countertrade requirements in the People's Republic of China. However, the general shortage of foreign exchange available on the market (as opposed to that in central government coffers) has made it necessary for some Chinese entities to resort to countertrade to finance imports. This form of trade has seen increased emphasis recently in China's current free wheeling trade and commercial environment, particularly in the power sector, where import demand far outstrips hard currency supply.

Countertrade can be difficult. Most companies that make a product attractive to foreign buyers will want to sell to foreign customers directly to earn their own foreign exchange, rather than sell, for local currency, to a foreign company. Success in this business requires a global trading network and a good deal of patience.

*How do I perform a credit check on a Chinese company?*

You don't. Very few Chinese companies disclose their financial reports, with the notable exception of those companies listed on the foreign stock exchanges. A better way to analyze the viability of a potential investment partner is to examine their network of contacts among local officials, trading companies and current customers. A well supported company will have access to the financial resources necessary to make the venture viable. A weak company will be unable to produce the official support necessary to meet your demands prior to signing the contract.

# INSURANCE IN CHINA

It is possible to gain insurance in China against both financial and political risks. The majority of insurance offered in China, including policies provided to foreign companies, is made available through the People's Insurance Company of China (PICC). By 1991 PICC had extended coverage to over $59 billion worth of international insurance business, yielding premium's of over $463 million.

## *What types of insurance can be purchased in the PRC by foreigners?*

Insurance in China offers protection against the following risks.

**COUNTERINDEMNITIES.** An exporter to China is required to pledge a counterindemnity to the (usually Chinese) bank that offers an advance payment guarantee against arbitrary draw down or unfair calling. Chinese insurance provides an on-demand bank guarantee indemnity that covers the exporter's counterindemnity risk.

**CONTRACT FRUSTRATION.** This insurance type covers the exporter's expenses when a contract is prematurely terminated for reasons beyond the exporter's control. Typically covered reasons include embargo, force majeure or rejection by the (Chinese) government buyer.

**EXCHANGE REPATRIATION.** This insurance option covers the exporter in the case of an arbitrary decision by the Chinese government to temporarily or permanently prohibit the remission of earned foreign exchange to the exporter's home country.

PICC's standard premium rates vary from 15 to 110 percent of the trading contract value. There is a wide range of premium rates because the standard rates offered by the PICC central administration are only guidelines for the company's 3,300+ subsidiary companies. In addition, PICC offers variable premium rates based on the foreign customer's country of origin. For many Third World countries rates will exceed those offered to foreign companies from the U.S. or Western Europe. Finally, rates will vary based on the products being traded or the business of the foreign joint venture. Despite the overwhelming size of PICC there is competition in China from other Chinese insurance companies. In addition, branch or subsidiary offices of PICC are often in competition with each other. As a result, quoted premiums in China are often negotiable, and foreign business persons should consider meeting with two or more insurance representatives while visiting the PRC.

**FOREIGN INSURANCE.** Although U.S. and foreign insurance companies may reinsure Chinese direct insurance on foreign risks, they are not permitted to do business in the Chinese domestic market or to insure foreign operations in China. Several foreign insurance companies currently have offices in the PRC. Foreign insurance companies may participate in China's insurance industry by entering into joint ventures with PICC, and several foreign firms, including industry giant American International Group, have entered into such joint venture arrangements.

American International Group, Inc.
Jing Guang Center #3407
Hu Jia Lou
Beijing 100020
People's Republic of China
Tel:5013388 x3407
Fax:5012878

# PART THREE

## Investing in China

# CHAPTER 12

# SMART STRATEGIES

# FOR INVESTORS

*"Beijing has been exploited by a parade of business suitors willing to indulge any local whim to romance local hosts to offer only the vague promise of further intimacies. At the same time, many foreign companies have waltzed into China, giddy about the prospects and ignorant of reality. The Chinese have a phrase for the resulting misperceptions: Tong chung yi meng—Same bed, different dreams."*

**—James Sterba**
**Wall Street Journal**

*A*n "appropriate" China strategy recognizes the potential (hidden and apparent) of China's market and indigenous industrial capabilities, embodies a long-term commitment, and is designed not only to exploit opportunities in Greater China, but to tie together other elements of the firm's Asia strategy. Assuming that China will continue on its apparent path to establish a highly visible presence in the global economy, firms should be seeking a long-term commercial relationship with China that can combine the various research and production assets of both parties to develop and manufacture competitive products to be sold in regional and international markets—and not just China alone.

American corporations pursue eight different corporate strategies in China, all of which you should consider before making a decision about how your company will participate in the region's economic take-off.

*What investment strategies can be pursued in Greater China?*

## 1. Manufacturing for Export

The ultimate objective of an "export platform" strategy is to increase price competitiveness by cutting the cost of producing goods by employing cheaper labor, renting cheaper land to place a factory and locating where taxes and duties are low. As taxation, as a percentage of production, has outstripped wage level in importance in this strategy, companies have been locating in Greater China increasingly on the basis of preferential regulations, such as taxes, fees and rental rates. Overhead may also be cut when firms locate close to their markets, since they can reduce transportation costs. In this way, they can also acquire cheaper, locally sourced raw materials. American companies have used this approach in Taiwan where "export zones" offer an extremely attractive setting for offshore subsidiaries and more recently, China where wage rates are the lowest in East Asia. Of course, firms have to make sure that the products they produce overseas are not sold to their current overseas and home markets behind their backs by the country in which they have set up operations. Few U.S. firms have set up in China *solely* to export to world markets on a large scale, though many firms have been forced to export a certain percentage of their production in order to gain market access in China. However, scores of very small Sino-foreign enterprises have been formed in Special Economic Zones with the objective of exporting light industrial products and foodstuffs for export via Hong Kong and Macao. Except in export zones, the Chinese are not normally accepting of a venture which utilizes only cheap labor and does not transfer any technology.

### Can you hire inexpensive labor in Taiwan?

Most Taiwanese and Hong Kong Chinese do not actively seek to be employed by a foreign firm, like the mainland Chinese do. Labor is in short supply in Taiwan and Hong Kong and the immigration of cheaper "alien" labor has been limited, especially in Taiwan. Educated Taiwanese desire to earn PhDs in the United States, after which they usually return to Taiwan to work; wages in Taiwan are thus high, and will be until immigration rules are relaxed.

## 2. Developing and Exploiting Natural Resources

Companies in resource-poor nations have made investments in Greater China as part of their quest for new sources of raw materials, like coal, oil, lumber, rubber, copper, and uranium. Lacking home sources of numerous essential raw materials, the Japanese are especially active in Greater China in this regard. Many of these projects find their funding through government loans and/or aid packages made available by the Asia Development Bank, the World Bank, and other international banking institutions. The added costs of pursuing this strategy usually involve infrastructural development to facilitate the transportation of raw materials from the interior of the source country to the receiving country.

For some U.S. companies, China offers a promising source of raw materials. Many firms involved in petroleum, coal, and mineral development have entered China as part of their world exploration and development endeavors. Yet because of infrastructure deficiencies these materials are not altogether a good bargain. For example, Occidental Company began work on the Antaibao mine in Shanxi Province, but it became too expensive to refine the coal because of the high ratio of unusable rock to coal, coupled with the high cost of transporting it inside China.

Because the Taiwan Basin of Xinjiang Province and the South China Sea are of the last frontiers of unexplored offshore resources, it is no surprise that oil exploration has attracted the foreign investment to China. Petroleum is China's most lucrative export industry. Since China opened up its sea tracts to a global sweepstakes, most of the major oil companies have entered into exploration China contracts. Unfortunately, no significant discoveries have been made in China's offshore oil tracts to this point. Many of these foreign companies entered into long-term contacts with China, obligating them to train Chinese workers and to transfer technology. The same is happening now in Xinjiang since the discovery of major oil fields there.

### 3. Sharing the Burden of R&D

Under this investment strategy, a firm usually forms a joint venture partnership with a counterpart that has the inhouse resources and/or government backing to share the expense of developing a new product that it cannot afford to develop—due to high cost and high risk—on its own. In Greater China, this strategy has grown in popularity as the cost of developing technologically sophisticated products has skyrocketed while unaccompanied by a lessening of the inherent risk that the new product may fail in the marketplace, even with a concerted R&D effort behind it. Also, increased "modualization" of global industrial systems permits more of this aptly named "technological cross- fertilization." Since the exorbitant cost of developing new airliners necessitates the support of cash-rich counterparts, at least one U.S. carrier is currently following this investment strategy in Taiwan. In the near term, the People's Republic will likely foster more sharing of R&D endeavors by alotting revenue earned from exports for cooperative projects that they are willing to help finance. Possible project areas could include: aerospace, satellite communications, nuclear power, and superconductivity. Opportunities may also arise in the development of software design to accommodate the Chinese environment. Wang and Visidata were early participants in this area in Shanghai. These same areas will be those that China will achieve technological capability that may interest foreign firms seeking to acquire technology from China in the future. Japanese companies are especially keen to develop new sources of highly trained, and less expensive, labor in Greater China since a scarcity of technicians in Japan is predicted to grow in the late 1990s. In

China you can hire a qualified computer system engineer in for
$200-250 per month. Motorola is following an R&D based strategy
by locating its new 326,000 square foot Asia-Pacific Headquarters
in Hong Kong, called Silicon Harbour Centre. The enormous complex is not only the company's corporate headquarters, but also
design, manufacturing, and computer center serving the Asian
region and employing highly trained technicians. The strategy is of
course, to be near the fast growing markets for semiconductor
chips, but also to utilize the talents of Chinese technical people.
As C.D. Tam, Corporate Vice President and General Manager of
Motorola's Hong Kong operations, told *China Trade* recently:
"When people talk about the Chinese-American businessman, you
can generally take it for granted that he's good. But what few people have thought of is that the Chinese are also very good technically—half of the people who work in Silicon Valley [in California]
are Chinese engineers and research people. So what we wanted to
do here in the Asia Pacific region was to bring together technology and business—the two strengths of the Chinese people—and
train people to become businessmen."

## 4. Holding Ground in a New Market

Due to the development of new technology and the acquisition of older, but not yet obsolete, technology by Chinese nations,
these once noncompetitive areas are quickly entering the fold of
the world economy as producers of manufactured products. To
maintain market share in the face of growing economies-of-scale
in Greater China, many U.S. firms have entered venture agreements simply to hold ground in these emerging markets where
before long, indigenous producers will have acquired similar technology to produce the products on their own. Many times this
strategy involves technology transfer via licensing. For firms that
have no presence in a burgeoning market, licensing may be a way
to lessen the negative effects of not participating in markets where
its competition may have a secure presence already. Licensing can
also generate cash flow needed to conduct the necessary R&D on
new technology that can put the parent firm in a more competitive position vis-a-vis its immediate rivals. Also by being on the
inside of a market, some firms believe they may be able to avoid
import restrictions that may be set up to offset the purchases of

foreign goods. A free market for commodities does not exist yet in China, or for that matter Taiwan, and these firms believe that their presence in the market may offer an advantage if import policies become even more severe in their products lines. This strategy might also be called "protecting against protectionism."

## 5. Acquiring New Technology

When the parent firm cannot afford to develop a new technology, it can opt to form a joint venture with an overseas firm that has already developed it, in an effort to acquire it. This objective may be intense if the newly developed technology represents a radical new breakthrough that threatens the competitiveness of the firm's present product lines. As technological innovation becomes more globalized, many firms will enter Asia simply out of technological survival, i.e., if they don't, their products will soon become obsolete. The trend will only increase as traditionally separate technological fields begin to merge, e.g., when genetic engineering firms link up in cooperative ventures with pharmaceutical firms in order to produce new drugs based on biotechnology.

## 6. Transplanting Corporate Rivalry into a New Market

In this investment scenario, competition between corporate rivals—for example, Pepsi and Coke, Xerox and Fujitsu, etc.—is superimposed on the Greater China playing field. Often these firms set up wholly foreign-owned subsidiaries as part of a "battering ram" approach that seeks a share of a new market relative to their competition. Companies following this approach are keen to protect their state-of-the-art technological know-how from spreading into the recipient country, creating an undesired competitor. Plus a firm with this strategy soley in mind is not comparatively attractive to a host Chinese company. Essentially, firms in this category have entered China to gain a foothold in the market before other firms in the same line of business do so. Also, some multinationals fear that if they do not enter China now, the best Chinese partners may be taken by their competitors. By seeking out a position in the China market they are responding to two possible types of competition: (1) home country competition—where

China becomes the site for the playing out of competition among other domestic firms and themselves. For example, Sanyo and Hitachi have entered China and are currently competing for shares of China's consumer electronics market. American computer firms such as Wang Laboratories and Hewlett-Packard are doing the same; (2) transnational competition—where competition among firms from different countries is transplanted into China. Many U.S. firms, for example, realize that Japanese firms are entrenched in the China market and, in the long-run, could prove insurmountable world export competitors if allowed to capture the China market, especially if China's modernization program develops to its full potential in the near term. Within this context, therefore, global competition is superimposed on China. The competition between AMC and Volkswagen is a good example; each firm is attempting to gain a strong foothold in China by agreeing to source components from China. Such deals are attractive to China because they encourage import substitution and technology transfer which eases the strain on foreign exchange reserves.

## 7. Co-opting the Competition

What happens when a company in Greater China acquires, steals, or simply develops a technology that is identical to that your firm currently bases its competitiveness? What happens when that company suddenly floods your markets with low-priced, high-quality goods produced with that technology? One investment strategy available is to acquire control of the Chinese company through stock ownership and/or equity joint venture. This strategy became popular among U.S. automakers losing ground to Japanese and Korean automakers; the General Motors joint venture with Toyota formed in part, so that GM could control—or co-opt—Toyota's share of the U.S. market. As Chinese companies begin to compete, a firm may want to acquire a controlling stake in them through partial ownership. Firms such as these enter China not only to compete among themselves or protect market share, but also to stay abreast of emerging Chinese industrial competitors. Recognizing that China's R&D and industrial sectors have made headway in certain areas, a select number of firms have decided to plug into these developments, hoping to build strong working relationships with the most technologically dynamic and advanced units in the Chinese economy. Both U.S. and Japanese firms have concluded that to be a part owner is a better position in the long run as China becomes more competitive in export markets. Also, in this way firms believe they can influence the course of future developments in their particular industry.

## 8. Penetrating a New Market

The most popular investment strategy pursued in the PRC aims to capture new markets by setting up operations in-country, behind tariff and nontariff barriers, via any number of different business forms. During the 1980s, most U.S. firms pursuing this strategy in China set up ventures in order to build a "low risk bridgehead" into China's domestic market. Such firms believed that they could eventually lock the Chinese into use of their product and its successors by entering the market early or by offering technology in return for greater market access. By making direct investments in the form of a joint venture or coproduction agreements, foreign firms could get closer to the Chinese market than by merely licensing their technology to a Chinese factory. In some cases the initiation of a joint venture even yielded a market access clause in contract. The same approach has become more pronounced in the 1990s as access to the market has widened. For example, the bulk of the venture capital currently entering the Shanghai area is coming in for the purpose of investing in ventures that will serve the huge local market. "Growth is the goal," investment project manager Dean T. W. Ho of UBS International told me in Shanghai, "Fast growth." (Mr. Ho's company was an original investment partner in the Great Wall Hotel in Beijing.) The common denominator in these deals is that the foreign firm must offer the necessary perks to gain market access. These concessions often include: offsetting a percentage of production to indigenous producers, sourcing supplies from domestic sources, exporting a certain percentage of production, and transferring advanced technology. These strategic investments may also take advantage of Chinese labor and inexpensive start-up costs and may be motivated by a desire to get closer to certain raw materials. Firms sometimes leverage a commitment to a joint venture in return for guaranteed supplies of certain materials.

As in other parts of Asia, U.S. firms have actively pursued the market by transferring technology. However, the Chinese are often unwilling to adequately pay for the technology and training they so badly need. Many American corporations in China have been selling for modest profit, sharing their technology with only limited compensation, and paying dearly for the opportunity to do business in the China market. In addition, many firms have established service-oriented businesses in China as a means of increasing market share, following their product sales or even joint ventures, into China to cultivate satisfied customers. Foxboro set up a sales and service arm in order to expand its market, but more important, to dispel any notion that dealing with a foreign firm would be a liability in terms of service and maintenance. Foxboro officials wanted to demonstrate that dealing with the Foxboro joint venture would be an asset in comparison with dealing with other foreign firms without an equity presence in the People's Republic.

Because the costs of participating in China's investment opportunities are high and the risks great, most of the pioneering firms which entered China and made financial commitments there were large multinational corporations that already had a worldwide network of subsidiary companies and factories. The majority of these firms pursued a strategy aimed solely at penetrating a new market. The same trend continues, except that the players have become smaller. Thousands of medium-sized and small companies have set up ventures in China in order to penetrate the local market and utilize cheap Chinese labor. Firms which pursue strategies in China other than an export platform one, or one aimed at exploiting the domestic market, are all too rare.

### What other ways can I invest in China?

As the pace of economic reform in China accelerates, new options are being created for foreign companies wishing to invest in the People's Republic. Companies could consider purchasing a stake in a state-run corporation and converting it into a joint venture. Firms may also enter the China market by purchasing shares of stock in Chinese companies. Foreign entities may purchase B-class shares on China's stock markets, H-class shares listed on the Hong Kong exchange, or shares of one of the few I-class, or international shares of Chinese companies, listed on international stock exchanges. Investors beware, however. Chinese companies that have issued B shares to foreign investors do not have to answer to Western board members. These are Chinese firms, and as such, they are viewed by many observers to be risky investments at best. The China Fund is currently earning a 15–30 percent yield during 1994.

### How many PRC firms want to go public?

Seemingly, they all do. Yet only the best performing and clout-possessing will ever actually get listed inside or outside China. Beijing does ensure in its selection process that a handful of competitive firms in all of China's provinces will be permitted to list. Even Tibet has its candidates, including the Tibet Shengdi Natural Mineral Water Company, which wants to issue 5,000 shares with its joint venture partner in Sichuan, to start up a project exporting Himalayan water. (Before you dismiss the potential, recall that people had doubts about Federal Express overnight mail in its inception also.)

### Are PRC companies listed on the Hang Seng stock exchange in Hong Kong?

Yes. The so-called "red chips" number is about 40 as of this writing. Chinese companies either buy a controlling interest in a publicly traded Hong Kong company and raise revenue through it, or state-owned PRC companies list on the Hang Seng exchange directly. The most prominent of the latter is Shougang Corporation, a steel maker that has the backing of Deng Xiaoping and a partnership with the Li Kashing group. Shougang has purchased a total of six Hong Kong companies, which operate, as the common phrase goes, under its "umbrella." More Chinese umbrellas in Hong Kong have been formed since, as PRC companies continue to claim an increasing degree of control over Hong Kong.

### *Are "red chips" a wise investment?*

Not for the faint of heart. China linked stocks fell in mid-1993 by 20 percent due to austerity measures announced in China. It was thought that PRC companies would have to return profits to the Chinese government to support an ailing yuan. Lolliman Holdings, under the CITIC umbrella fell 37.7 percent. Tung Win Steel, listed by Shougang Corporation, lost 28.6 percent of its value. "China plays" are prone to every rumor of policy change that eminate from the Mainland, not to mention the fragile health of Deng Xiaoping. On the other hand, companies in Hong Kong that successfully tap a rich vein in the China market, like Goldlion in 1993 have watched their stock fly up by a factor of 4 in less than a year. Tsingdao was the first state-owned PRC firm to be listed directly on the Hang Seng. Shougang is the PRC's most active dealmaker in Hong Kong. Its annual foreign exchange earnings jumped 76 percent to US$340 million during the first seven months of 1993 as it set about on a spree of takeovers in Hong Kong. A recent mainland company to "seek a back door" listing on the Hong Kong stock exchange is China Metallurgical Import and Export Corporation (CMI & E), which runs steel mills and employs 240,000 people. The state-run mega corporation paid HK$140 for a 39 percent stake in Chee Shing Holdings from the family that owns most of the company's shares.

Investors must remember that most PRC companies have dubious export potential; they are vulnerable to incoming foreign competition (especially if China becomes a member of GATT), they often are subjected to high and unpredictable tax rates, and they often carry enormous worker welfare obligations.

You might also consider the U.S. company "China play," one which stands to profit big by entering the China market. Singer is such a firm, with one store open in China and eight more on the way, with a two-thirds stake in a sewing machine manufacturing venture in China that will serve a market of an estimated 8 million potential unit sales. Suppliers of "the four essentials" in China could also be candidates. Look for internationally oriented companies entering China with a clear market strategy based both on the strong initiative of the CEO and a long-term commitment to success.

## China's listed companies in Hong Kong

Major Chinese firms listed or to be listed on Hong Kong stock exchange

| COMPANY | SHAREHOLDERS |
| --- | --- |
| Ka Wah Bank | China International Trust and Investment |
| Union Bank of Hong Kong | China Merchants Holdings |
| Guangdong Investment | State-run firm in Guangdong Province |
| CITIC Pacific | China International Trust and Investment |
| China Overseas Land & Investment | China State Construction Engineering |
| China Resources Enterprise | China Resources Holdings |
| China Travel Int'l Investment Hong Kong | China Travel Service Holdings |
| Shougang Concord Internatinal Enterprises | Shougang Corp. |
| Eastern Century | Shougang Corp. |
| Continental Mariner Investment | China International Trust and Investment |
| Onfem Holdings | China National Nonferrous Metals Industry |
| Public International Investments | China Venturetech Investment and Shanghai International Securities |
| China Everbright International | China Everbright Holdings |
| Santai Manufacturing | Shougang Corp. |
| Paragon Holdings | China National Petroleum |
| Shougang Concord Grand | Shougang Corp. |
| Hoi Sing Holdings | Shougang Corp. |
| Tsingtao Brewery | State-owned |
| Shanghai Petrochemical | State-owned |
| Guangzhou Shipyard International | State-owned |
| Beiren Printing Machinery Holdings | State-owned |
| Maanshan Iron & Steel | State-owned |
| Kunming Machine Tool | State-owned |

### *Can the Shanghai, Shenzhen, and Hong Kong stock markets coexist after reunification?*

Shenzhen is likely to be absorbed into the Hong Kong financial market, but Shanghai will raise capital for the economic region of the Yangtze River Delta while Hong Kong does so for the economic circle of Guangdong, Hainan, Guannxi, and Fujian.

### How do stock investors get information about the performance of Chinese companies?

Information about Chinese company performance is hard to come by in the West. The shareholder relations departments of the firms provide investors and reporters information that is deemed appropriate for public consumption. The foreign securities companies issue English and Chinese reports including daily news about the listed companies, but these reports are not readily available outside China and Hong Kong. Call your broker to find out about report availability. In China, stock "salons" have sprung up, especially in Shanghai, where so-called stock experts provide hot tips to the local investors, and are known to manipulate the market by spreading strategic rumors about listed companies. Their paying audiences are typically unsophisticated speculators who stick to playing the momentary rise and fall of stocks rather than looking at company performance data. "They would not know how to use good information about the listed companies if it existed," says Claire Cheng, a reporter for the Shanghai Star, an English-language newspaper owned by the China Daily which covers the Shanghai Stock Exchange.

### Does an index of China-related stocks exist?

Yes. The Peregrine Greater China Index averages 30 components including "B" shares on the Shenzhen and Shanghai exchanges, ten Hong Kong companies with 20 percent of their sales, assets or earnings from China, and a PRC company listed on the New York Stock Exchange.

### Can a foreign company "go public" in China?

With the growth of capital markets in the PRC some foreign companies are now exploring the option of offering shares of stock to investors on one of China's stock exchanges. At this time only new or preexisting equity joint ventures are permitted to issue shares on China's stock markets. Wholly foreign-owned enterprises may not convert to companies limited by shares. The establishment of a company limited by shares offers access to increased capital through additional investors, although the venture's capital reserve requirement (35 percent) is higher than an equity joint venture. This investment option also allows for the cross-holding of shares between the legal entities of multinational investors, thus securing links with other components of a company's investment network in China or allowing ties between more than one foreign company. A company limited by shares also has limited liability under Chinese law. The company's liability for its debts is limited to the extent of its assets, while the liability of the shareholders is limited to the value of the subscription price of their shares. It should be stressed that China's capital markets are still in their infancy, and clear rules regarding the flow of capital from stock markets into foreign-invested enterprises have yet to be published. Companies should expect a lengthy approval process when deciding to establish this form of joint venture.

**FORMING AN UMBRELLA COMPANY.** Companies wishing to increase their visibility and impact in China may wish to consider trying to establish an umbrella company in the PRC. Also known as holding companies or investment companies, umbrella companies are currently not permitted under general Chinese investment law. However, the Ministry of Foreign Trade and Economic Cooperation (MOFTEC) has granted special permission to a number of well known international companies to establish umbrella companies.

An umbrella company unites two or more existing Sino-foreign joint ventures into a single company. This company can then conduct integrated sourcing, manufacturing, sales, and service activities to Chinese customers, and can also export a percentage of its production abroad. This investment option allows for the full exercise of a foreign company's management skills and overcomes problems of coordination and distribution. In many cases it has been an effective response to China's limited transportation system and lack of marketing and service expertise. Umbrella companies also offer significant foreign exchange and tax advantages to potential investors. Foreign exchange can be balanced between different operations and renminbi profits can be consolidated prior to being swapped for foreign exchange and repatriated. Umbrella companies may also allow the parent company to defer taxes on profits from its China ventures if those profits are reinvested in the PRC.

# REAL ESTATE MARKETS

Investing in Chinese real estate has been a boom to foreign investors who had the foresight to get in early. Though foreigners can only lease but not own land in China, literally hundreds of foreign-invested real estate companies have been launched near the opened land markets throughout China. Unfortunately, a crackdown on many of these offices is expected because often they are capitalized with loans from Chinese banks rather than a foreign partner. Another complaint is that the foreign partner tends to kick in less than 10 percent of the contracted capital with its own funds.

Increases in capital construction peaked at the end of 1992, growing by 75 percent over the previous year. The result was rapidly escalating property values that made several Chinese developers millionaires overnight and caused rents in urban areas to skyrocket. Foreign companies were especially hard hit, as office space dried up in Beijing and Shanghai and waiting periods for new offices grew to six months or more. The Pudong Economic Development Area in Shangai is an instructive example. When the Shanghai Municipal Government first began transferring property rights to the Area in 1991, local officials were leasing space to foreign companies at $61 per square meter for a fifty-year lease. At the beginning of 1993 the charge had been raised to $97.

Since Vice-Premier Zhu Rongji imposed partial restrictions on property development the price of land has fallen in many parts of China, although office space is still hard to come by in Shanghai. Estimates now project a slow decline in property values over the next several years, and some analysts predict the surge of projects currently under construction will yield a glut of office

space by the turn of the century. Two-to-three bedroom apartments in Shanghai now sell for $250,000, while in 1993 they were
selling for only $100,000. Although rapid construction of houses
should produce a real estate glut in the near future, at least in
Shanghai, the city is still a landlord's market as of this writing.
Keep in mind when considering real estate investments in China
that your market is mainly Taiwanese and Hong Kong Chinese
buyers. Given that Taiwan and Hong Kong are potentially to be at
odds with China politically, you could be exposed to significant
risk of losing your customer base should political winds shift. Plus,
the Chinese government can choose to open up huge new tracts
of land to foreign ownership at any time causing the price of existing real estate to fall. Another risk to calculate.

### What has been the strategy of Japanese firms investing in China?

Unlike European and American firms, which are often willing to enter cooperative manufacturing agreements and transfer
technology, Japan's business interests in China have depended
mainly on direct sales of goods. Japanese corporations have been
spearheaded by their representative trading firms (soga sosha)
which help them source raw materials throughout China and sell
a vast array of Japanese manufactured products. Acting as responsive middlemen in a burgeoning market, many Japanese trading
firms arrange billions of dollars worth of China trade each year;
they are also well placed to set up countertrade agreements, structure creative solutions to pricing and payment problems on the
Chinese side, and strike quickly when new marketing opportunities arise. The first soga sosha in China, Nissho Iwai Corporation
(NIC), focuses on setting up extremely complex transactions
involving China, Japan, and third countries. In one deal, NIC
shipped processed marine products from third countries to a
Chinese factory, from which they were exported to the Japanese
market.

The second, less intense phase of Japan's approach has been
to transfer into China its competing manufacturing firms that produce high-demand household consumer goods. This move has
been made in response to rising tariff barriers imposed by Chinese
trade authorities on imported consumer goods. Many Japanese
firms that produce restricted items are now positioned inside the

tariff barriers. Some of these equity-based ventures include Hitachi, set up in 1981 and producing color television sets; Sanyo Electric Company, with ventures in Shenzhen that produce radios, televisions, and tape recorders; and Canon, which has been furnishing parts for copiers in Guangzhou Province.

Although other Japanese firms, including Ricoh, Toshiba, and Matsushita Electric Industrial Co., Ltd., established joint ventures early on in China, the Japanese generally showed an aversion to setting up joint ventures there until recently. The Japanese pursued a strategy of reduced operations and patiently waited for the most critical problems in the market—problems in conversion of profits, insufficient patent laws, and inaccessibility to the domestic market—to be improved. By the mid-1990s the Japanese have moved more quickly. They have set up roughly 4,000 investment projects in China as of early 1993 worth $6.5 billion, focused primarily in Shanghai, Tianjin, and Dalian. As in the United States, Japanese firms are quickly forging integrated business relationships between their companies in Japan and throughout Greater China—synergetic tie-ups between manufacturing, R&D, and marketing companies, guided to some extent by the Japanese government, and (as in the U.S.) closed to non-Japanese players. Soon, observers will likely be talking, and writing, about the domination of the region by Japan's "Greater China *keiretzu*."

# CHAPTER 13

# BUILDING

# PARTNERSHIPS

# IN THE PRC

*Many times we find business people in China trying to mold their transactions to the requirements of an equity joint venture, when they should be doing exactly the opposite. They should take the requirements of the transaction and find a legal relationship between the parties that best suits the situation. We find the legal and business environment is becoming much more flexible and is allowing technology transfer or cooperative production in different legal relationships that would not require a formal joint venture.*

**—An American Lawyer
in Beijing**

$O$nce the decision has been made to enter the market in the form of a venture (as opposed to direct exports), where does a firm begin in its search for the proper partner on the Chinese side? Of all the potential entry points, which ones offer genuinely beneficial connections with a viable counterpart in China? No golden axioms or hard-and-fast rules exist for locating the "perfect" partner. However, by looking at the past experience of firms in China, one can begin to surmise the appropriate items to consider and the relevant questions to ask during a firm's search for a counterpart in China.

## BUILDING PARTNERSHIPS IN THE PRC

Sino-U.S. business partnerships often originate in an unorthodox manner because of China's provincial, fiefdom-like organizational structure that puts a premium on personal connections. A number of American companies have simply stumbled into China by coincidence or by accident. The catalyst may have been a company executive meeting a Chinese economic official at a trade convention, and then running into him again later at another location, perhaps in China. Or it might have been a Chinese-American in the firm, through a connection with a relative in a remote Chinese province, who brings an opportunity to the attention of his or her boss. Or a telex arrives one day from a Chinese factory expressing a desire to visit the company's facilities and discuss possible cooperation in a venture. Many of the early pioneering deals were put together as the direct result of the personal motivations of American executives who saw great promise in the China market. Some of the early firms were led into China by veritable crusaders who boarded the first plane to the mainland the day the door was opened. Some American executives (e.g., John Marshall of 3M, Armand Hammer of Occidental Petroleum, and Todd Clare of AMC) had been enthusiastic about the mainland for years, especially if they had previously dealt with East Asia and had since become top executives with the power and position to usher their firms into China. Interestingly, the Chinese had similar true believers on their side. These individuals, either through their educational training or by having relatives in the United States, served as advocates of strengthening links with American industry.

### *What entry modes exist in China for initiating a venture?*

Until 1979, only very formal, highly controlled channels existed for the foreigner to approach the Chinese. For years, the

Canton Trade Fair was the sole mode for introducing your company to China. As recently as six years ago, foreign companies had to choose among the various foreign trade corporations under MOFTEC to gain access to China's economy at all. With time, and the ratification of China's investment statutes, the process of entering China's economy has grown more standardized and systematic. Today, multiple paths exist for foreign firms seeking partnerships with Chinese industrial enterprises.

High-level corporate diplomacy has served as a stimulus behind some Sino-U.S. joint projects. In 1985, Hewlett-Packard opened a joint venture that had its origin in talks held between former Premier Zhao Enlai and former U.S. Secretary of State Henry Kissinger. Other agreements were linked to the ongoing bilateral science and technology cooperation accords between the two countries. Coca-cola began its involvement in China in 1927 when it started selling coke there as well as setting up bottling plants in Shanghai and Tianjin. Two years later, it set up a plant in Tsingdao. The company returned to China after the Mao years in 1979. Coca-cola now controls 12 percent of China's soft drink market, selling 1.8 billion bottles of Coke there in 1992. Its ten bottling plants posted a RmB 300 million pre-tax profit in that year, its second straight year of profitability in 12 years operation in the PRC. The company has invested $100 million dollars in bottling plants and a joint venture soft drink maker, and plan to invest $150 million more by 1998. Maurice Greenberg, the CEO of American International Group (AIG), the only foreign insurance company as yet allowed to operate in China's potentially lucrative insurance market, worked in AIG's Shanghai offices on the Bund before the Communists took over in 1949. AIG has been in China since 1919. Greenberg also founded the International Business Leader's Advisory Council, which assisted they mayor of the city, Zhu Rongji.

Today, contacts can be made at a variety of different levels. This makes the selection process much more complex, but it does allow for more intimate working relations between the foreign firm and its specific Chinese counterpart. In spite of a certain reimposition of control by the central authorities regarding foreign economic and investment relations, MOFERT no longer coordinates all of the access routes. For better or worse, the cast of characters grows daily as those provinces and cities in the interior compete with China's coastal cities for attracting potential investors and foreign partners.

An entry-mode decision must take into account the size and type of project to be undertaken as well as the specific organizations that have responsibility for the implementation of the venture. A project involving extensive infrastructural improvements or multiprovince coordination of Chinese government agencies requires a myriad of approvals from central and local officials. From the outset, such a project should have the backing of an influential government-entity counterpart that will facilitate all project-related activities. If the project requires large inputs of foreign exchange on the Chinese side, an investment entity such as CITIC or one of its provincial counterparts might be an appropriate point of contact, since these agencies control large sums of foreign exchange and have close ties with the Bank of China.

### *Is it necessary to open an office in Hong Kong or in the PRC?*

To begin to establish a network of business connections and create a good reputation among Chinese customers, Western companies typically set up an office presence in the China market. This is done at the very beginning if a firm needs to position itself close to its prospective end-users. Trading firms, for example, require a more visible presence than others because trading involves constant interaction with suppliers, distributors, and a variety of other entities. Office presence, however, is expensive and not always the most cost-effective use of resources. Thus, the majority of firms doing business in China still do so from their Hong Kong or Tokyo offices. Most small firms merely selling to China still operate from within the United States. Obviously, while operating from outside China may be sufficient for some firms, it may also prevent them from staying current on the latest business scuttlebutt or maintaining the maximum attention of their Chinese counterparts. Many U.S. firms are penetrating the China market, as well as other burgeoning Asian markets, from their comfortable offices in Hong Kong, and will continue to do so at least until 1997, when Hong Kong becomes part of the People's Republic. For the average firm, an office in Hong Kong does hold several advantages. First, Hong Kong offers office space that is less expensive than in China. Because of the high costs in China, some firms simply base their operations in Hong Kong and make frequent trips to the People's Republic. For the same cost of renting an office in Beijing and stationing an expatriate there for a year ($250,000-300,000), a firm can send a small team into the People's Republic from the United States twice a month for the whole year at $10,000 per visit. In addition, appreciable profits continue to be made by foreigners who ally with Hong Kong businessmen to invest in cooperative ventures in the People's Republic. This sort of venture has gained in popularity as China has decentralized economic decision making and the special economic zones have developed a more functional business infrastructure. Second, the role of Hong Kong may be more important to foreign firms as a next-door source of management personnel, financial services, and components, which can be utilized in operations within the People's Republic. In addition, Hong Kong reigns supreme as a way station for re-exports from China. Hong Kong will remain a conduit for goods exported by joint ventures in China to other nations in Asia. Heretofore it has also served as a vehicle for facilitating China trade with Taiwan, Japan, and South Korea, especially on the import side.

### *Will maintaining an office in China help me find a better partner?*

Office presence in China certainly does not represent a panacea for finding the right venture partner. This can be accomplished through a number of avenues. A proven method is the direct communication of proposals to potential Chinese counterparts who are introduced by a Chinese consulate business officer in the United States, or a U.S. consulate business officer in China. There are numerous examples of Chinese-American firms in the United States being approached directly as potential business partners. This was especially true for small firms that produced machinery or parts and components for manufacturing processes. Evidently, information concerning their products and technologies had been previously obtained as part of an intensive, orchestrated effort by Chinese factories and/or technology import corporations. The Chinese also frequently purchase space in major periodicals and newspapers to advertise projects open to foreign participation and invite foreign executives to attend technology and product fairs throughout China. In some instances, these advertisements go unseen by U.S. firms, which is unfortunate because these fairs differ from exhibitions in that they are specifically joint venture fairs in which Chinese municipalities and provinces solicit foreign partners directly. In the case of Cummins Engine Company, the China National Technical Import Corporation (Techimport), an agency under MOFERT, invited a Cummins delegation to China in July 1978 to discuss a technology transfer project. It was no coincidence that the China National Machinery Import and Export Corporation (MACHIMPEX), another subordinate to MOFERT, had purchased ten Cummins engines from the company's Manila office a few months earlier. In 1979, soon after the Cummins delegation visited China, the Chinese contracted with the Japanese firm Komatsu to license their technology to produce bulldozers in two factories in China. The connecting link in the strategy of courting both of these firms was the Komatsu powers its vehicles with Cummins engines, which it licenses from Cummins Engine Company. Because Komatsu could not sublicense the Cummins diesel engine technology in China, the Chinese were highly motivated to offer Cummins preferential treatment to entice the company to transfer their engine technology. This case also points out the importance of monitoring the finished products and components China purchases and what products come under licenses to be manufactured there. Certainly, a vast number of U.S. firms fail to realize that some of their products and technology are currently being sold to China as part of finished goods assembled by other companies around the world.

### Would hiring a Hong Kong trading company give me an advantage in locating a partner?

Though Hong Kong offers the foreign firm many benefits and comforts, there exists a widespread misperception that by going into China through Hong Kong representatives, a U.S. firm will gain an absolute advantage. Indeed, some Hong Kong representatives can offer valuable connections in the People's Republic. However, if a U.S. firm enters the China market through a Hong Kong subsidiary or partner, it may offset some of the clout that the firm, through its reputation, may wield among Chinese leaders. The Chinese greatly respect American businesspersons and engineers, and consider an American presence in China a sign of great sincerity and commitment. A firm should not assume that a Hong Kong negotiator's common culture link can necessarily overcome the regional loyalties and idiosyncrasies of various parts of China. Officials working in the central government in Beijing are not always impressed by the use of Hong Kong negotiators. For one thing, Cantonese speaking traders from Hong Kong do not always make the best speakers of putonghua (Mandarin Chinese). In fact, there is a traditional Chinese saying: Don't be afraid of the heavens; don't be afraid of hell; just be afraid of a Cantonese trying to speak Mandarin! Another drawback to using Hong Kong negotiators concerns the past dealings between Hong Kong businessmen and their Chinese counterparts. There may arise certain doubts in the minds of Chinese officials regarding the integrity and reliability of the Hong Kong representative. While there is often no basis in fact for this kind of perception, it nonetheless may be a problem worth considering. Another common practice that frequently leads to problems is the use of a Hong Kong trading firm as an intermediary between potential foreign and Chinese partners. One firm made the mistake of transferring the main responsibilities for supervision and control of its manufacturing contract with China to a Hong Kong trading company that had no experience with either the specific equipment in question or the qualifications for selecting the Chinese factories that would manufacture the equipment. The U.S. firm, therefore, was not involved directly with the end-user in the People's Republic, leaving quality specifications largely unmonitored. As one would expect, the ensuing equipment malfunctions led to the collapse of the enterprise with concomitant losses to both the U.S., Hong Kong, and Chinese companies. This is not to downplay the value of contacts with trading entities; they are often useful in establishing initial contacts. Including them in the implementation of a contractual agreement and plant operations, however, generally spells trouble later on.

### *Is using a Chinese government-operated investment broker a good strategy for U.S. firms seeking Chinese partners?*

If the Chinese press is any guide, more and more investment companies in the People's Republic nowadays exist primarily as brokers for U.S. firms seeking Chinese partners. These companies differ from their counterparts in the West in that they are government operated; however, their income is based on commission. If they have a direct link to the potential Chinese partner, they may have a vested interest in selecting that partner, even though it may not be the most ideal one available. On the other hand, such companies make good potential business partners if they are close to the decision makers in the People's Republic and have access to foreign exchange, such as an "ITIC" and its subsidiaries. For foreign firms that are unfamiliar with these new business entities, caution should be observed. They should avoid being drawn into a partnership billed as quick and easy. These silver-lined opportunities quickly tarnish when the Chinese partner does not deliver all that the liaison has said that the partner has promised. Some of these newborn brokering entities include foreign trade companies able to form joint ventures with foreign firms; investment and trading corporations seeking revenue-creating partnerships; and consulting companies specializing in linking up foreign firms and Chinese partners. Some of China's larger factories also have been granted the power to seek foreign investors unilaterally. As long as these enterprises have approval from their superiors, this may be a channel worth considering—though do not ignore the need to establish and nurture the partnership network.

## EVALUATING THE CHINESE PARTNER

*How do I choose an appropriate Chinese partner?*

The selection of an appropriate venture partner, whether for a joint venture or a nonequity-based venture, is quite simply the most important factor in the successful implementation and operation of a project in China. Locating potential partners has become less difficult than in the past and the foreign company has more choice in the matter. Nowadays, most firms initiate a concerted search for a partner rather than depending on a Chinese introduction. Before making an official tour of China, foreign firms should feel under no obligation to commit to one or another Chinese partner. Do not be pressured into a commitment prior to making an assessment of the alternatives. Keep agreements simmering with 5 or 10 potential Chinese partners simultaneously. Sift through a number of options before deciding on a specific partner, avoiding the glossy trade brochures being published by various Chinese organizations that offer one-stop services to the China market. Remain flexible until a Chinese partner emerges who possesses the appropriate qualifications or which can at least meet the basic conditions for success. The rules for locating a good partner in China are not firm, yet some useful guidelines do exist. To begin with, finding an ideal, high-quality partner remains problematic since many of the factories chosen to be partners with foreign companies are nearly always deficient in several critical areas, e.g., management, worker skills, shop-floor technology, and sourcing. All partner alternatives involve tradeoffs of one sort or another. An initial set of questions to ask are:

**WHAT TYPE OF ACCESS DOES THE PARTNER HAVE TO CHINA'S DOMESTIC MARKET?** A foreign firm should request a marketing history of the Chinese enterprise to ascertain the prevailing market for the enterprise's products and how much this market might be expanded if higher quality products are introduced. Market access frequently remains circumscribed even for enterprises that have upgraded production using foreign technology. Firms should not assume that new markets in distant provinces will automatically open up for joint venture enterprise. They should attempt to find out the potential for attracting new customers given prevailing market boundaries. They should also be sensitive to the existence of economic blockades, which prevent the free exchange of goods and services.

**IS THE MARKET THAT THE ENTERPRISE SERVES LIKELY TO REMAIN STRONG?** It is essential to remember that changing government policies and changing consumer preferences can significantly alter the nature of current and future demand. A good example involves a project in Shanghai that uses American technology to produce glass bulbs for black-and-white television tubes. With the rapid upsurge in demand for color televisions, and the government policy of establishing domestic manufacturing for color televisions, this project is in trouble even taking into account demand from the rural sector.

### Are Competing Enterprises Planned and Does Your Partner Wield the Political Clout to Keep These Enterprises Out of This Area?

Also, be aware of the existing distribution system the partner relies upon. Because of the premium China places on both partner diversification and developing indigenous capabilities, it is quite possible that a domestic source of the same or a similar product will appear in a short time. In one extraordinary case, a zipper manufacturing joint venture formed by China and Hong Kong— Lanzhou Xinglong International Enterprise Co.—carried out an initial feasibility study and found that in 1983, only 11 zipper factories existed in China. Both partners predicted huge sales. Two years later, 105 zipper factories (20 of them Sino-foreign joint ventures) had driven up supply of zippers in China eleven fold, saturating the market and bankrupting the venture in 1987, two years after start-up.

### How Much Weight Does Your Partner Have in Securing Needed Supplies and Raw Materials?

It is often assumed by many foreign firms that necessary manufacturing inputs will be readily available or easily acquired. In many instances, neither assumption is true. Even if the needed inputs can be acquired, they may not meet U.S. specifications.

### How Far and How Fast Has the Enterprise Moved in Keeping Step with the Economic Reform Program?

Will its leaders move forward decisively in this effort over the long term? Foreign firms, for the most part, should seek out Chinese enterprises with a high degree of autonomy in place. These enterprises can maneuver more easily within the structure of China's emerging industrial economy. If supplies or raw materials do not materialize from traditional sources, these enterprises have the ability to go elsewhere to obtain needed inputs. Clearly, not all of China's enterprises share equal enthusiasm for the new economic reforms. Some are reluctant to break the iron rice bowl because for them this represents security and minimizes much of the uncertainty that tends to be associated with the reforms. While at one extreme there are enterprises led by exuberant entrepreneurial managers, there are also others at the opposite extreme who are basically ignoring the reforms.

**IS THE ENTERPRISE RUN BY "IDEAL" MANAGERS?** The ideal manager not only understands the expanded autonomy offered to the enterprise but is willing to capitalize on it. Is he, or she, familiar with multiple points of access to the supply and distribution system? A Chinese manager must be sought and can be found that has a vested interest in building an alliance with a foreign firm and is open to having a direct relationship with the people on the foreign side.

**DOES THE GENERAL MANAGER HAVE A TECHNICAL EDUCATION BACKGROUND?** Has he any conception of Western corporate management? And, in some cases, a joint venture director may not even have been a factory director in the past. The appointed director may have little grasp of corporate management in a Western sense.

**DOES A UNIFIED RELATIONSHIP EXIST AMONG THE CHIEF ENGINEER, THE PARTY CHIEF, AND THE FACTORY MANAGER?** If so, this unification represents the smooth synthesis of the political, organizational, and technological aspects of the management in the factory. Look carefully at the interplay between the de facto and the de jure leaders of the enterprise. Who controls the day-to-day operations of the factory and where it gets its operating budget?

**WILL THE CHINESE FACTORY BE ABLE TO SMOOTHLY ASSIMILATE THE FOREIGN TECHNOLOGY PACKAGE PLANNED?** Evaluate the technical competency of the chief engineer. This individual is primarily responsible for the technological aspects of the enterprise, which will include manufacturing, quality control, research, and maintenance. The chief engineer also helps prepare the feasibility studies for technology importation. Solicit the potential partner for help in conducting feasibility studies so as to gain a better appreciation for how the Chinese assess the key elements needed to make the project a success.

As noted, Chinese officials tend to introduce foreign executives to enterprises most in need of technical upgrading; they may be incapable of absorbing advanced technology for lack of managerial experience, poor infrastructure, or a dearth of skilled workers. Chinese unwillingness to divulge all the necessary details about its specific capabilities and resources makes the process difficult. Obviously, repeated investigative visits by foreign technicians should be conducted. Rockwell International had to shop around until it found a technically competent plant for its textile machine project. The plant Rockwell chose had been building high-precision parts for weapons, and therefore was capable of fine tooling and meeting precision requirements.

Investment partners are judged both in terms of manufacturing prowess as well as marketing know-how. "No longer can the Chinese manager put the product at the front door and find it gone the next morning," says venture capital manager Dean T. W. Ho in Shanghai. "The wholesale system of the past remains but a new system is emerging quickly, at least in the Shanghai area." The object of the wise investor, says Mr. Ho, is to locate the partner. And the best partner is the company with the best manager—the best *manufacturing marketer*, if you will.

### Which is better investment form—a joint venture or a wholly-owned company?

In appearance, while foreign investors are offered more decision-making power and less Chinese interference in wholly-owned factories, they experience no greater ease of access within the bureaucracy. In theory, the management of a wholly owned China venture appears rather simple, often three managers handling sales, finance, and production, respectively. However, such ventures are not protected by joint venture tax treatment. In many respects, the Chinese consider them representative offices, and, as such, assess them at a tax rate far above what joint ventures must pay. Wholly owned factories are in the 20-40 percent bracket plus 10 percent. The endeavor of going at it alone in China generally brings worse problems and higher costs than joint ventures. Marketing and distribution tend to be more arduous. Without the leverage and influence of a local partner, many local Chinese will take advantage of foreigners, charging them higher rates for factory space, services, and labor, and then competing with them for export sales. Nonetheless, owners of wholly foreign-owned enterprises do experience more independence over setting wages, hiring and firing workers, and other production details.

### Will a joint venture gain me more access to the Chinese consumer?

In a growing number of cases, foreign joint venture partners have successfully negotiated contracts stipulating that a significant percentage, if not all, of their production may be marketed in China: Coca-cola markets soft drinks, Kodak sells film, Gillette markets razors, Nabisco sells food, Foxboro sells industrial controls, Volkswagen sells automobiles, and Hitachi sells television sets. Often, ongoing sales of parts and components can be made to the factory where licensing of technology takes place. Although foreign firms without China ventures can more readily contact Chinese industrial end-users directly, a pro forma contract between a foreign firm and a government-controlled import/export agency is still required.

Remember, however, that part of the Chinese approach to joint ventures with foreign firms is to require that they balance foreign exchange payments. For this reason, they encourage joint ventures to export a large percentage of their production, sometimes leaving little to sell to the domestic market.

### Will the Chinese pressure you to enter a joint venture deal rather than merely buy your product?

You can count on it. Government-backed pressure on foreign suppliers is one of the long-time features of China's business scene since the door was first opened. Here's an anecdote about a case which is still unfolding. A U.S. manufacturer of a portable industrial vacuum cleaner realizes that a sales opportunity may exist in the PRC. The product is based on 5 hard years of research and development. A team goes to China and demonstrates the vacuum. The response is favorable; the Chinese perceive specific applications for the product in China, especially inside textile mills. But the Chinese aren't interested in buying the product; they want to assemble the vacuum and thereby lower its cost for the Chinese enduser. The U.S. side balks. The Chinese side announces that it wants to duplicate the vacuum and sell it itself! "But we want to first invite you to invest in the joint venture as a partner."

The U.S. side is appalled and hires a U.S.-based consultant to ascertain whether the Chinese company could, indeed, reverse engineer the vacuum. The consultant concludes that the Chinese could do this and sell it to the internal market, lowering the products' patentable technology. As of this writing, the United States is scrambling to determine the minimum cash investment necessary to lock down the Chinese counterpart and protect their product in a joint venture. For the Chinese company unable to attract investment through an equity joint venture, issuing stock is the best option. They might also form a company in a foreign country, or purchase one there, then infuse it with capital and take it public to raise additional cash.

You will no doubt discover how tough it is to sell goods in China without discussing your investing in China, forming a joint venture, and transferring technology. I recently assisted in introducing the Mayo Clinic to China, with the intention of helping the U.S. hospital sell its medical publications to Chinese consumers. But such information and consulting services were of little interest alone; the Chinese whom I met with wanted Mayo to participate in a venture to build a hospital!

In some sectors, Chinese trade officials have made it a condition of direct sales from U.S. firms that they assist China in localizing a portion of the cost of such sales within China. Auto manufacturers have also found that a key leverage device in entering agreements involves the localization of parts and components manufacturing in China. This form of leverage requires extremely prudent planning because China's industrial environment does not facilitate the production of high-quality parts on schedule.

The art of venture leveraging can take yet other forms. Some U.S. firms have found they can get closer to the China market by offering services and training to the Chinese. Perkin-Elmer has utilized its service center to make direct sales of its products. Service centers have other direct benefits, such as increasing product applications, facilitating software exchange, and developing a larger customer base.

### *What is a cooperative venture?*

The cooperative venture affords a more flexible arrangement than a joint venture because of its simpler legal structure and its informal business environment. Generally, the nature of these ventures is impermanent and not as precisely defined as an equity joint venture. A cooperative agreement is often treated as a preliminary stage of technical transfer. In manufacturing, it may be best to establish a cooperative venture at the beginning. This arrangement is well suited to foreign investors because they can minimize their equity at risk and are not solely involved in trying to manage the business.

### Are government partnerships a good idea for a joint venture in the PRC?

In some cases, success in China may depend on whether the venture includes, as either a formal or informal partner, a Chinese government entity such as an industrial bureau or department. At times, high-level local officials serve on these government bodies; their involvement in the business relationship lends clout to the project, and cuts communication time with the government to a fraction of the norm. Forming a partnership with a Chinese government entity may offer certain strategic advantages, especially if it is brought in as a minor third-party partner for the purpose of gaining clout among Chinese decision makers. Third-party partners often contribute foreign exchange or provide a mechanism to swap Rmb for foreign currency. Hewlett-Packard, for example, focuses its energies on developing a direct working relationship with one of China's most powerful industrial ministries, the Ministry of Electronics Industry (MEI), which is joined in the partnership by the municipal electronics bureau of the Beijing city government. Hewlett-Packard credits the preferential treatment it receives to the company's cooperation with a highly subsidized factory. In this case, high-level officials from MEI organize, plan, and attend meetings. This partnership affords Hewlett-Packard direct access to high-level government officials. Who should be the third party and how much equity should they be required to bring to the venture? While equity contribution is important, knowledge and political clout are even more valuable. A third party can bring all three to the venture. For example, the joint venture involving Volkswagen of West Germany and the Shanghai Automobile Corporation includes minority participation by the Bank of China and CITIC. Both of these organizations bring to the venture needed foreign exchange and high-level access to officials should problems arise. Their presence has helped rather than hindered the operation of the venture, proving the strategic advantage of including them from the start.

# SUBSTITUTING IMPORTS TO PENETRATE THE MARKET

Foreign firms pursue an import substitution strategy in hopes of selling to China's domestic market for foreign exchange rather than Rmb. However, as outlined in the Measures Concerning the Substitution of Imports with Products Manufactured by Chinese-foreign Joint Ventures, ratified in 1987, the foreign exchange input by the Chinese will only be issued on a temporary basis. Import substitution status is guaranteed to 12 products that China will need over the long term, including acrylic, pig iron, and aluminum, among others. Other products require approval by the State Planning Commission at the central or local level. The Chinese also insist that these projects localize production progressively and source some supplies from China while ensuring that the goods produced meet international standards in price, quality, and service back-up. Criteria applied to import substitution proposals include long-term need for the products and advanced technology. As with other forms of special status, import substitution certification could be retracted if Chinese entities began producing similar products.

### How do I set up an import substitution deal?

In pursuing an import substitution deal, U.S. firms should also (1) prove to the Chinese side that significant savings can be made, and (2) show that the manufacturing process can be localized rapidly. An exhaustive investigation stage should culminate with a feasibility study to gauge local-level interest in the project. Once a local partner is secured, get a local FTC behind the project. Then go about convincing local government official to push for approval at the central government level, where most of the red tape is involved. In 3M's import substitution approach to the China market, China manager John Marshall outlines several guidelines that bear consideration by those companies planning to sell in China.

- Select products that fit China's pressing needs rather than those promising easy exportability. (3M ascertained that electrical generation, distribution, and telecommunications were serious priorities in China; hence chose to manufacture electrical tape and connectors.)

- Select products from company divisions that have international orientation. (3M chose product lines, in part, because managers associated with them sold the products around the world.)

- Select products already produced in the Far East by your company, and from which you may draw experience.

- Select products, as 3M did, that are simple to start up, easy to scale up, and require minimal front-end investment.

3M's initial approach to China involved assessing the investment climate, defining objectives, and presenting a proposal that had little regard for such Chinese priorities as exporting and technology transfer, or the fact that China had ratified no law governing wholly foreign-owned ventures in China. The company proposed a wholly owned factory that would sell 100 percent of its production to the domestic market, and transfer no technology. They reached an agreement by leveraging the company's solid management reputation, which meant offering management training, and because the product to be manufactured in the People's Republic represented an import substitute. Holding to these requirements, the firm nailed down a successful agreement. The 3M China entry strategy followed a bold, three no's approach: no technology transfer, no export guarantee, and no Chinese ownership.

# CHAPTER 14

# ORGANIZING FOR

# VENTURE START-UP

*O*rganizing a venture in the People's Republic requires a high degree of preparation, in-house organization, and sensitivity to Chinese capabilities and deficiencies. More than in other places, China demands that additional preparatory work must be conducted before start-up. Not long ago, the Chinese were unconvinced of the value and necessity of feasibility studies, although this has changed. After their problems with Baoshan Steel Works, Beijing Jeep Corporation, and Fujian-Hitachi, China realized that feasibility studies are essential. Since then, the debate now centers over who should pay for them. The feasibility study has grown in importance in terms of getting the overall venture approved, with Chinese partners having to justify both partner and technology selection. Feasibility studies should be undertaken by qualified institutes and consultancies, particularly on larger projects. The Chinese now require that a joint feasibility looks into raw material supply, expenses, labor availability, profit projection, foreign exchange needs, and return on investment. In short, the study should contain all the relevant information one would expect to find in a western-style business plan.

### Where should I locate my venture?

In China's fast-paced developing economy, individual localities and provinces are in competition for foreign investment. Foreign investors should anticipate that a given locality will offer a series of investment incentives to entice foreign capital to their region. A company considering investing in China should base their site selection decision on the package of investment incentives offered by the locality and the confidence the company feels towards the local government to deliver on its promises.

*Tax Holidays.* Most investment zones will offer a standard tax holiday of three years for an investment project, followed by two years of taxation at 50 percent of the normal rate. Some localities may offer more attractive tax holidays, but officials should be pressed on the source of their authority to exceed national guidelines. The tax holiday should begin on the first profit-making year of the enterprise, however what constitutes a profit may vary from location to location.

*Tax Waivers.* Investment zones are also authorized to waive taxes on venture profits that are put to a specific use. Most commonly a locality will waive taxes on a foreign partner's profits that are reinvested in the China enterprise.

*Fee Waivers.* Many localities will waive import fees on imported goods for use as inputs in the manufacturing process. Localities may also waive special surcharges on repatriated profits and expatriate salaries, as well as port and licensing fees. In general, any fee that seems extraneous or unusual can probably be negotiated away for an extended period.

*Donated Land and Equipment.* Some municipalities may offer to donate land and equipment to a potential investment project. Land ownership is not granted, but de facto property rights in the form of long-term, subsidized leases may be offered.

*Donated Services.* Occasionally a locality may offer access to office space, office equipment, staff and interpreters. Economic development agencies can also assist with domestic travel arrangements and absorb the cost of domestic travel and accommodations.

Investors should carefully evaluate the ability of local officials to deliver their promised package of investment incentives. Companies considering investment in a given region should consult with the managers of other foreign-invested enterprises in the area to evaluate the region's track record with foreign companies.

### What are the specific attractions of setting up in a Special Economic Zone?

Economic zones now dot the entire country; in 1991 there were only 191 of them—now there are nearly 3,000. Only a handful of these zones wield central-level political clout and the autonomy to approve large deals quickly and independently from outside government interference. Two of the most well-known and well-endowed are located in Shanghai and Tianjin. Fifty U.S. firms have located in each zone as of this writing. The following is a list of just a few of the attractions in the SEZs: Foreign firms can employ foreign staff managers; foreign personnel pay no taxes. They are exempt from import/export duties and from after-tax profit remittance. Access to Chinese partners is facilitated by various industry-specific development companies, which assist foreign investors. Tax rates in SEZs are 15 percent versus Hong Kong tax rates of 18.5 percent in Hong Kong. Wages in SEZs are 75-80 percent lower than in Hong Kong; they range between 600 and 1,000 Yuan per month in TEDA, for example.

> **WARNING:** Many self-proclaimed 'investment zones' in China are special economic zones in name only. These regions or municipalities may offer tax holidays, low tax rates and other incentives to foreign investors without central government permission. Efforts to crackdown on these investment zones have achieved mixed results to date, however, the risk remains that a potential investor could be left with a factory producing in an area that requires them to pay the full tax rate.

### Where are the major manufacturing centers in China?

Manufacturing has grown exponentially across China's coastal regions over the last five years, and has also significantly increased in the inland provinces. The largest share of manufacturing is centered in Shanghai and its surrounding provinces, which collectively comprise the lower delta of the Yangtze River. Historically this area has been China's most productive and the center of its most intensive capital investment.

The Shanghai region is closely followed by Guangdong in South China, particularly the Pearl River delta cities of Guangzhou, Guangdong's capital, and Shenzhen, China's first Special Economic Zone. Southern China has benefitted from an enormous influx of investment capital from nearby Hong Kong, and is now the center of a booming region of light, export-oriented manufacturing. Investment in China's technology sectors has migrated north to Beijing, taking advantage of the large number of engineers and researchers produced by Beijing's leading universities. Other areas of intense manufacturing development include Fujian province, which sits across the Straits from Taiwan, and Shandong province, once occupied by Germany and long a center of heavy industry in China. In the industrial North, China's third largest city of Tianjin, formally called Tientsin, is fast becoming the northern gateway to the China market. U.S. firms such as Motorola, Coca-Cola, and Otis Elevator have joined 2,500 other foreign companies which have set up joint ventures in the city's investment zone started in 1984. The city features China's largest container port facility and train yard; land is plentiful and much less expensive than in Shanghai's Pudong industrial zone.

## *What is the availability of raw materials for manufacturing?*

China has large reserves of unexploited natural resources that feed its industrial growth. As yet undeveloped oil reserves in Northwest China continue to be explored by joint Sino-foreign efforts, while hydropower efforts center around the massive Three Gorges Dam project. China has a well developed coal industry, and coal is currently the leading source of energy in the P.R.C. Large untapped mineral deposits are centered in Southwest China, particularly in Yunnan province. Timber is one commodity in seriously short supply. Three thousand years of intensive agriculture has deforested the vast majority of China's natural landscape, with its remaining timber reserves centered in Heilongjiang province, in the far Northeast.

An increasing number of joint venture production companies are able to source their raw materials locally, as China expands the utilization of its natural resources and improves its distribution systems. Regional sourcing is also becoming a more important trend in China-based manufacturing, as material inputs are imported from Japan, Korea, Russia, Vietnam, and even Mongolia.

### *What is the availability of energy in China, and cost and reliability?*

China's power industry has grown at an annual rate of 10 percent over the last several years, yet lack of available power continues to frustrate the modernization of other sectors of the Chinese economy. By some estimates, power shortages have held back industrial production by 20 to 40 percent since the late 1980's. Brownouts remain common and up to 120 million Chinese continue to live virtually without electricity across the country.

The cost of power should be estimated by local authorities when negotiating a joint venture or applying to open a wholly owned-foreign enterprise. Managers should budget for productivity losses due to brownouts and the occasional blackouts, but should heavily lobby local officials for priority treatment when such cases do occur. Frequent power failures can be confirmed by other joint venture representatives in the area, and compensation for these problems in the form of tax breaks or rebates may become an issue during negotiation sessions.

### *Who ultimately decides where the plant will be located?*

The Chinese usually bring foreigners to prospective existing factories or sites that are in great need of upgrading. Negotiators should make serious inquiries regarding the location of the proposed venture. All too often, the foreign partner has little say in the choice of an appropriate site for the factory. The decision is commonly made by central and local bureaucrats. Yet the selection of a site is vital and should include the foreign party and other experts who can objectively judge potential locations. Begin the process by asking to visit several separate possible locations and use the following criteria in making a final decision:

- Does the city have a well-developed industrial base that could manufacture Westernized in the area?

- Are local factories and business entities exposed to Western companies and business practices?

- Does the area have any historical linkage with the outside through trade and other contact?

- How open are local decision makers to new business forms outlined in foreign investment policy and what application of these techniques exists in the area?

- Are city leaders, especially the mayor, positive about foreign investment and will they actively assist enterprises with foreign participation?

- Does the city offer the necessary infrastructure?

- How does the area compare with others in terms of privileges for foreign firms such as tax exemptions and access to market?

For example, by locating in the Minhang-Shanghai Economic and Technological Development Zone (called an ETDZ for short), Xerox was allowed to sell 100 percent of its copiers to the domestic market for the first five years of the venture. Officials of Tianjin's TEDA claim that many of the foreign companies which have located in that industrial zone sell exclusively to the domestic market on an indefinite basis. "The more a foreign company sells to China," one official of TEDA told the author, "the more money they make, and the more tax they pay to TEDA."

### *What questions should I answer before agreeing to a physical plant site?*

- Is there sufficient infrastructure at the site?

- Does the existing factory suffer frequent power outages as do the majority of Chinese plants?

- How much additional electricity will the joint venture require and will that amount be available?

- What is the status of surrounding communication, road, rail, and port transportation systems, and what demands will the joint venture have on them?

- What will the total costs of improvements be and will local Chinese agencies be willing to contribute?

- What is the current availability and quality of raw materials in the site area?

Obtaining verified answers to these questions will reduce unanticipated costs. Seeking such information, however, may entail asking questions that fly in the face of Chinese assurances. One case illustrates the prudence of early information gathering. A Sino-American joint venture was designed to manufacture pharmaceutical capsules utilizing water from a nearby lake that the Chinese guaranteed was clean. It was not, however, and the U.S. partner was forced to install a water purification plant. Then the company discovered that local power outages were common, which soon jeopardized the manufacturing process. The U.S. partner was compelled to install the appropriate back-up generating equipment. Both problems resulted in unanticipated higher costs to the U.S. partner, yet both, it seems, could have been avoided.

## DECISION MAKING ON A FOREIGN PROJECT

The process for securing approval from Chinese authorities for a proposed joint venture will vary from locality to locality and from industry to industry. Nevertheless, the majority of all approved joint ventures have passed through the following stages:

The potential partners sign a **letter of intent,** outlining the scope of the project, the activities to be conducted, and the financial structure of the new entity. While the letter is not a binding contract, many investors recommend that a letter contain no reference to financial obligations between the parties. Such obligations, if not fulfilled, could serve as a basis for a suit for nonperformance under Chinese law. Note that a letter of intent often serves as a basis for the subsequent contract, and articles in the contract may be limited by the contents of the letter of intent.

The Chinese partner submits a **proposal** and a preliminary feasibility study to the relevant Chinese authorities. The foreign investor should ask for a copy of this feasibility study prior to continuing the joint venture process.

The partners conduct a **full feasibility study** after the Chinese partner receives preliminary approval from the overseeing administrative agency. The feasibility study should contain all relevant information one would expect to find in a traditional business plan. During this period the foreign investor should be meeting with the appropriate representatives from the local or municipal government, economic planning agencies, tax agencies and banks.

The partners draft and sign a **contract.** The foreign partner should ensure the Chinese partner keeps the relevant government officials updated on any changes made during the contract negotiation.

Both the feasibility study and contract are submitted to the relevant authorities for **official approval.** Which authorities have the authorization to approve joint venture investments varies from project to project. Particularly, the authority of local governments to approve independent agreements between Chinese entities and foreign investors varies from industry to industry and province to province. Investors should seriously consider the risk of central authorities overriding local governments and rescinding agreements on investment incentives or even the entire authorization for the project. The best way to prevent this occurrence is to familiarize oneself with the perceived impact of the project on China's national economic development. The relevant industrial ministry should publish up-to-date guidelines on the type of projects that are currently encouraged to employ foreign joint venture partners.

A joint venture proposal should receive an official decision within three months from the time of submission. The joint venture must register with the appropriate local office of the State Administration for Industry and Commerce (SAIC) to obtain a **business license.** In addition, all joint ventures must register with the Ministry of Foreign Trade and Economic Cooperation (MOFTEC). The foreign investor should not assume that just because a local agency has granted approval for a joint venture that these steps have been completed by the Chinese partner.

In recent years the traditionally lengthy approval process for joint ventures in China has shortened dramatically. Just as different states in the United States have streamlined licensing and regulatory processes to attract investment, these localities and regions in China are in direct competition to attract foreign capital. While the average time from the start of negotiations to the establishment of the actual venture was once one to two years, many companies are now reporting an average period of six months. Occasionally a Chinese business partner may ask for a transfer of cash up front to 'obtain a business license'. Investors should independently confirm the cost of a business license in a given locality prior to signing a contract. Compare the cost to comparable localities.

### *What decisions must be made before approval of a venture will be given?*

There are two types of decisions that are made along the path of getting a China venture approved. The first type involves those of a *technical* nature—for example, logistical issues of technology choice, building site, training of workers, and so on. These are working issues which are resolved at the local level, often within the enterprise itself. At worst they must also involve a local ministry, a financial entity, and an FTC. The second type of decision is purely *administrative*, and involves the ratification of the venture by bureaucratic entities independent of the enterprise. American companies tend to be adept at obtaining approvals for the first type of decision and not too effective at interfacing with local bureaucrats to obtain the necessary second type. On the other hand, the Japanese appear quite adept at obtaining both types. (See the chapter on Negotiating for more about influencing Chinese decision makers.)

### *Do the ministries in Beijing and local authorities have the same priorities in approving a project?*

No. The government ministries in Beijing decide which enterprises should be upgraded or be the recipient of a package of imported technology. Selected enterprises are termed *gugang,* literally, "backbone." The firms not in the ministry's plan will have a difficult time getting the ministry to approve its own technology acquisition plans. However, provincial and municipal authorities don't care whether the enterprise is gugang or nongugang. They judge a proposed venture in terms of the revenues it can earn for these local entities in the form of taxable income, and how many local people it will provide jobs for. The central government ministries in Beijing want local end-user enterprises to buy from the state-owned enterprises under their jurisdiction. On the other hand, provincial authorities want local enterprises to buy goods at the lowest possible price regardless of whether the supplier is a state firm, a foreign joint venture, or a company located overseas (as long as the end-user has the foreign exchange).

### *Why do Chinese bureaucrats involve themselves in Sino-foreign projects?*

For the foreign firm, it is critical to know both *why* a Chinese official wants to involve himself in a deal with a foreign firm, and *what* would motivate him to do so. His or her possible motives might be first, to bring benefits to their organization, in the form of regulatory privileges which accrue to organizations which have partnered with foreign firms. Second, to bring in foreign exchange is a common motive. Third, any official with a foreigner in his pocket will gain clout over higher-level officials where once he enjoyed none. Next, an official who has been reluctant so far to respond to market reform might want a deal merely to exhibit a commitment to cooperating with foreign firms. Lastly, the official may be in line to receive reciprocal favors from related organizations if a cash-rich foreign partner can be lassoed.

### *How do you measure enthusiasm for your project?*

First of all, *don't* be sucked in by public displays of enthusiasm for your project. Americans often visit Taiwan, for example, and are received well, only to find that enthusiasm dies the moment they leave the island. Part of this is a face issue—it is impolite to outwardly reject another company's idea and proposals. That doesn't mean, however, that a deal is being seriously considered.

### *What, if any, financing is available for Chinese joint ventures?*

The majority of joint ventures seek their funding through Hong Kong banking institutions because the People's Bank of China (PBOC) has shown a reluctance to share the financial risk of initiating joint ventures. The PBOC is not keen to lend to joint ventures for initial assets; instead, it concentrates more on short-term working capital loans. Typically, international banks want a guarantee from the PBOC or other Chinese financial institutions authorized to guarantee loans. The PBOC will only guarantee the portion of joint venture equity share held by the Chinese side; the foreign side must find its own guarantor. However, 75 percent of all Sino-foreign joint ventures have received some PBOC funding. Equity investments by the PBOC are made in ventures as well, under the auspices of the bank's investment arm, the Bank of China Trust and Consulting Company. Between 1983 and 1994, the company has invested in joint ventures. The China Investment Bank and the provincial "ITICs" (including CITIC) are other Chinese organizations that the foreign firm should solicit.

### *Are European and American banks exhibiting a willingness to fund some U.S. joint ventures in China?*

European banks are exhibiting a willingness to fund some of the largest U.S. joint ventures in China. More American banks may also choose to fund projects in the China market through subsidiaries set up in Hong Kong rather than setting up operations in Beijing, where many U.S. banks have gutted their operations for lack of business. Only a handful of U.S. banks directly finance U.S.-China joint ventures. The few that do, attract hundreds of applications for joint venture projects, most of which are already beyond the negotiation stage with the Chinese. At present, a funding range of $50,000 to $100 million is available to U.S. firms with joint venture agreements already signed with the Chinese that meet a relatively stringent set of risk-reducing criteria. Of course, these criteria vary according to the amount of funding required, the past experience of the bank or institution in China, and the idiosyncrasies of the personnel in its Asia affairs department.

*What is the criteria for potential financiers of Chinese joint ventures?*

**FIELD OF ENDEAVOR.** Potential financiers view technology transfer projects as high-risk ventures for two reasons: (1) technology venture products are too expensive for sufficient numbers of Chinese customers to purchase, even when authorized to do so; and (2) the questionable quality of high-tech products made in China makes them difficult to sell to export markets.

**LOCAL BUSINESS ENVIRONMENT.** U.S. banks want to know whether the local business environment is sufficient to support the joint venture. They make this determination based on a series of questions: Is the joint venture practical within this specific locale? If skilled employees are not available in the factory's locale, do municipal regulations in the area allow employees to be located by way of labor advertisements? (The difficulty of this varies as to location.) Finally, does the area possess the export capability to transfer production to outside markets?

**MARKET: DOMESTIC AND INTERNATIONAL.** Creditors take a hard look at the markets the parent company already serves in the United States. A firm's market projections must indicate ready markets for the projected percentage of export product from China. Unless the parent company's reputation is extremely strong, a firm producing China products without ready markets will find potential creditors unwilling to finance their production. Also under consideration is the attractiveness of a product line to China as either a potential export or an import substitute. Firms involved in joint ventures producing import substitutes for the China market have an obvious advantage in ready markets, and thus can project instantaneous sales. In this case, creditors will consider the percentage split between production for domestic sales versus export sales.

**CREDITOR'S EQUITY PERCENTAGE.** Are other financial institutions involved on the U.S. or Chinese side? If other creditors are involved, their experience and history of funding joint ventures in China will be a consideration.

**PROJECT SIZE.** There is an inclination among U.S. creditors to avoid overambitious projects and concentrate on joint ventures in the $1-10 million range.

**BUSINESS BACKGROUND.** Creditors will investigate the background of the specific type of business and its interrelationship with the province and municipality in which the joint venture plans to produce and market its products.

**ENDORSEMENTS.** The level of Chinese approval and the number of significant endorsements is also given some weight in the creditor's decision.

**PROPOSAL PREPAREDNESS.** The great majority of proposals from U.S. firms soliciting funds for joint venture projects in China contain a general description of a production idea, but little detail on China's business atmosphere. Most market projections are based on the firm's experience in other, less difficult overseas investment climates. Surprisingly, interviews with banking executives indicate that many of these corporate ideas are ill-conceived in terms of China's unique market, often containing totally exaggerated sales projections for the locality in which they plan to sell in China. Many cases exist in which the venture plans of a U.S. partner receive rapid approval by an overenthusiastic Chinese partner, who views the venture as an easy way of obtaining foreign exchange and foreign technology, without serious consideration of product salability or the venture's future ability to repay its creditors. The U.S. side, excited by the quick hit, approaches the financial institution ill-prepared. The downfall of many proposals is that market projects rarely contain verifiable market information about the marketability of production in specifically defined areas of China, down to the municipality level. Financiers interpret this fundamental problem as a lack of understanding of the China market on the part of the U.S. firm. With few exceptions, proposals for funding contain letters of approval and signed contracts between joint venture partners, but few of them show that a significant number of Chinese managers and officials from many different levels of local and central leadership—endorse the project and plan to actively generate support for it. This may be acceptable in SEZs, where approval by one aggressive city mayor or other high official may be sufficient to unify and mobilize local suppliers, labor organizations, export transportation companies, etc., to ensure the success of a young joint venture, but this is rarely the case in areas outside the SEZs. Without the energetic support from a large number of Chinese up and down the local administrative hierarchy, the venture may fail simply because of its isolation and neglect in the business infrastructure. In any viable proposal, local and regional support should be confirmed by the inclusion of letters of endorsement. To many firms, the high cost and frustration of selling the joint venture concept to relatively low-level, nonessential players is perceived as superfluous. Many of these same firms, however, discover later that their joint ventures suffer from time-consuming operational problems because they failed to secure the outside support from local officials, suppliers, and other entities affecting the efficiency of the venture. Thus, another criteria could be added to the list: How well has the U.S. partner performed so far in influencing the Chinese business system through the ground-laying of guanxi relationships? Proposals should indicate how many Chinese approve, endorse, or are involved positively in the project. The great majority of proposals usually contain Chinese approval at two levels only: (1) one high-level approval, such as a mayor of a city; and (2) an approval from the head of the factory entering into the joint venture. These two levels might be enough in a SEZ, but in cities such as Wuhan, Xian, Urumchi, etc., two-level authorization and endorsement would not be enough. In these places, multilevel approval and assistance will be necessary from Beijing through provincial and municipality levels.

### Should I shop around for financing?

Bank officials take a hard look at the investigative work U.S. firms carry out before they sign a joint venture contract. Loan officers, in their own research, ascertain how many potential Chinese enterprises were considered before choosing the best one. They research such questions as:

- Did the U.S. firm contact U.S. embassy commercial officers in China in order to solicit potential partners?

- How many factories did the U.S. firm tour?

- Has the firm taken full advantage of U.S. government assistance, consultants, and trade liaison services on both sides?

Bank research supports the notion that many firms find a single partner and hold steadfast. This occurs, perhaps, because the Chinese foreign trade corporations tend to promote specific factories which need foreign help in promoting their exports. To counter this steering, foreign firms should demand to see as many potential partners as possible. The challenge is to obtain financial and market information from factory managers, who may be instructed not to divulge sensitive figures. Before this information can be collected, however, U.S. firms have to build a bond of trust between themselves and their potential partners. This takes time, but it is essential to obtaining funding from risk-averse lenders.

# CHAPTER 15

# INSIDE THE

# CHINESE

# ENTERPRISE

$W$hile the Western press exalts China's capitalist reforms, Western corporate executives must still forge workable partnerships within the state-controlled sector of the PRC economy. One should not ignore the tremendous changes that seem to be moving China closer to Western modes of enterprise management; at the same time, they must realize that no matter how market-oriented China becomes, the foreign investor will still have to engage with a Chinese firm which is only one of many actors with an interest, direct or indirect, in a particular project or initiative.

## WHAT IS CHINESE ENTERPRISE?

Foreigners are seldom prepared for what they find inside the noisy, cavernous Chinese industrial plant: the apparent chaos on the shop floor, workers asleep at their positions, and the dilapidated factory buildings. Interestingly, working conditions in China's factories closely resemble the conditions in American and European factories during the early 1900s: dimly lit, the air choked with dust, the noise sometimes unbearable. While tightly packed with machinery and workers, the bulk of the equipment in Chinese factories appears dormant and large numbers of workers seem to be just standing around. Under pressure to conserve electricity, plants are often rather dark and lack any effective air-cleaning or anti-pollution apparatus. To their surprise, foreigners often find outdated and obsolete factory machinery kept in immaculate condition by poorly equipped repair personnel, a vestige of Mao's promotion of factory self-sufficiency. All in all, it is difficult to imagine after visiting a series of state-run Chinese industrial facilities how China has entered the ranks of the industrialized nations.

### What kinds of enterprises are there in China?

China's industrial base consists of over 450,000 state and cooperative enterprises. Of the country's total industrial output, about 50 percent is generated by state-owned enterprises. Virtually all of the remaining output is produced by collectives, and their local hybrid called "township and village enterprises" (TVEs), of which there are now over 20 million in the country. Collectives and TVEs together make up over 45 percent of China's GNP; their combined output is growing at a rate of 18 percent annually while the figure for the state sector is only 8 percent. The so-called "privately owned enterprises" still account for only a few percent of total productive output in the People's Republic.

The fundamental difference between state enterprises and collectives is their pattern of ownership and mode of administration, explained in more detail below.

### What constitutes a state-owned enterprise?

State-owned entities, such as enterprises and research institutes, are theoretically owned by the people. The largest Chinese factories in terms of both size and output (though not necessarily the most efficient) are administered by the state. These are generally considered the most important enterprises and have first call on skilled workers, foreign exchange, material inputs, and so on. The near total social and job security these enterprises offer workers, however, tend to minimize labor productivity and innovation. As discussed earlier, Chinese leaders would like to stimulate improvements and technological progress in these enterprises, and thus have begun a movement to release a sizable number of them from direct state control. While some enterprises have clearly prospered under these new conditions, others have not. As one enterprise manager remarked during an interview, "There are just too many factors still outside our control to allow us to produce at a higher level."

The lines of authority above an individual enterprise can vary drastically. Heretofore, most ministries have managed a series of state-owned enterprises directly; local governments have also had management authority over a set of enterprises as well. If led by a ministry, the operation of the enterprise, including the planning, distribution resources, and sales of the enterprise, have been controlled by various components of the ministry. The ministry asserts its control directly from Beijing. If led by a locality, the enterprise comes under the auspices of a bureau at the provincial or municipal level. Some enterprises, however, are under joint control (shuangzhong lingdao). If dual-controlled, the enterprise, in effect, is under the authority of both the central and municipal government. Under such circumstances not only does friction occur, but it is often difficult to understand where the real locus of decision authority lies.

### How do collectives operate?

Collective enterprises grew in number from about 300,000 in 1983 to 370,000 in 1985. Until that time, the proportion of state enterprises to collectives was about one state enterprise per four collectives. In the 1990s, collectives and TVEs have literally multiplied. Jointly owned by groups of citizens, collectives are sometimes aided by bank loans or government subsidies. They offer the participants some of the security of a state-run business along with the profit potential of a private enterprise. At present, hundreds of new collectives and TVEs are being established each month, producing everything from foodstuffs and fodder to soft drinks and rice wine. Though TVEs are supposed to be collectively owned by a group of people, they are typically set up, financed, and operated by a small partnership of local officials who benefit as private owners of the enterprise. In many small towns, TVEs account for over 70 percent of economic output.

Another recent manifestation of the push toward industrial collectives has been the development of the so-called "minban" companies. In essence, these are joint stock companies organized by a few persons with special competence. A good example is the Stone Computer Company, which was founded by a small group of engineers from the Chinese Academy of Sciences.

Over the past few years, a substantial amount of discretionary power has moved into the hands of factory managers within these collectives. In certain facets of their day-to-day operational decision making, however, many of these managers still must consult local bureaus of supervising ministries for assistance in obtaining commitments for supplies, transportation of goods, etc. Nonetheless, in response to the problems associated with the multiple administrative bottlenecks throughout the economy, the Chinese government has encouraged the spread of collective enterprises. Their flexibility in terms of both organization and decision-making allows more timely responses to emerging opportunities.

Since state enterprises receive the majority of government preferences, collective enterprises are often hard-pressed to compete. For example, state enterprises possess better access to investment capital, especially if the funds are coming from Beijing rather than a local province or municipal organization. Because the state authorities wish to retain tight control over capital investment, they tend to focus their investments on enterprises that the state owns. Moreover, Chinese banks generally lend money far more readily to state enterprises since these enterprises maintain a higher, and more consistent credit rating; they are perceived by banks as more accountable borrowers, while they view collectives as virtually unsecurable.

Because state enterprises have greater access to foreign exchange via loans from state-controlled banking institutions, it follows that, in most cases, the level of technology is higher in state enterprises. So too, state enterprises tend to be better endowed with skilled personnel and production resources. Heretofore, they have gotten first choice of promising graduates, who first are made available to the military, second to the university system, and third, to the ministries (i.e., the state enterprise system). Only recently have collectives been allowed to bid for Chinese youths entering the job market. Similarly, state enterprises also are placed first in line for needed supplies and raw materials, having the power and leverage to circumvent red tape to rapidly obtain allocations of critical supplies.

### How important are China's privately owned enterprises?

A relatively small number of Chinese, less than 1.5 percent of the total national employment, have started more than 170,000 private, mostly small businesses with annual revenues of 33.4 million yuan. For the most part, these businesses have not made a significant contribution to the country's economic development, though they receive the dragon's share of foreign press coverage of China's economy. Examples of private ownership include restaurants, travel bureaus, tailors, doctors, law firms, food stalls, service shops, transportation specialists, and handicraft makers. The overwhelming majority of these enterprises involve services such as catering, commerce, and the supply and marketing of goods including household wares. They have had their greatest impact on the Chinese economy in the distribution sector, for example, when local entrepreneurs purchase a truck and facilitate local transportation of agricultural goods to the free market. A handful of these private entrepreneurs are becoming rich, at least by Chinese standards. Yet, because some reforms have been delayed in the urban areas, most of China's "10,000-yuan households" are in the countryside, as are 90 percent of the private enterprises.

Apparently, the main purpose of private enterprise promotion has been to put the rural unemployed back to work and increase agricultural production. China's modernization agenda does not include—as the international press often suggests—widespread privatization of large-scale industry in the near term. In other words, capitalist free enterprise in the People's Republic is accepted by most as a short-term response to specific social and economic problems, rather than as a long-term cure-all for the country's economic ills. Undoubtedly, the Chinese economy is much less centralized and less planned than a few years ago.

Nonetheless, planning remains as an important part of the economy, even as the locus of planning has shifted to the local level.

## CHINA'S MANAGERIAL REVOLUTION

In 1978, China's leaders inaugurated a broad program to push Chinese enterprises into the forefront of Asian manufacturing efficiency. During the late 1970s, and in contrast to previous thinking, Chinese leaders realized that productivity could best be increased by implementing managerial improvements along with introducing new technologies (hardware and software) into the enterprise setting. In this context, the Third Plenary Session of the Eleventh Central Committee of the Chinese Communist Party held in December 1978 was a milestone in the evolution of industrial management in the People's Republic. At the meeting, China's top leaders revealed a willingness to reconsider many of the policies that in the past were considered inviolable principles of the socialist system.

Beginning with the introduction of new management techniques in 4,000 Sichuan enterprises in 1979 (and in a fewer number of enterprises in Yunnan and Anhui provinces), a new industrial responsibility system was inaugurated, and later introduced in over 36,000 industrial enterprises. These enterprises, while only 16 percent of the total number of state-owned enterprises in the People's Republic, account for a remarkable 70 percent of total profit making among state enterprises. Party Secretary Zhao Ziyang outlined four major tasks for the reform of industrial enterprises: (1) to strengthen the economic responsibility system, improve management in enterprises via better planning, control, and business accounting; (2) to promote capable people to leading posts and overcome overstaffing problems through reorganization of work units; (3) to increase worker discipline by implementing a strict reward and penalty system; and (4) to tighten financial control.

In essence, the reforms altered the ideological foundation of what a Chinese enterprise was within China's socialist economy. The enterprise was no longer merely a production entity fulfilling quotas and turning profits over to the state. Many enterprises became fully activated business as well as production entities, formulating their own marketing targets and distributing their output without direct government control. They now issued full profit and loss reports. For the most part, they could also set wages and gained greater control over the hiring and firing of their workers. They could reward good worker performance to a much greater extent than in the past. They were given the means for independent expansion and growth, more control over depreciation funds, and more power to procure their own equipment and technology from abroad. Some could even negotiate directly with foreign firms. Taken in its entirety, the management reform program was designed to bring into practice, in most areas, new systems of accounting, quality control, strategic planning, and market forecasting.

### *What was enterprise organization and management in China like before the reforms of the early 1980s?*

After the Chinese Communist Party (CCP) took control of China in 1949, it introduced a system of enterprise management patterned after the Soviet Union. The system was characterized by the strong role attached to the CCP. Almost every economic and social aspect of the enterprise, came under the purview of the Party. At the same time, the factory also felt the administrative influence of the government bureaucracy. Production "mandates" were assigned to enterprises and goods were handed over to the state to be distributed. All profits and losses incurred were the responsibility of the state, not the enterprise.

With little in the way of competitive pressures to conduct their manufacturing processes efficiently, most Chinese factories fell victim to a host of operational and organizational problems. Many of these problems continue to exist today. To begin with, they suffer from an array of shortcomings associated with poor shop-floor management techniques. Quality control, product testing, and inspection are incomplete; complicated products are often not tested until assembled. Moreover, most Chinese factories do not operate under any statistically based process control systems. Since there is not inventory cost associated with factory production, there is little concern about excess inventory and no tradition of inventory systemization. In addition, the infrastructure and technology associated with transportation of goods prohibits quick response in the shipping of products. Thus, as one China scholar has suggested, most Chinese factories are run with a "just in case" mentality rather than a "just in time" mentality. Chinese factories also have trouble managing high-volume and high variety manufacturing endeavors. Widespread production redundancy causes long lead times from the design to the implementation stage of a new product. Often four or five years is necessary to bring a new product onto the market.

### How are state enterprises being restructured to increase efficiency?

A state enterprise can take advantage of China's industrial reforms in a number of ways to increase its bottom-line profits. First, it can form new companies within its own corporate structure that can operate with heightened entrepreneurial autonomy; the profits these smaller ventures earn are used to cover their overhead and then flow back to the parent firm. For instance, the Institute of Science and Technology Information Corporation in Chongqing (CB-ISTIC) is a large state-owned publishing company—one of the premier information gathering and publishing houses in all of China. Because the state is increasingly unwilling to pay so much of the Institute's overhead, it has been forced to either make money the old fashioned way, or cease to exist. In response, the institute formed four separate entrepreneurial companies within itself (and more are on the way), all jpursuing bottom-line profits by addressing the needs of the domestic and international markets. The four experimental companies are involved, quite typically, in the rather incongruent activities of: selling pet food to foreign markets; developing and marketing new Chinese technologies domestically; marketing various pharmaceutical products; and collecting and selling business and technical information in China and abroad. (Anything goes at a state firm that has the potential to generate income to keep the lights on.) One of the new companies at the institute is called VIP Information Company. VIP is mandated to sell the institute's databases and distributes foreign-made products in Southwest China. One of the institute's best young managers—Mr. Chen Yuanshu—has been put in charge of the company; he's in his mid-forties and worked his way up the hierarchy from Chief Librarian to Vice Director. Rather than hire VIP salespeople from within the firm, Mr. Chen hired young people just out of college. He found a new marketing director through a help-wanted advertisement and hired on the basis of a contract that specifies exactly how the person must perform in order to keep his position. The result was recently startling for the visiting author, who had been dealing with this institute since 1987. Accustomed to dealing with the institute's stodgy Party-types and meeting in musty negotiating rooms with a committee of note-takers, I found myself whisked from the airport to a rotating skyscraper restaurant for a power lunch with two twenty-something VIP salesmen who talked about hot stocks and multimedia hardware sales in China. Profit-making is clearly the top priority for this fledgling micro-entrerprise conceived and nurtured from within a state firm.

A large state enterprise which employs many thousands of people and in need of complete overhaul may be restructured from outside, by its controlling ministry. The ministry normally begins the process by bringing in a new management team of professional directors and managers, though the term "professional" is used loosely here since most will be Party-affiliated people with clean political records, and some will be people on the receiving end of favors whose function will be largely titular. It contracts the team ostensibly on the basis of performance. The appointment of new managers is often part of a larger plan to take the firm public on a stock exchange in order to raise capital for upgrading. If stock is issued, however, the government will remain the primary stockholder and thus the firm will remain under de facto state control.

### What must an enterprise do in order to go public in China?

The Chinese government has decided that by allowing enterprises to issue stock they can siphon off some of the 1.2 trillion Yuan that Chinese citizens save in banks or inside the proverbial mattress. Officials surmised that enterprises could raise funds from stock issues rather than continuing to depend on government bailouts. I visited a large state-controlled textile enterprise to find out how a firm goes about getting listed on a stock exchange, and what that means for the management of the firm. Dragonhead is a large textile company located in the Yangpu textile manufacturing district in Shanghai. It was formed 70 years ago and employs 10,000 people. It is a state enterprise and ranked third in size among China's textile companies. The company's biggest challenge, says its managers, is "making the transfer to a market economy." As Manager Xie described: "Before [the reforms] there was no worry. State-run trading organizations would supply what we needed and would sell what we produced. Now, we have to locate both our suppliers and markets to sell to." The firm was going deeper and deeper into the red. In August, 1992 the company began to issue stock under the name Dragonhead on the Shanghai Stock Exchange.

The process of getting listed involves a number of steps on the part of an enterprise's management. First, the company must apply to the government for permission to privatize. Second, the government engages with the firm to conduct a complete financial evaluation of the company. Next, the firm organizes for transfer to a shareholding system, which entails having workers sign performance contracts that, if unfulfilled, may result in worker dismissal. Fourth, board members are elected at a shareholder's conference. Their biographies are published in a company prospectus along with information about the company's assets, structure, annual growth, profits, etc., and this is made available to the public. Finally, the accounting procedures used to operate the company are changed to Western practice. The issue of stock is announced in the newspaper, along with all pertinent information about the company. Dragonhead sells only "A" shares, those sold in Renminbi currency. "To gain approval to sell "B" shares (which are foreign exchange-denominated)," says Manager Xie, "you must be export oriented. If you are approved to issue "B" shares the company will enjoy joint venture status, as long as it sells a certain amount of "B" shares to foreign entities."

Dragonhead issued 55 million shares, of which the company owns (that is, the state) 70 percent; in other words, the company is now 30 percent privatized. When the firm first listed on the Shanghai Stock Exchange, 200 million Yuan flowed in, which the company invested wisely. The board of directors makes all investment decisions. They put 50 million Yuan into the purchase of new equipment, mainly spinning machinery from Switzerland and Italy. They invested another 50 million Yuan in other companies involved industries such as construction materials, taxi services, materials processing, restaurants, and real estate. They sunk the next 50 million Yuan into stock holdings in *unlisted* companies.

These are companies that sell their stock but are not yet listed on any exchange—a business activity that is theoretically illegal but everyone seems to be doing it. "When the state allows this stock to be traded," said one manager, "it will mean *big* money." The company also sells this form of stock to its staff, holdings that will not be redeemable for another year, says Manager Xie. The final 50 million Yuan awaits a home. Managers mentioned that the money may be invested overseas, most likely in offshore textile companies.

### *What changes have the reforms made in the operation of Chinese enterprises in the 1980s and 1990s?*

China's management reforms have provided many new freedoms to factory managers, but the ideal of "enterprise autonomy" has not yet been fully realized, especially in the areas of R&D, training, distribution, technical renovation, and importation of technology, all of which are still governed by state mandate. This is not to suggest that major adjustments in enterprise operations have not been carried out. In fact, many significant and highly promising changes have been put in place.

For example, in the past, most working capital was allocated by the state. Governmental agencies simply paid out to enterprises what they believed the enterprises needed in relation to achieving the targets set in the central plan and in light of negotiations with the enterprise directors. Investment capital was doled out in a similar fashion to enterprises by the state. Nowadays, earnings, loans, and even stock issues have become the primary sources of funds that can be used by the enterprise for investment. By retaining earnings and obtaining bank loans, enterprises directly make decisions related to the accumulation and expenditure of capital.

Enterprises also have obtained a great deal more power to conceive and carry out expansion plans, in part, because of additional depreciation funds and a new enterprise fund derived from enterprise profits. With greater control over its finances, enterprises are able to procure equipment and raw materials better suited to their production requirements. Unfortunately, these funds also are being used to engage in unauthorized capital construction—a problem that has grown extremely serious at times despite Beijing's efforts to curtail such investments.

Because of the increasing availability of bank loans, enterprises now have a better position opportunity to carry out factory renovation. Renovation projects are undertaken for the principal purpose of modernizing both the plant and equipment of the enterprise. Projects can originate from four different sources: the central government, local governments, a foreign trade corporation, and the enterprise itself. In order to compete, many enterprises pursue multiple avenues of equipment improvement, often buying foreign machinery and know-how to create new or more sophisticated products. From the perspective of foreign firms, the technical renovation program offers a chance to reshape both the structure and operation of a particular Chinese production facility.

New links between foreign trade corporations (FTCs) and producers have fostered more efficient and direct connections between enterprises and the distribution system. Raw materials and component sourcing were once largely the responsibility of the state; serious delivery problems were incessant due to internal diversion of supplies and chronic shortages. Now, enterprises have some discretion over from whom they obtain supplies; they can go outside of their regional system to acquire needed inputs, sometimes with the help of the local government. This helps speed up production, lower costs, and remove unwanted bureaucratic interference in the sourcing process. However, to import raw materials or components, enterprises must for the most part, buy from local FTCs, many of whom charge double the rate for imported items compared to the international market price. Increasingly, manufacturers can sell their product directly into the Chinese market. In the past, state supply agencies received products from the factory for distribution. Today, enterprises producing consumer products, for example, are largely responsible for initiating collaborative arrangements between themselves and retailers. Ideas regarding product design have been changed as well. In the past, the ministry would gather product ideas from factories under its control; sometimes these ideas would come from the reverse-engineering of a foreign product. After consultation with the ministry, each factory manager would return to his factory to produce the item, ostensibly the same way in each factory. Today, factory managers can initiate the design and production of new products in response to emerging market demand. Thus, the trend is for enterprises to respond to, and deal more directly with their customers.

## The Organization of a Chinese Enterprise

The Chinese organize enterprises to emphasize vertical, rather than lateral, communication. The typical state-owned large enterprise has five functional levels: (1) administrative, (2) workshop production, (3) shift leaders, (4) team leaders, and (5) workers. The enterprise is under the auspices of a party committee and is administered by three deputies working under a factory director.

Of the factory's three organizational "trees," only one deals with actual production; the other two handle supply, marketing, and worker service. Thus supply and marketing remain divorced from manufacturing operations. This overburdens Deputy Director #3, who has to organize R&D, product design, quality control, and technology acquisition as well as ameliorate constant shop-floor problems brought to him by all four workshop directors. His responsibilities befit two deputies – one in charge of production; the other, R&D.

Below Deputy Director #3, the presence of shift leaders and team leaders implies middle-management redundancy. Workers need to be brought into more direct contact with workshop directors.

Source: Adapted from Martin Lockett, "Culture and the Problems of Chinese Management," *Organization Studies*, Sept. 4, 1988.

Therefore, quality is improving. Historically, quantity rather than quality has been a top priority in Chinese industry. "Mao jacket philosophy" (it doesn't matter what a product looks like as long as every citizen can have one) continues in China today, even though the current five-year plan emphasizes the need for higher quality in Chinese products. In China, the inherent quality problems of domestically produced products are accepted as part of the risk of buying Chinese; domestic merchandise carries no consumer guarantee. As such, enterprises now advertise their products, especially consumer goods, in order to boost sales. Foreign competition in the domestic market also encourages Chinese firms to promote their products.

### *What is the new role of the Chinese manager in the enterprise?*

China's reformers recognize that the enterprise manager is the turnkey for China's industrial modernization. Articles often appear in the Chinese press about managers succeeding in the marketplace in the face of numerous obstacles, the "manager-hero" who takes over a factory in debt, gathers market information, comes to understand the demands of his consumers, finds a niche for his products, acts quickly to get the product into the market, works to become "number one" in his township, and eventually succeeds in exporting his production. However, until now, the Chinese manager has occupied a relatively low position in the Chinese decision-making hierarchy. Typically, prereform enterprises were headed by a factory director who worked with several deputies, including a chief engineer and a senior accountant. The day-to-day operational responsibilities were distributed between a number of staff departments: finance and accounting, labor and wages, training, planning, personnel, and general administration. In some respects, management reforms have forced the factory director to assume a greater role in shaping the operation of the factory. In all likelihood, he now chairs a committee composed of his senior deputy, chief engineer, chief economist, chief accountant, CCP committee secretary, trade union president, secretary of the Communist Youth League Committee, and a representative elected by the Workers' Congress. This committee has a great deal of influence on identifying a range of managerial alternatives and options.

The enterprise responsibility program is best viewed as a system of informal *contracting* between selected Chinese managers and government entities in charge of factories. The process often begins with the solicitation of bids from numerous managers on specific manufacturing projects. After winning a bid, theoretically on the basis of ability and past performance, the manager agrees in contract to meet certain production targets and quality specifications over the life of the contract, usually 3 to 5 years. A number of different contract forms are used depending on the nature of the enterprise in question. If the enterprise succeeds in meeting the stated requirements, the manager typically can earn a bonus equal to one year's salary; if the factory misses the target, the manager can be expected to receive a reduction in salary of around five percent. Often, the newly contracted manager of an enterprise will subsequently sign contracts between himself and middle managers and even workers, forming multiple levels of "responsibility" contracts within an enterprise. In effect, the factory director responsibility system has replaced the party leadership system: it has now been implemented in all of China's major cities.

### Does the Chinese manager wield real control over the operation of an enterprise?

The new system gives managers greater control over everything from product mix to advertising, product development, and marketing both the quota portion as well as the surplus portion of production. In the past, production schedules were traditionally established on the basis of directions from the state. A ministry would inform its factories, either directly or through the channel of a local industrial bureau, as to the amounts they were responsible to produce for the next year. Factory managers could negotiate for a lower quota, if need be. Today, in most industries, no quotas are issued as such. While the same decision-making hierarchy exists and sets informal expectations, these are seen as "guidance plans" by the factory manager. At one time, factories would produce and deliver production to a wholesaling bureau, never selling to or even seeing their customers. Most managers had little idea who were their customers or what were their specific requirements. Nor did they know the final selling price of their products. Today, factories produce against an adjustable quota, but the factory has to find the customers itself.

The road to better management in China, however, has not been without its potholes and cul de sacs. Many managers have found it extremely frustrating taking advantage of their new freedoms, basically because of the incomplete and uneven nature of China's economic reforms. The structurally entrenched problems of pricing, taxation, and distribution remain a serious impasse to true factory autonomy. In many ways, the vitality of an enterprise still strongly depends on the guanxi relationships held by the factory director. A manager may have all the technical skills as his foreign counterpart, but the one with fewer personal connections will not be as effective. Although the Chinese manager is being forced to address new issues like technological innovation, performance-based incentive systems, and production of new products that are responsive to fast-changing world markets, guanxi relations are still important, if not more important, as new competitive pressures emerge. To a large extent, the fact is that the success of the enterprise reform package depends on the enthusiasm, technical skills, and leadership ability of the Chinese manager. This pivotal role lends a certain amount of prestige to the role of the manager, albeit, also a great deal more vulnerability.

### *How have Chinese managers responded to market-oriented reforms and carried out real changes?*

Essentially, the growing competition among Chinese enterprises has led to a new emphasis on creating products that can dominate domestic markets as well as successfully enter export markets. Enterprise managers have responded to the growing role of the market in a variety of ways. Some managers actually gather market information and formulate long-term market forecasts. When products emerge as high-demand items, numerous factories may mobilize to produce them on their own. Possession of good market information allows managers to improve product quality, produce new varieties of products, and offer more extensive customer service. In their effort to target new markets, enterprise managers now carry out fairly sophisticated sales forecasting and customer-demand investigations. Inventory problems in selected factories are starting to disappear as managers are able to move products into the marketplace without state interference. Product lines are being improved and diversified, and more attention is being paid to aesthetics, warranties, and service backup. Greater technical innovation has also come into play as enterprises seek production advantages. Many plants are producing closer to capacity and are utilizing their machinery and labor more efficiently. Recent trends in patent registration confirm that the evolving system is encouraging Chinese enterprises to innovate, and protect their discoveries via patent protection.

Unfortunately, the enterprise reforms have not resolved all marketing dilemmas for factory directors, especially when one considers the marketing of Chinese products abroad. Managers remain principally concerned with maintaining market share within their own domestic market rather than the export market since the monetary rewards for doing so are greater. Even when an enterprise succeeds in exporting production for foreign exchange, 50-75 percent of those earnings must be returned to the central government or local governments. Of the limited percentage that the enterprise is allowed to retain, such foreign exchange must be placed in an account with the Bank of China, and must be used under the auspices of the relevant bureau. The legacy of direct state control over enterprises, combined with the fact that the domestic market in China is so hungry for products, encourages the Chinese manager to maintain a rather short-term perspective. As such, the Chinese manager admonishes export schemes and emphasizes selling to domestic endusers—much as American manufacturers behaved during the 1950s and 1960s. Since the domestic consumer and capital goods markets are impulsive, managers pursue short-term goals, and may limit spending on R&D and foreign know-how. In addition, short-term enterprise performance evaluation (in the form of quarterly assessments) encourages short-term behavior on the part of management. The lessons of the past and the uncertainty of the future seem to dictate a "quick fix," short-term managerial mentality.

### How well do Chinese enterprises fare in the international marketplace?

Based on interviews in the People's Republic, many Chinese managers perceive producing for export as a risk rather than a surefire benefit. In considering the opportunity to export production, they seem to fear losing domestic competitiveness, and perceive they are vulnerable to fluctuations in the international market as well as pressures from foreign exchange-seeking Chinese government agencies. In many respects, the Chinese manager's response is a rational one, especially given the far easier task of addressing the local market. Accordingly, most Chinese managers still possess less than full knowledge or appreciation of the international market. Since some enterprises can literally sell everything they produce domestically, they often can ignore the task of understanding overseas markets. They take it as an affront that international prices fluctuate. Many factory managers refuse to export their production since foreign distribution of their products remains largely the task of the relevant FTC, which are not particularly reliable as distributors. Production may sit in warehouses for long periods of time, while the FTC delays payment of foreign exchange owed to the factory until the FTC gets paid from abroad. Because of the rapid turnover rate in the domestic market, most factory managers try to avoid dealing with FTCs any more than necessary.

Surely, part of the international marketing problems forced by Chinese management have their origin in the lack of exposure to the world economy and a dearth of educational programs geared specifically to training management to operate in a globally competitive economy. Blame does not fall solely on the managers, however. As indicated, many obstacles stand in the path of the manager who desires to utilize enterprise autonomy to maximize production—and sell abroad. These obstacles are built into the Chinese industrial system. Their efficacy cannot be overemphasized as primary causes for both Chinese enterprise inefficiency as well as their unresponsiveness to foreign markets. Nonetheless, as decentralization of the Chinese economy spreads, the market mechanisms now in full swing in selected areas will come to play an important role throughout the entire production and distribution network. This will clearly necessitate the emergence of internationally-oriented managers, in China on a broad scale.

### *What forces outside the enterprise impinge upon its ability to perform?*

Chinese enterprises are simultaneously administered from inside as well as outside, by internal managers, directors, and cadres, as well as local bureau and central ministerial officials. The vertical structure within the enterprise is an extension of the vertical structure of the bureaucracy that surrounds the enterprise. Each department within an enterprise must report to the general manager of the enterprise as well as its corresponding municipal bureau. For instance, the import department of an enterprise will, of necessity have links with the local foreign trade commission. Hence, the enterprise is not only regulated, in the Western corporate sense, but it is "checked" at every level of its organization by numerous external forces. Enterprises must contend with various types of government controls, usually enacted through government-issued directives, *and* local government prerogatives and priorities that are most often based less upon carrying out Beijing's wishes than allocating as much production and foreign exchange for its own needs. Thus, with the enterprise reforms, while the central government may play a reduced role in individual enterprise decision making, local bureaucratic entities seem, to some extent, to be taking advantage of decentralization to meddle in the affairs of the enterprise even more than before. The implication of this for foreigners is to seek partners with clout at the central level.

Often the ministry, bureau, and other government units are all pulling the enterprise in different directions. The manager remains largely powerless to extricate the enterprise from the state's administrative clutches. Multiple government entities are likely to wield influence over the internal functioning and decision making of the enterprise, making it nearly impossible for managers to implement, let alone fully actualize, their new plans and programs. If their plans fail, demotion, or at least ostracism is quite possible. Directives emanating from outside can be both conflicting and redundant; the Chinese enterprise manager is often forced into a position of trying to please various bureaucrats rather than concentrate on taking full advantage of his enterprise's pronounced autonomy and responsibilities.

### *Are Chinese managers bogged down with matters pertaining to non-operational issues?*

Because some of the lines of managerial authority and responsibility are still unclear, Chinese managers spend a great deal of time and energy on issues that seem arcane and irrelevant to their economic role. Since all problems, including maintenance issues of a relatively obscure nature, must be approved by several layers of management, high-level managers find themselves quickly overloaded. Managers must not only oversee their enterprise efficiency and output, but also attend to worker welfare issues such as housing, safety, and family policy. That is, managers find themselves constantly bogged down in dealing with personnel issues such as worker housing, pension funds, and the education of workers' children. The Chinese manager typically describes the danwei production unit under his auspices as a "family"—a Big Family. I have a good friend in Chongqing who has recently been promoted to Vice Director of a large state enterprise that is in the throes of privatizing itself and performing on a bottom-line basis. Next year my friend will take over as director of the enterprise. Does he like his new job? No way. As director of the enterprise and its danwei, he is now saddled with arduous and tedious tasks such as "caring about the family planning program" and "working out a fire prevention program." Such social welfare tasks siphon away nearly all of his time and energy. And this is a 44-year-old English-speaking highly trained professional person who might otherwise be able to manage his enterprise into the black.

### *What role does the Communist Party play inside the company?*

Along with the vagueness of authority, the position of the CCP represents the most formidable obstacle to direct managerial leadership. Under the current reforms, enterprise managers and party secretaries have in theory, entered a dynamic relationship of "shared leadership" over factory operations. The CCP no longer solely governs decision making that concerns the economic administration of enterprise operations. This is not to imply, however, that political considerations no longer affect the functioning of the Chinese factory. The CCP secretaries still play an important role in decisions concerning wages, worker welfare, worker rewards, and political consciousness-raising, though its energies are increasingly focused on raising production levels rather than raising the political consciousness of workers.

### *Are Chinese enterprises ever to be free to operate autonomously?*

With the Chinese economy still characterized by high levels of state inducement and intervention, no matter how much freedom the enterprise may have on paper, its choice of alternatives, for example, in articulating new production techniques, is still greatly restricted by the economic requisities imposed upon it from outside. In effect, the state still controls enterprises through the pricing of imported goods, the imposition of import tariffs, the delivery of critical inputs, and by manipulation of the amount of revenue enterprises can keep after taxes. The state accomplishes this through a complex system of quotas, taxation, remittances, and state purchases of production. The state's continued influence on the criteria for allocation of revenue by banks for enterprise renovation, and its control of most major distribution channels all run against the independent functioning of the enterprise, thus limiting its ability to respond to new demands or shift production into new areas.

Acknowledging this, it must also be noted that direct economic control over enterprises by the central government has been reduced with decentralization of enterprise management. While under this situation, the enterprise still has not been freed from the financial fetters one associates with a socialist economy—production quotas, high taxation, and government controls over product pricing, though it has gained some discretionary authority. The crux of the problem, however, is that all of these restrictions represent serious impediments to enterprise directors seeking avenues for production/marketing flexibility, responsiveness, and competitiveness. Since state-led economic control ensures the government a continuous supply of revenue to fund the country's modernization, Chinese reformers have experienced much trepidation and even resistance to their attempt to disengage the financial aspects of enterprise management from the governmental organs of economic administration. Too much financial freedom for the enterprise, critics claim, is a threat to China's economic stability.

### *Does the Chinese enterprise have control over its profits, or does the State take everything it earns?*

A system of taxation-against-profit (li gai shui) has recently been applied to industrial enterprises in order to turn over more control of the financial aspects of factory management to enterprise employees. In the past, factories simply remitted all their earnings to the state. Administrative authorities would then issue the factory an operating budget for the following term. In fact, the largest source of income to the state came from factory remittances; it is this revenue that is being replaced by factory taxation. Taxation, however, is not seen as a sure method of guaranteeing the state the revenue it is accustomed to receiving. Profits are difficult to predict and remeasure, and can be manipulated. Officials fear that factories will skim profits, falsify rates of production, and hide sales figures in order to avoid paying their share. Furthermore, with increasing competition among enterprises, some extreme inefficiencies associated with poor implementation of reforms, and the possible diversion of funds to factory-planned investments, the collection of enterprise taxes could be fouled and tax revenue lost. The result for management: government officials lack trust in managers to honestly remit their factory's profits in the form of taxes.

## MOTIVATING WORKERS: THE INERTIA OF DANWEI

*What systems have been used in China over the years to motivate workers?*

The Chinese have extensive experience with motivational schemes to enhance worker productivity. Since 1949, China has employed numerous incentive programs in hopes of increasing output, running the gamut from group incentives to individual rewards, from moral suasion and emulation campaigns to piece rate and stock options. Mao Zedong promoted labor volunteerism based on "emulation drives," which in turn, inspired the formation of emulation committees in most of the country's factories. Awards were given for successful imitation of highly propagandized model factories. Since Mao's death, emphasis on material incentives has been increased. Thus, incentives based on moral encouragement and those based on material rewards have been, in effect, combined.

Unfortunately for workers, there have been no significant pay raises in the state sector since 1966. With some exceptions, recent wage reforms have been mostly remedial. Within the state sector there still exists little job mobility. The challenge now is for China to create a new incentive structure so that worker motivation rises and output increases.

### Does a free labor market exist in China?

There remains restrictions on labor mobility in China due to restrictions on migration within the country. When the Communists took political control of China in 1949, they organized human resources into a system that evolved into the household-registration system called danwei. In the system, workers and managers are placed (often permanently) in a specific production unit directly out of school. In effect, a Chinese person's workplace and home tend to be one in the same; a place to live, raise children, socialize, grow old, and die. A production unit may be part of a commune, a state farm or factory, or a collective. In general, it is extremely difficult to transfer to another production unit. To change units, a person must have the approval of the new unit as well as that of the old. Furthermore, getting out of a unit is even more toilsome if one is technically skilled, as that unit will resist allowing a much-needed worker or manager to leave. To leave an enterprise, a worker might be labeled aberrant, and find it nearly impossible to locate a better position in another factory. Though there now exist more ways of leaving a unit and moving to another one, workers must still obtain releases. A woman wanting to relocate in Beijing describes her ordeal: "Getting my residence permit transferred to Beijing was difficult... had to move on several fronts at once. There is the official... that looks after entry to and exit from the city, and there's the unit in Beijing that you want to work for ... you have to find somebody who wants to exchange with you. There are a few people who want to leave Beijing. I found some ... working in the track maintenance department of the railway bureau ... These two people made a couple of conditions: firstly, one of them wanted me to help him find a job, a good job, in [my] little town. The other one wanted a flat there. I managed all of this but then the personnel department wouldn't let them go. So I had to think up some way to overcome this new problem ... It's no good just spending money: you have to make sure you spend it the right way. The thing to do is to see what they need for their families—you have to use your eyes or make inquiries."

In a nutshell, the danwei system is China's welfare system. The danwei provides residents with 90 percent of their medical costs, and provides housing such that their rent only amounts to 5 percent of their income. In addition, says one danwei resident in Chongqing, "In winter, the danwei gives us money to buy fuel or clothes or anything we want." The decimation of the danwei—an ongoing process that should be a case study for a sociologist—is underway, at least in the large cities. People are removed, move into their own apartments as tenants or owners, some remaining dependent on the danwei while others become entirely self-suffi- cient with salaried positions. Perhaps 85 percent of Chinese fac- tory workers remain members of a traditional danwei.

### *Do Chinese managers have an equivalent to traditional western "hire and fire" powers?*

In the mind of the enterprise manager, the danwei system prevents workers from being easily dismissed, thus largely depriv- ing him of the power to hire and fire. Generally speaking, jobs in China are guaranteed—lifetime employment has existed since 1949. Also, workers will not readily leave their jobs to relocate, making recruitment of appropriately skilled workers difficult. As a result, some industries have too many workers clogging plants and factories and draining off capital into unnecessary wages, while sectors such as the service industry experience underemployment because of a lack of capital and equipment. This overabundance of workers, in relation to work to be completed, leads to rampant worker idleness, absenteeism, low morale, and spreads disrespect for management. Ultimately, overstaffing inhibits a manager's efforts to offer individual incentives, to streamline production activities, or to reduce the ranks of middle managers. Because workers are now hired on a labor contract system, more and more of them can be dismissed if they violate work rules.

### *How are Chinese workers recruited?*

New forms of worker recruitment represent an attempt to cir- cumvent the traditional obstacles of the danwei. Another approach involves employment quotas in selected youth categories, such as youths sent to the countryside, recent graduates of secondary school, and other groups not yet rooted to local work environments. These youth groups are often solicited through recruitment advertising. The most successful approach, however, is for individual factories to organize their own new-employee recruitment and then establish ex post facto approval by the labor authorities. In this manner, temporary workers are hired, graded, and paid daily rates. Some of the temporaries may become regular workers after on-the-job training. Because workers are now hired on a labor contract system, they can be dismissed if they violate work rules. Referrals for new workers may be obtained from relatives of workers already employed, by off-site employment offices, or by word-of-mouth networking (the grapevine). In addition, there appears to be a pattern of informal job inheritance, wherein a job may be guaranteed for one child of each retiring worker.

As noted, the danwei system enables enterprises across the economy to provide services and welfare to their employees. Most Chinese are attached socially and psychologically to the security offered by the production unit system. In spite of the recent influx of labor into China's special economic zones, luring them away from their danwei to work for more money or a better job may be problematic. In some cases, Chinese workers choose to remain at a secure job rather than take the risk of leaving it for a higher paying one, especially if they hold a position in a state-owned factory where benefits and stability are greatest. On the other hand, workers in major cities like Shanghai seek employment in higher paying foreign-invested ventures; job hopping from one FIE to another has resulted recently in many foreign managers hiring only workers *without* a history of working in a FIE. Luring talented workers from one JV to another is also common practice.

### How many days a week do Chinese employees work, and what are their wages?

Workers usually work a six-day week, nine-hours a day. By January, 1995 laws will be in place which set minimum worker age at 16, a minimum wage, and a maximum work week of 44 hours and six days per week. Wages for workers are based on an eight-grade scale, grade one being unskilled, grade eight, highly skilled. Worker promotions once followed this scale: the higher the worker on the scale, the higher his wage. Critics claimed the system rewarded worker seniority but failed to reward actual performance. By 1978, a points system that rated an individual's performance, skill level, and labor attitude had been developed to supplant seniority as a condition for promotion.

More problems ensued with this system and, in 1982, a system of bonus-giving was adopted in a new effort to link wages to performance. Net profits now go to bonuses, under a system of "distribution according to labor," thereby linking worker reward directly with the profitability of the enterprise. Since skill levels differ across various sectors of the same industry, the bonus system becomes a means to tie wages to performance. Workers who perform well receive a bonus of 10 to 25 percent of their basic wage. Continual raising of the bonus ceilings has been underway since the program was initiated. Bonuses stand at 12.9 percent of basic wages. The state encourages bonus-giving by offering favorable taxation structures. However, if an enterprise fails to produce a profit, workers may only receive 80 percent of their base pay and forgo bonuses altogether. While good for workers, this may deprive the enterprise of investment capital, which may work against everyone's interests over the long term. Danwei has worked against the idea to base worker wages more on performance rather than prestige and seniority. Traditional and informal hiring arrangements associated with danwei—based upon kinship and personal references—remain in use. Recent efforts to base the hiring of workers more upon skill level and other achievement criteria are meeting with some success, though obstacles still remain. In 1986, the labor contract system was instituted in state-owned enterprises. Two forms of contract system are currently gaining acceptance: per unit output, and per unit of labor. Both contract systems tie wages directly to performance. These new forms of labor contract promise to enhance worker performance in ways that "moral" campaigns have not.

Currently, wage structure in state enterprises consists of four different levels:

1. basic wage which is guaranteed across the country;

2. supplemental wage based on piece rate and extra shift work which rewards individual performance and seniority;

3. welfare subsidies, which includes housing, food supplements, utilities, transportation, day care, and hospitalization; and

4. performance wages, which are rewarded in the form of "floating" bonuses.

These wages are normally grouped for workers in foreign-invested companies located inside investment zones. There, total wages paid range from 600-1,500 yuan per month, or the equivalent of $70-160.

### How are managers appointed and promoted?

The appointment of managers was once an area exclusively assigned to the state through the local economic commissions at the municipal and provincial level. Managerial appointments were made from among the workers who were both politically sound (i.e., red) and, secondarily, technically competent (i.e., expert). Their promotion involved recommendation and discussion among workers, managers, and Communist Party committee members. Today the appointment of managers depends more on a balance of both "redness" *and* "expertness," yet it is clear that the latter is now much more critical than the former; the entire system has moved toward examination and merit as a basis for achieving management positions. Although most managers are still appointed by local economic commissions, the State Council has decreed recently that managers must come up for election every five years. And it is the task of local workers' congresses to decide—by holding elections—whether managers should be reinstated. Herein lies the tension. Bemused by inconsistent policies imposed from the outside, many workers have become disillusioned with their directors and have voted against them in director elections. No clear-cut regulations exist to deal with the worker-manager dichotomy. Factory directors are hamstrung. They promise workers high bonuses only to discover that red tape at a higher bureaucratic level reduces the factory's income. Bonuses fail to materialize and workers blame the director, putting him in jeopardy at the next director election.

Educational systems have been employed in a system of manager "certification." Factory managers are now being asked to pass national exams before being installed as top managers, even though choosing managers via examination runs against the long-held belief among veteran managers in China that managerial experience should be valued more than formal business-oriented education. This may be changing, however, with the management certification policy taking hold. Managers are being motivated to seek more training and increase their skill levels. Younger, well-educated managers are getting top positions. More formal skills among new managers is resulting in the introduction of more scientific management practices in greater numbers of enterprises. Potential managers are increasingly appraised in terms of technical competence and leadership abilities; in fact, it would not be premature to suggest that a professional managerial class is emerging in the People's Republic.

### What is the relationship of managers to workers in China today?

Full financial responsibility for enterprises has placed workers and managers in a new relationship. In the old days, Soviet "one-man" leadership, wherein the factory director answered to a government body rather than the party, had been implemented. The system gave prominence to the factory director, who could then work up the ranks to a position of sole decision maker. By 1956, the system was rejected and the party divided powers among management cadres. The rationale was that leadership by one individual was incongruent with Maoist egalitarian ideology. The new emphasis on democracy in Chinese management was designed to keep management from exploiting or abusing the rights of workers.

The change started a tradition of worker influence in the factory through various labor organization bodies such as the workers' and staff congresses, labor unions, and the party within the enterprise. The sharing of control over the administration of such things as production plans, annual budgets, and labor management, while beneficial to workers in terms of seeing that their wages are fair and the workplace is safe, is one reason, however, market-driven decision making is today so difficult for the enterprise manager.

### What is the status of worker safety, and are workers' interests represented?

Workers are represented by the All-China Federation of Labor Unions (ACFLU), a government-controlled union criticized because it tends to side with management in most disputes.

Beijing would like to set up branches of the union in all Chinese-owned and foreign-invested enterprises before illegal unions get further organized and gain a real voice in labor policy making. Pressure has mounted on Beijing to facilitate the building of an organization to protect workers in the wake of increasing numbers of accidents and injuries in Chinese and foreign-operated factories in China. Forty-five thousand industrial accidents occurred in Guangdong Province alone in 1993, killing 8,700 workers. Enterprises with over 50 workers in Shenzhen are now required to hire safety officers, modelled on the Hong Kong practice—a first in all of China; where large state firms have safety units but where small companies and foreign-invested companies rarely do.

### Does China have an enterprise bankruptcy law?

The Enterprise Bankruptcy Law of the People's Republic of China was issued in December 1986 to punish inefficient enterprises in a setting that includes systemic inequalities. By ratifying a bankruptcy statute, the Chinese are attempting, as they have numerous times in the past, to create incentives for workers and managers to revitalize the enterprises in which they work. The law outlines the conditions upon which an enterprise can be declared officially bankrupt. Debate over earlier versions of the law showed that many decision makers felt strongly that it was simply too early to punish enterprises that fail to perform against a profit criteria without consideration of the manifold negative influences that impinge upon the profit-making capability of underprivileged enterprises. Indeed, the reasons cited in forcing the first enterprise bankruptcy (of Shen Yang Welding Equipment Factory) included: a lack of skills among workers, large numbers of pensioners to support, frequent changes in management, corruption, and high taxes—not all of which can be blamed directly on the enterprise or its director. Certainly, the danwei labor system and outside bureaucratic meddling play key roles in factory efficiency and inefficiency. Only a handful of large state firms have been allowed to go under; most continue to be bailed out with "working loans" and subsidies.

# CHAPTER 16

# TRANSFERRING

# TECHNOLOGY

# TO CHINA

*A new technological revolution.... presents both an opportunity and a challenge to the economic development of our country. We should seize this opportunity and make selective use of the new scientific and technological achievements so as to accelerate our modernization and narrow the economic and technological gap between China and the developed countries.*

**—General Secretary Zhao Ziyang, 1984**

*"To steal a book is an elegant offense."*

**—Chinese Proverb**

*I*n the mid 1980s, the first Chinese translation of Alvin Toffler's book *The Third Wave* caused quite a stir. In response to the book a debate ensued among Chinese leaders over what China's response should be to the growing importance of the "third wave" technologies: biotechnology, microelectronics, information technology, and new materials. Several Chinese leaders argued that unless China is able to make significant advances in these four key areas, the technological gap between China and the West will grow even wider. Since the present leadership has based much of its credibility on its ability to close the gap and position China as a major force in world economic and technological affairs, anything short of its goal would be politically unacceptable. At the same time those party leaders still committed to the self-reliance principles often associated with the Maoist era argue that China has gone too far and too fast in importing foreign technologies.

Most Chinese have come to realize, however, that China will have to commit a larger share of its domestic market to foreign firms to attract the capital necessary to develop China's resources and consumer market, as proponents in China of the so-called northward strategy have advocated. Under this strategic imperative, China's inland markets would be opened to induce foreign capital to expand northward, easing shortages of domestic capital, introducing advanced technology, and promoting "technical advancement in the national economy."

### What has been China's approach to engaging with foreign technology vendors?

One of the characteristics of China's "transformation" in the 1980s was the desire of Chinese entities to enter into licensing, training and other technology transfer arrangements in order to gain access to foreign "know-how" in both product and production process technology. As part of this effort, provincial government and commercial entities have been granted greater decision-making authority in selecting the types of equipment to be imported and the necessary training to accompany the technology transfer. Such licensing agreements have often included significant fees for foreign companies willing to share their experience and technical expertise. However, in recent years Chinese authorities have come to believe that many enterprises have acquired unnecessary or redundant technologies. The need for absolute "know-how" is declining and both buyers and approval agencies are becoming more sophisticated in their purchasing preferences.

Today, Chinese authorities are employing a new bargaining technique in the negotiation of technology transfer arrangements. Recognizing the allure of the China market for foreign companies, many Chinese entities are demanding "trade and technology" arrangements, which ask foreign companies to transfer technology for free in exchange for continued or expanded access to the China market. Companies receive compensation for equipment, components and parts, rather than from royalties or fees.

### *What are the technological needs of state-owned enterprises in China?*

An estimated 25 percent of the state-owned enterprises in the industrial sector actually require complete renovation, which entails revamping both plant and equipment. Yet, even with more than eleven thousand contracts signed with foreign companies since China opened its doors, the short-term results of China's foreign technology acquisition program, in the opinion of many Chinese leaders, have not been satisfactory. Though China's leaders have decided to pursue a more gradual approach for fear of the risks inherent in adopting a more ambitious course, the priorities contained in the current state plan evidence no less of a high level commitment to massive technological development. The program contains three fundamental objectives: (1) the renovation of outmoded and inefficient factories; (2) the improvement in process and product technologies; and (3) more efficient use and substitution of raw and processed materials.

Unfortunately, the task of updating production equipment, product designs, processing technologies, and quality control capabilities is a major undertaking for which the Chinese are largely unprepared. The Chinese complicate this task by refusing to depend on one firm or country any more than necessary. This means, of course, that numerous foreigners are transferring technology into Chinese industry simultaneously, which creates serious equipment compatibility problems.

### *What are China's indigenous technological capabilities?*

Technological innovation in China outstripped that in Europe until the 1600s. Maintained chiefly through the trading of luxury goods via the Silk Road and missionaries residing in China, scientific contact between China and the European continent was continuous since Classical Greek times. The old Jesuit Observatory still stands in Beijing, where Father Verbier was commissioned by the Chinese emperor in 1674 to build a set of astronomical instruments, including an azimuth theodolite and an altazimuth. The arrangement was one of the earliest official technology transfers to China. Before this, however, innovation flowed in the opposite direction. The Chinese discovered gunpowder in the tenth century; the printing press in the eleventh century; and the magnetic compass was invented in the twelfth century, when a Chinese mariner discovered that a chunk of the naturally magnetic lodestone, when floated on a stick in water, pointed to the polestar. These inventions had revolutionary impacts on the European continent, though their origin went largely unrecognized and unappreciated.

Because early Chinese society distrusted merchants and inventors, the development of new technology was confined to the country's bureaucratic organizations. This hampered the pursuit of the practical arts flourishing in Europe. Given China's Confucian/Buddhist conception that an inner harmony pervaded the natural world, it was to be expected that Europe's Galilean science, which is founded on mathematical explanations of dead matter, did not fall on open ears in China, and thus was not accepted. China's isolation from outside innovation and scientific research was intensified by the events emanating from the European occupation of the country in the mid-nineteenth century, about the time Japan embraced Western technological progress wholeheartedly.

Throughout the twentieth century technology has entered China through a number of conduits, including high-technology trade, technology licensing, acquisition of turnkey plants, joint venture enterprise, scholastic exchange, literature collection, and study abroad by Chinese students. Following the virtual technology blackout imposed on the country during the fanatical years of the Cultural Revolution (1967-76), the role of technology in the economic development of the country—especially foreign technology—was completely redefined.

In 1975, at the Fourth National People's Congress, Zhou Enlai announced the modernization of China's organizations, industries, national defense, and science and technology. By the late 1970s, scientists and intellectuals who had been ravaged by the Red Guards were being rehabilitated and conscripted to pursue research under the Outline Plan for the Development of Science and Technology, promulgated at the National Science Conference in 1978. In 1979, China purchased $2.5 billion worth of foreign technology and equipment; by 1986, the country signed over 744 technology and equipment import contracts worth $4.45 billion.

### *Where are the Chinese areas of technological excellence?*

Though it is doubtful China will become a major exporter of third wave manufactured goods in the near term, there are signs of real achievement within certain sectors of the country's industry. The Maoist policy of developing technologies locally in order to promote village self-sufficiency has given way to one promoting regional technological excellence in strategically selected high technologies (e.g., integrated circuit boards in Shanghai, aerospace technology in Xian, and computers in Beijing). S&T planners hope to establish new research centers in robotics, biotechnology, and new materials, as well as 50 new national laboratories utilizing larger budgets and more numerous research grants. Scientific innovation and coordination of R&D efforts are present in chosen cities and industrial sectors that enjoy central government nurturing. This is particularly true of defense-related industries, such as military electronics. There have been outstanding examples of research achievement: the successful connection of telephone substations with optical fibers; the artificial synthesis of crystalline bovine insulin as early as 1965; the creation of 900 automated units on factory production lines; and the production of laser products for export, including sealed carbon dioxide lasers and electro-optical modelers.

The electronics industry was selected as the first to be modernized at a national industry conference held in Beijing in 1977, because of its importance as a for the four modernization. Today the focal point of the Chinese electronics industry is Shanghai. China's ultimate intention is to create a version of Silicon Valley in the city. To attain this goal, China has promoted the rapid development of "the magnificent seven" technologies: microelectronics, fiber optics, lasers, bioengineering, marine engineering, new materials science, and robotics. So far the transformation has indeed produced important research results, most notably involving semiconductors and integrated circuits, and all seven of these emerging industries evidence a high degree of initiative and performance potential. To play a role as a producer in the age of "informatics," and to reduce imports of components necessary to build computers, a major effort is being focused on upgrading semiconductor and integrated circuit (IC) production. China can produce 53 million ICs annually, but because only 4 percent of total production are medium-and large-scale ICs, China will have to import advanced ICs for some time.

Major accomplishments have also been achieved in the field of computer development. As a national priority, official directives state that the application of computers has been emphasized in every industry where their presence will help achieve economic goals. Although China's domestic computer production lags behind end-user needs, a concerted push is underway to increase computer research, manufacturing, and educational programs designed to offer computer-related training. As early as 1983, over 90,000 Chinese were involved in computer research, production, application, and education in over 130 institutions.

### *How have foreign firms approached technology selling opportunities in China?*

Savvy foreign companies have found numerous, profitable responses to China's changing market for high-technology. The overwhelming strategy for technology transfer in the 1990s seems to be joint venture arrangements. A joint venture offers the foreign company greater management control over the use and dissemination of its technology, and may allow for long-term profits from the sales of its products to third parties in the PRC.

Foreign companies have also profited from the transfer of technology bundled with extensive service contracts. Telephone switching systems, for example, offer lucrative service arrangements in which the system's software is upgraded twice yearly. In addition, companies have transferred technology with the expectation of further sales due to technology system expansion in the future. A recent sale of a cellular telephone system to a major city in central China was accompanied by a contract clause that extended preferential treatment to the company when the city's province began to expand the system to secondary and tertiary markets.

Technology transfer is often effected to ensure first access to future market opportunities. This is particularly important in China's highly regulated high-tech market segments. In another province, an American company recently entered into a joint venture to transfer pager technology to a Chinese company. In the process, the company made extensive contacts with the local and regional telecommunications authorities, as well as regional politicians, planners and economic development officials. In the next two years the region is expected to grant an exclusive license to a foreign company to develop and assist in the management of a cellular telephone network. The American company feels it is well-positioned to take advantage of this opportunity.

Finally, "trade and technology" arrangements can still be profitable to foreign companies from the outset through markup practices. Although Chinese market research capabilities are clearly improving, foreign suppliers of high-technology will still be in position to source the lowest-cost equipment and add a significant markup prior to transfer to the PRC.

Between 1950 and 1980, over 90 percent of China's foreign exchange expenditures on technology imports went for whole plant imports rather than the licensing and acquisition of know-how. These years were followed by a decisive move away from whole turnkey plant imports, to a sharper focus on the import of key technologies employing alternative forms of acquisition. The three most popular modes of technology acquisition include countertrade, compensation trade, and the so-called "one purchase—three cooperations", in which the foreign vendor participates in a joint venture, accepts produced products as partial compensation, and is willing to trade off a percentage of the production process to a Chinese manufacturer in return for purchase commitments.

This policy is nowhere more prevalent than in China's civil aviation market. With most of the world's largest aircraft manufacturers targeting China for increases in export sales, civil aviation has become the most competitive market in the People's Republic. A willingness to offset production gives the foreign firm an edge, but given that Boeing, McDonnell-Douglas, Short Brothers, and

Messerschmitt-Boelkon-Blohn (MBB) of West Germany, have all entered co-production ventures in exchange for sales of airplanes, foreign aerospace firms are having to offer more; like exclusive training centers, auxiliary high-technology projects, and commitments to participate in future joint ventures on newer model airliners. Moreover, the China National Aeronautic-Technology Import and Export Corporation (CATIC) is now required to disapprove aviation contracts with foreign firms if they do not agree to offset part of the purchase price with purchases of components made in China.

With China's general shift away from plain-and-simple technology acquisition has come a movement away from the simple expansion of plants and factories to the intensification of the country's existing capabilities. Often, older and cheaper technology is utilized rather than state-of-the-art equipment. To encourage the transfer of technical expertise there has also been a turn away from the acquisition of semi-knock-down (SKD) technology; foreign firms are now encouraged to import complete knockdown (CKD) packages that allow the Chinese to achieve a deeper understanding of the internal functioning of the technologies that they purchase. Overall, while China's technology acquisition program has not necessarily had an impressive beginning, results in certain areas have been appreciable.

### How do foreign suppliers structure technology transfer agreements?

While technology transferred as part of the capital contribution of the foreign partner in a foreign joint venture is governed by Chinese joint venture law, most foreign companies demand a separate technology transfer contract with their joint venture. The terms of such a contract must comply with China's technology import regulations, which were updated in 1993.

Technology contracts are typically limited to 10 years unless longer terms are granted by Chinese authorities. Typically, the confidentiality requirement of the technology transfer agreement will correspond to the overall contracted length of the joint venture. Exceptions may be offered when the licensor offers regular and ongoing improvements or systems upgrades in the technology.

All technology transfer agreements will be subject to MOFTEC approval or the approval of its designee. Import contracts that exceed $5 million must also be authorized by the State Planning Commission. Approval should become automatic if the parties' application is not acted upon within 60 days.

### How is the decision making on a foreign technology project handled?

The negotiation and agreement process is also likely to involve other entities, including MOFTEC's China's National Technology Import-Export Corporation, also called Techimport. Techimport may actually take the lead in seeking out foreign suppliers and arranging negotiation meeting times and sites. One may also encounter representatives from the local municipality, provincial officials, ministerial officials from the industry in question, as well as banking and tax representatives. One should definitely expect the participation of officials from regional planning and technology commissions/agencies, and should question any negotiation setting in which they are not present. Many of these entities will review the proposed venture's or trade deal's feasibility study, and will have a say in the approval of the technology transfer agreement.

Foreign suppliers can save themselves unnecessary time and headaches by following a simple checklist when approached by a potential importer of foreign technology.

1. Is the technology importer authorized to deal with foreigners?

2. Does the importer have access to foreign currency to pay for the technology?

3. Has the importer already conducted a feasibility study and received authorization from local planning authorities? Ask to see the project authorization certificate.

Alternative (i.e.: nonlocal Chinese and foreign) financing for technology transfer arrangements is available from a variety of sources both within and outside of the PRC. Two of the most common sources of external financing are foreign concessionary or soft loans from the government of the supplier and international development agencies. Consult the chapter on Banking and Insurance for more information regarding alternative financing sources.

### *What restrictions exist on the transfer of technology to China?*

China is limited in its ability to purchase technology from the major industrialized suppliers because of its status as a Communist country. Restrictions on Chinese imports is imposed by a multilateral organization called the Coordinating Committee for Multilateral Export Controls (COCOM). The organization was founded in 1949 to prevent the flow of dangerous dual-use technologies with potential military applications to the Communist powers.

COCOM's membership includes the United States, Japan, the industrialized countries of Western Europe and Canada. The organization reserves the right to review proposed technology transfer arrangements and to block the sale of those goods or equipment seen as posing a potential dual-use threat. COCOM's regulatory regime encompasses direct military/defense items, atomic energy-related technologies and a general list of industrial goods. For most exporters to China, potential problems related to COCOM will fall in the latter category.

In recent years COCOM has significantly reduced the limitations on products that could be exported to China. However, the changes in the COCOM regime have been complicated by the existence of additional national export license restrictions. U.S. companies' technology exports, for example, are covered by a separate control regime that was tightened following the Tiananmen Crisis of 1989.

It is worth noting that the Clinton Administration's new China policy of "Comprehensive Engagement" may offer additional liberalization of the U.S. trade regime. The Administration has indicated a desire tde-emphasize trade restrictions as a method of influencing Chinese policy-making, and the President has personally suggested that the United States' evolving policy towards China will include liberalizing technology controls over U.S. exports to the PRC.

### How does China's approach compare with Taiwan's approach?

The Taiwanese government requires that suppliers by the holders of the patents of products sold, not merely a licensee of the product. Thus, to structure a deal in Taiwan, the foreign company must enter joint venture agreements with the patent holders included in the deal. This drives up the costs because the patent holder will desire an interest in the project, which the deserve because it is being asked to take on risk—that is, they must guarantee the technology. They are also directly bond to service the contract rather than just license their technology through another company.

I spoke to Mitch D. Dudek about this, an American lawyer working in Taipei. "Taiwan hurts itself by giving in to public pressure to avoid dependence on a single foreign supplier on large infrastructural projects," a core part of the country's sixth five-year plan and a potential boon to U.S. companies. "Thus, the dormant rapid transit system that cris-crosses the city was built by companies from France, the United States, and elsewhere. The stations and tracks and cars don't match! All coordination is done by government ministerial entities that do not effectively communicate with the suppliers. It's a mess." Walking the city, I saw that the stations were idle and the pillars holding up some of the tracks are cracked. It is, indeed, a mess.

### What are the appropriate technologies I should bring to China?

A central dilemma foreign firms encounter when transferring technology to China is one of trying to satisfy China's desire for state-of-the-art technology while supplying technology that is appropriate to specific Chinese environments. Chinese factory managers request the most advanced technology from foreign firms as a matter of protocol during initial negotiations, whether or not sufficient foreign exchange, trained personnel, or adequate infrastructure are present to support such technology. American firms are often pressured into offering their most advanced technology—often displaying blueprints and conducting technical seminars—only to see the contract go to a European or Japanese firm offering technology a decade old and at half the price. With some notable exceptions, the reality is that the Chinese may talk quality and sophistication but they tend to base their buying decisions on price.

Japanese, European, and U.S. firms pursue different approaches to this problem. The Japanese have taken advantage of their proximity and historical links with China to penetrate interior provinces and offer technology closely tied to existing Chinese capabilities at the factory level. However, the Japanese suffer a reputation among many Chinese of not being forthcoming with even basic technological know-how, often described as "more talk, less do." Yet Japanese firms offer consistently lower prices and seem to be better prepared to interface their newer technology with older equipment inside Chinese enterprises. In contrast, European firms are said to be more willing to transfer their highest technology, and do so rapidly and straightforwardly. They also enjoy the concessionary government financing typical in Europe. Chinese leaders have courted European firms throughout the mid-1980s, stepping up competition with the United States for technology transfer projects. Lastly, the U.S. firms have pursued a direct approach to technology transfer, though they have been neither as flexible in sharing high technology as some of the Europeans nor as able to offer the low prices of the Japanese firms.

A foreign firm's competitive edge in renovation projects depends on a combination of factors. Chinese trade officials in a position to approve contracts often consider price and credit terms more important than appropriateness, quality, and service backup. Also, technology acquisition decisions made by enterprise directors and official decision makers are often influenced by the place of origin of existing equipment in the importing Chinese enterprise. For instance, Shanghai steel factories were installed with German equipment in the 1930s, so when it came time to renovate, new German equipment was installed. Service backup and management training are considered important in terms of China's larger objectives to achieve self-reliance in key industries. The Chinese insist that foreign firms not only sell technology but also provide for its successful assimilation within a reasonable period of time, including the transfer of necessary expertise for the Chinese to manufacture it independently under license or freely. Although it is common for factory managers to want only the latest technology, representatives of foreign firms must remember that selling what the Chinese end-users desire may not be as prudent as it sounds.

### What happens if the technology proves to be too advanced for the Chinese factory?

If the technology proves to be too advanced for the Chinese factory, or the equipment is inadvertently damaged or ruined by workers whose training level is not commensurate with the level of technology, the reputation of the foreign firm may be seriously damaged. Although the president of Otis Elevators Company, Francois Jaulin, told a Chinese reporter at a press conference heralding Otis's joint venture in Tianjin that the company's Chinese partner would have the same access to Otis technology as other Otis subsidiaries, the company soon discovered that the notion was out of line with Chinese workmanship. Colin McDonall, then president of the joint venture, realized this when he found Chinese workers in the factory drilling holes in steel while other workers held the material in place, rather than use clamps. And instead of using mechanical measuring devices, workers were bending sheet metal and measuring by hand. Half-assembled pieces were being dragged from station to station, causing damage along the way and fatiguing the workers. Otis began by reorienting the shop floor so that raw materials enter at one side of the factory and undergo assembly in steps as they move through the factory. Before, a steel cutting saw used during the first steps of assembly stood in the center of the factory. The Chinese have come to recognize problems associated with the assimilation of foreign technologies and have begun to request technology more closely geared to the local environment.

Unfortunately, foreign firms must negotiate licensing contracts with people and organizations other than the factory managers and technicians who operate the destination factory, such as a local FTC or ministerial bureaucrats. The unfortunate aspect is that the decisions concerning the organization of construction and the implementing of technology in the Chinese factory are made on the Chinese side without ample consideration of the compatibility of the transfer technology to the Chinese setting. For example, in a case study by William A. Fischer, negotiators from Global Multinational (fictitious name) found that during their negotiations to sell a turnkey chemical plant to China, the firm dealt mainly with a Chinese technology import agency. Personnel from the ministry, bureau, and the recipient chemical factory merely sat in on the negotiations. Officials from the factory were consulted on construction and production matters only. Because the import agency operates under the incentive to keep foreign exchange expenditure to a minimum by importing as little foreign equipment as needed, the decision was made to exclude the purchase of water treatment equipment for the project. The import agency accepted assurances by its technicians that local river water was clean; however, it was not. The corrosion caused by the high turbidity of the water led to long production delays associated with resolving the problem and 33 production shut-downs over a 14-month period during the start-up of the project. There are also many cases in which Chinese technicians fail to insist that technical specifications be met by workers under their authority. The foreign partner should plan on maintaining a presence on-site for at least a year. For example, in one venture between China and Japan that is called a model for emulation, the Japanese partner stayed ten months after start-up for the purpose of implementing a managerial and technical system in training the Chinese how to utilize it.

Both parties must ensure that compatibility exists among the foreign technology, the product line, and the conditions at the Chinese recipient factory, even to the point of providing backup systems to guarantee that production continues when breakdowns occur. Further provisions, such as installing supplementary generators, may be necessary to deal with all-too-frequent power outages and surges. Local water problems may require installation of water purification equipment. In general, serious consideration must be given to the modification of production equipment according to the local Chinese environment to avoid unnecessary delays and costly mishaps associated with technical incompatibility.

### *What are some priority areas for foreign investment in China's high technologies?*

Microcomputer and compatibles (co-production).

Digital telecommunications equipment production

Laser typesetting and printing equipment (co-production)

Polyethylene cable materials manufacturing technology

Coal mine exploration, liquefaction and gasification of coal, and pipelines to transport coal gas

Metal deposit exploration including iron and copper, and the production of iron, lead, aluminum, and other metals

Compound fertilizer and pesticide production, especially those less toxic and more effective

Power generator design and production

Construction and building materials production including glass, cement, asbestos, marble, and ceramics

Used electric cable manufacturing equipment, especially copper/aluminum conducting wires and cables

Offshore oil platform and equipment production

Automaking and heavy truck design; tractor parts manufacturing (especially bearings)

Antibiotics and ultrasonic medical equipment production

Technology for extracting plant proteins and freezing techniques for exporting foods

Agricultural processing equipment, especially for sugar and fruits

Deep-sea fishing techniques

Passenger airplane parts (co-production)

Diesel engines (co-production)

Artificial leather production line

Carpet-making equipment

Peripheral equipment for jet looms

Used equipment for manufacturing dyes

Used water glass manufacturing line

Used petrochemical manufacturing equipment

Used baking soda manufacturing line

Optical fiber production line

## *What investment activities do the Chinese plan to curb?*

Radio, television, and videotape recorder production

Van and taxi rental, and vehicle repair

Photographic film processing techniques

Shopping arcade operation

Household appliance repair

Liquor, cigarette, and soft drink production

Camera, vehicle, bicycle, elevator, wristwatch, refrigerator, sewing machine, and electronic calculator production

## *Can attending trade fairs help my company "plug into" Chinese R&D?*

In planning China ventures, foreign companies should acquaint themselves with the most technologically dynamic sectors of Chinese industry. They should make an effort to pinpoint those areas (with Chinese assistance) where pockets of excellence are likely to emerge. One proven method has been through cooperation and interaction in China's R&D sector. This may involve participation in one or more of China's numerous trade fairs, collaboration with a Chinese research institute, or sponsoring technical seminars. All three of these activities should be considered essential in a firm's long-term strategy in China.

The biannual Canton Trade Fair is the most famous of the trade fairs, once estimated to foster half of China's annual export trade. Its main goal, however, has been to sell and buy commodities and manufactured goods. Since 1979, the fair has become much less important as an entrepot for foreign technology. Out of the S&T reform effort, however, has come a new and increasingly important institution, namely, the local science and technology fair. Today, a multitude of annual technology fairs are being held around the country, each focused on a different industrial sector. Successful market penetration could begin with participation in an applicable technology fair. This low-cost project ($15,000-25,000 total expenses) may be part of a firm's initial market investigation of business opportunities. The trade fair offers a firm the chance to ascertain the broad goals of the Chinese participants. If the visiting firm is well-prepared (with company brochures, portfolios, etc.), the Chinese will have an opportunity to understand the objectives and business philosophy of the foreign firm as well.

As a next step, companies are advised to visit and initiate interaction with the Chinese research institutes working in related fields. A firm's active participation in this way will help to determine the level of technical sophistication already present in the industry. The interfacing of the foreign firm and the Chinese R&D institute could reveal specific and mutually beneficial forms of cooperation. In addition, the nature and extent of foreign competition in the sector can be investigated. To be sure, knowledge of past projects in the sector involving foreign firms, the types of foreign technology already acquired, and the business approach used by other firms are essential in formulating venture options.

An effective third step in the process might be to sponsor a technical seminar. At this event, foreign firms describe and display technological ideas and engage in discussions and negotiations with participating Chinese ministry officials. Relationships are fostered between foreign and Chinese engineers in an informal atmosphere. Particular technical problems can be discussed directly with researchers or the R&D managers. With the right partner and workable licensing agreement, a relatively uncomplicated and low-risk form of cooperation can get a start and serve as the base from which a full-fledged relationship can blossom. The Chinese partner will feel comfortable in soliciting the foreign company for bigger projects, and the foreign company will feel at ease in developing additional ventures with his Chinese counterpart.

## INTELLECTUAL PROPERTY RIGHTS AND TECHNOLOGY TRANSFER

The 1979 United States-China Trade Agreement requires both parties to protect the patents, trademarks, and copyrights belonging to citizens of the other. China has adhered to the Paris Convention for the Protection of Industrial Property since 1985.

### *What is the status of copyright protection in the PRC?*

Under the International Property Rights Memorandum of Understanding, China's mandatory registration requirements are waived for American software; that is, American books, films, sound recordings, and software will be protected despite lack of "first publication" in China. The PRC has acceded to the Geneva Phonograms Convention and the Berne copyright convention (under which software will be protected as a "literary work", and video tapes and recordings will also be protected).

### *What is the status of patent protection in the PRC?*

China's patent law, which came into effect in 1985, applies to inventions, utility models, and designs. Patented inventions are protected for 15 years from the date of filing, and utility models and designs for five years, with a possible renewal for three more years. The Chinese law protects the first to file with the Chinese Patent Office, rather than the first to invent. It differs from U.S. law in excluding pharmaceutical products and chemical compounds from the scope of protection.

The Chinese Patent Office under the State Economic Commission registers patents. U.S. companies and individuals not resident in China may request the Patent Agency in Shanghai, the Patent Agency for the China Council for Promotion of International Trade in Beijing or Shenzhen, or China Patent Agent (H.K.) Ltd. to represent them in the application process. The addresses of these organizations may be founded in the Appendix.

In the case of chemicals and pharmaceuticals, China's existing Patent Law provided only process patents, not product patents. Under the MOU, China will extend patent protection to pharmaceuticals and chemicals (including agricultural chemicals). Existing American drugs and agricultural chemicals also receive special administrative protection for seven years if the products have not already been produced or marketed in China and meet other criteria.

The amendments to the Patent Law also extend the duration of patents from 15 to 20 years, and restrict the granting of compulsory licenses.

### What is the status of trademark protection in the PRC?

China's Trademark Law is based on the principle of "first-to-register." With the exception of well-known marks, China does not recognize the common law concept of "first use." A company receives the legal protection for the use of a trademark if it is the first firm to register the trademark in China, even if the mark belongs to another entity.

However, the Chinese government has shown an ability to act quickly and firmly when infringement of properly registered trademarks has been shown. Infringing products have been seized and destroyed, and infringing practices enjoined. Generally, the trademark owner must initiate enforcement action. Foreign companies may register their trademarks with the Trademark Registration Bureau of the State Administration of Industry and Commerce. The patent agencies referred to above will generally represent foreign applicants. The address of the Trademark Registration Bureau is found in the Appendix.

### Has the PRC enacted laws concerning unfair competition and protection of trade secrets?

China does not currently have a trade secrets law. Any recovery for disclosure of a trade secret must be based on breach of contract. Because unauthorized use of another company's unregistered trademark and "trade dress" (i.e., package design and shapes) are not actionable under current Chinese law, American companies look forward to the promulgation of an unfair competition law by January 1, 1994. China is already obligated to protect against acts of unfair competition which tend to confuse the consumer ("passing off") under the Paris Convention. While lack of domestic legislation has complicated matters, foreigners have successfully obtained protection in some cases of trade dress infringement.

The U.S. government also expects that the unfair competition law will protect trade secrets. Lack of protection for "know-how" which is normally disclosed through licensing agreements and joint venture contracts is a disincentive to invest in China. Because it is difficult to enforce non-disclosure clauses in such contracts, promulgation of an unfair competition law may discourage unauthorized use of foreign trade secrets.

Experience has, on the other hand, shown that when foreign companies establish joint ventures in China, and subsequently license proprietary technology to the venture, the Chinese venture partners typically take a strong proprietary interest in protecting against the "leakage" of technology to other Chinese competitors. While these new laws and agreements provide a legal framework for the protection of intellectual property, the procedures for enforcement are still unclear. Foreign firms must initiate action to protect their intellectual property.

# CHAPTER 17

# OPERATING

# A VENTURE

# IN CHINA

*The challenge for multinational corporation managers in China is to disentangle the Chinese factory from its web of bureaucratic supervision and transform it into a corporation.*

**—*Steven R. Hendryx***
Former Manager
Otis Elevators, Tianjin
(as quoted in the Harvard Business Review)

*F*oreign-invested enterprises do not, and cannot, exist in a vacuum in the People's Republic, free of the constraints and hardships experienced by the Chinese factory. To grow and prosper in the People's Republic, a foreign-invested enterprise (FIE) must be constantly on the alert to avoid crisis. The manifold problems and dilemmas that impinge on FIEs can be best managed if a foreign company can consolidate leadership within its China venture, and gain the support of administrative entities affecting the venture externally. Preventative joint management in the People's Republic requires team work and communication between partners as well as a system of planning and production geared to avoiding mishap. The foreign company must dovetail its objectives as a free enterprise with one in a state-controlled, bureaucratized socialist system—no small feat for foreign managerial personnel.

### *Will it be difficult or even possible, to synthesize managerial objectives in a sino-foreign joint venture?*

Joint venture management cannot be founded on Western management concepts or corporate strategy right at the outset. The Chinese factory will be unprepared to break with standard Chinese management practices. Though the differing objectives of each partner are not always inherently in conflict, they can lead to contradictory expectations and operating procedures. The table below, based on numerous discussions with both foreign and Chinese joint venture managers since 1985, presents an overview of divergent priorities within a China venture that the foreign manager can expect to encounter. Obviously, firms are well advised to begin discussions with their Chinese counterparts regarding all of these points early in contract negotiations.

#### DISPARATE PRIORITIES IN JOINT VENTURE MANAGEMENT

| *U.S. Side* | *Chinese Side* |
| --- | --- |
| desires clear-cut timetable | desires loose schedule |
| reduce work force | employ more workers |
| reduce number of middle managers | maintain number of middle managers |
| set up team/task force management | retain cadre management system/managers are often replaced unexpectedly |
| initiate pay raises based on performance | pay raise for all workers and increased bonuses |

| | |
|---|---|
| plans to fulfill contract and expects Chinese to do same | wants to renegotiate agreement when project becomes constricting |
| keep technology hidden | share new technology |
| emphasis on constant interaction between managers and directors | desires single point of contact between foreign partner and China plant director |
| increase domestic sales in China | distribute production overseas to earn foreign exchange |
| quality control assurance | rapid utilization of local sources |
| pro forma profit and loss to indicate real costs to foreign partner | expects ongoing "favors" from foreign side in the form of training, tech and so on. |

The key to success is to create a management structure that promotes integration of operational systems as well as the cultural characteristics of Chinese and Western enterprise. Hewlett-Packard has transferred Western-style management from the shop floor up. A tour of its joint venture in Beijing begins with a typically Western reception room, open-bay work areas, dust-free electronic testing rooms, and even a Western-style rest room. Every department has a deputy manager in charge of operations. Workers are managed by American expatriates and Chinese managers who "work as a team," says former China Hewlett-Packard Manufacturing Manager John So. On the other hand, the factory maintains a low profile and fosters good relations with its adjacent Chinese neighborhood. The factory is considered as much Chinese as it is American.

### How do I achieve management control of the venture?

It seems intuitive that a significant majority share in a joint venture brings with it a large measure of control over the venture's management. Yet this often fails to be the case in China. The degree of independence from central authorities and the extent of management control in China is often less than what a similar stake would obtain in other countries. Holding the largest single share percentage, for example, does not guarantee control over the venture's operations. An investor with 40 percent equity, in partnership with two Chinese partners each holding 30 percent, may find himself outflanked on critical issues by the other partners working in tandem. To most foreign executives in China, a "large" majority means equity of 60 percent or more.

Big stakes make things move more quickly in an operation— the foreign partner is not required to justify its actions to its Chinese partner or to go through protracted negotiations. This "do it my way" attitude is being heard more frequently in China today, in contrast to the early 1980's viewpoint that consensus is key to a venture's success. The latter views hold that the difficult road to achieving harmony yields better management results. However, many foreign executives now believe that Chinese parties have become more interested in profits, and are therefore willing to accept a smaller stake in a profitable venture and follow the lead of the foreign partner.

There are examples of foreign companies that have held a minority stake, but have still managed to control a joint venture's operations because they brought management or technical expertise not possessed by the Chinese partner. Companies can build into joint venture agreements mechanisms for assuring an adequate measure of control:

- Agreeing to a separate management contract, in which the foreign partner agrees to run the venture and gains a greater degree of managerial authority for a specified time period.

- Structuring the joint venture's Board of Directors.

- Specifying issues permitted for discussion at Board meetings.

- Limiting the number of issues requiring unanimous agreement (eg. mergers with other organizations, dissolution of the venture, increases in registered capital).

- Determining (and limiting) the number of annual Board of Director meetings.

- Ensuring that the position of general manager remains with the foreign investor throughout the duration of the joint venture.

- Stipulating that the foreign investor assume responsibility for sales and marketing, thus gaining access to important marketing information.

### What entities outside the joint venture will have partial or indirect control over it?

Although the various authorities that assume approval control over joint ventures will vary, they typically include: the local partner factory, the larger corporation of which the factory is a part, the provincial bureau in the related industry, the municipal import/export office, MOFTEC, and, depending on the size and type of project, certain top government authorities in Beijing. The figure on page 299 illustrates the web of relationships a joint venture will find it must contend with and manage.

### How is a joint venture's management structure decided upon?

Organizing the management structure of a joint venture begins with a power struggle over the venture's board of directors. Joint venture partners must write their own articles of association, which vary according to the complexity of the venture and the nationality of the foreign partner. The board establishes the organizational structure of the venture, sets up its departments, appoints a general manager and deputy managers, selects a chief engineer, accountants and auditors, and stipulates their responsibilities and the extent of their authority. The board governs annual expenditure, distribution of profit, formulates production plans, and conducts all significant operational activities. Its members stay apprised of Chinese regulations affecting the venture, monitor labor, and welfare contracts, as well as initiate financial and production strategies for the long term. Typically, boards consist of eight members, four foreigners and four Chinese. Operational decisions are usually carried out by two managers—one foreign and one Chinese—under the auspices of the board. Equity share usually governs each partner's degree of influence, although the

## The Organizational Bureaucracy Surrounding
## a Sino–Foreign Joint Venture

# Bureaucratic Entities Surrounding
# the Foreign-Invested Joint Venture

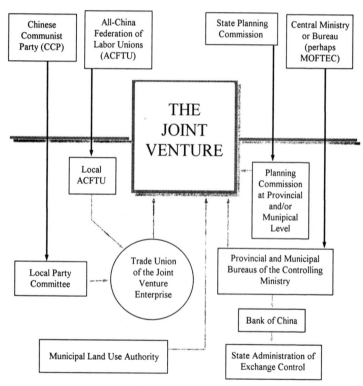

Source: Adapted from John S. Henley and Nyaw Mee-kau, "The System of Management and Performance of Joint Ventures in China: Some Evidence from Shenzhen Special Economic Zone" in Joint Ventures and Industrial Change in China, edited by Nigel Campbell and John S. Henley (London: JAI Press, 1988).

chairman, as noted above, must be Chinese. Where more than two partners are involved, the structure of the board grows.

Foreign firms can enhance their influence on the joint venture board by delineating in articles of the original contract exactly how the board will govern itself. Early on, joint venture partners must decide how board decisions are to be made, and how voting will be structured. Clear governing rules can help to prevent the Chinese board members from being influenced by organizations with which they are affiliated. External government agencies can wield direct influence over the joint venture by changing Chinese board members without notice. The Chinese board members may merely serve as figureheads. Many are retired senior cadres who lack business experience. Their positions on the board may have been awarded them by the state for past service rather than because they have the skills needed. Second, board voting procedures can be varied according to the type and importance of the decision; that is, one decision may require a consensus, another a majority, while an extremely crucial one might require unanimity.

Even after a degree of management control is achieved over the venture's top executives, the foreign company may still be challenged when attempting to implement its management style through the ranks of middle management and workers. Successful joint ventures have found that an incremental approach to diffusing Western management practices through a Chinese enterprises is most effective. This often means delegating decisions over when to implement a new management practice to middle-level Chinese managers.

Ventures have also introduced Western management practices through reformation of the enterprises accounting and control practices. By assigning cost responsibilities to individual section or division managers, the venture's leadership can instill a new sense of accountability to the Chinese enterprise. Many joint ventures now rely on incentive schemes that link financial benefits to manager and worker performance to help Chinese employees adjust to a Western management system.

Recent amendments to China's 1990 joint venture law offers more flexibility to foreign companies involved in Sino-foreign joint ventures:

- Joint venture partners may now determine the Chairman of the Board of the venture by appointment or election; previously the Chinese partner automatically appointed the Board's chair.

- Some investment sectors now permit the establishment of joint ventures with an indefinite investment period.

- Firms may now use other banks besides the Bank of China, including joint venture and foreign-owned banks, to oversee their foreign exchange transactions.


## ORGANIZING CHINESE WORKERS AND MANAGERS

The Chinese often view a new China venture as an opportunity to employ workers and managers from the production unit associated with the Chinese partner company. Because the Chinese will be responsible for hiring workers and managers at all but the highest levels of joint venture management, the country's archaic system of management tends to get transferred into joint ventures, much to the distress of the foreign partner. Too many middle-level administrators populate the joint venture, which results in productivity slowdowns. In theory, the middle managers can be fired, but that rarely happens. Otis Elevator's Tianjin initial joint venture started with a ratio of 70 percent administrative employees to only 30 percent workers. Smith-Kline succeeded in reducing the number of administrators in its joint venture to 30 percent by agreeing to export 30 to 35 percent of their production. Such tradeoffs may be necessary in order to shave off redundant layers of middle management that can hamper efforts to fortify a managerial system even remotely resembling what the foreign manager may be conditioned to expect from his experience in other Asian settings. Once entrenched, the old system in which many unqualified managers get hired, proves hard to dissolve. Foreign firms can push to get an expatriate placed in the position of personnel manager, but this issue should be agreed upon during negotiations. The benefit is that a foreign personnel manager, unlike a Chinese manager, hires objectively rather than out of loyalty to old friends, family members, and past co-workers.

Furthermore, foreign managers have to contend with the fact that a Chinese worker's loyalty will continue to flow toward his, or her, Danwei even after becoming a worker at an FIE. Under the auspices of various party, union, and welfare entities associated with the Danwei system, a worker's loyalty tends to flow out of the venture toward the Danwei, driving a wedge between a joint venture's management and its labor force. As a foreign counterpart, attempts must be made to align the interests of the Danwei with those of the venture in order to fortify the venture's authority over its human resources.

### How do you evaluate a Chinese manager?

Chinese managers must confront a new array of responsibilities, anxieties, and fears. Their reaction to their current predicament directly affects their willingness, and capability, to carry out the management tasks according to the guidelines proposed by foreign business partners. The ranks of good managers in the People's Republic is certainly expanding, yet foreign firms will still have problems finding the ones who first have the training, clout, and initiative to break the parasitic relationship between the factory and local government, and second, are willing work to build independent linkages between their factory and its foreign business partner.

The most desired characteristic in a Chinese manager is a recognition of the changes underway in China's industrial system. Does the manager know what's going on with enterprise reforms, with changes in the distribution system, and does she/he appear to be able to articulate them? A stagnant manager who is only holding on to yesterday's management system—or who feels uneasy about or incapable of changing his habits—may deflect questions about the reforms and their impact on his working style. A promising manager responds to his new freedom and incumbent responsibility with courage and vigor. He can foresee problems to be encountered in the attempt to fully implement the enterprise reforms. Good managers have learned to delegate some of the worker welfare issues to subordinates, and concentrate more effort on working directly with technical people and engineers in the firm. This is absolutely critical, given that most managers have not been able to free themselves from tasks related to worker welfare, and thus do not have the time to concentrate on product development or production. Managers who are tied to sponsors in the outlying government bureaucracy may have a modicum of clout, yet they may also be hamstrung in their efforts to innovate. Lastly, you need to measure the density of contract links maintained by the manager with the bureaucratic entities that surround the enterprise. This is normally accomplished by a go-between through informal meetings with local officials. The higher the number and level of contacts (guanxi) enjoyed by the manager the more effective he or she can be in obtaining outside support.

### Can the foreign manager reduce the size of the venture's work force?

Almost all joint ventures suffer from overstaffing. These residual workers create an obvious conflict because the foreign partner often brings substantial amounts of new technology into the venture that requires a smaller, more skilled work force. The foreign manager should not act on his first inclination, which is usually to slash the size of the work force. Since the workers in a joint venture typically are members of the Chinese partner's unit, the Chinese partner will act as the labor contractor. Decisions regarding worker incentives, hiring and firing, and discipline will be handled by the relevant labor union and the local chapter of the CCP. Overstaffing can be ameliorated, but the task will require worker relocation to other units, rather than firing. A growing number of cases exist, however, where foreign firms have reduced over-staffing and have secured scarce competent workers. Foxboro, for instance, halved its original labor force by transferring workers to another enterprise under the jurisdiction of its Chinese partner. Gillette reduced its joint venture work force to 60 from 240 employees, and now requires new workers to pass exams. Hewlett-Packard broke new ground in China by completely sidestepping FESCO. Hewlett-Packard wields total control of its workers and has no labor deal with either FESCO or the government. The Hewlett-Packard joint venture maintains its own salary structure and has tied wages to performance, increasing worker incentives. Taking advantage of close relations with its official government partner, Hewlett-Packard has acquired the right to an allotment of Chinese graduates from various service schools, filling slots on a yearly basis. By conducting recruitment seminars at such schools, the firm attracts top-quality applicants. According to one of the firm's managers, the reasons for this success are "good management techniques that the Chinese want to assimilate and high-level interfacing with Chinese officials who can get the seemingly impossible approved."

### How are employees recruited by Sino-foreign joint ventures in the PRC?

The Chinese government has published extensive regulations regarding the recruitment and management of Chinese employees in foreign invested joint ventures. Foreign companies should consult with the local Foreign Enterprise Service Corporation (FESCO) and the local Labor Bureau for more detailed information.

Employees are generally hired for foreign-invested enterprises from one of three sources:

1. Previous employees of the venture's Chinese party or sponsors.

2. Local employees of ventures unrelated to the business of the foreign-invested enterprise.

3. Recent graduates of universities, colleges and institutes.

Foreign employers and joint venture enterprises generally have their employees referred to them by the local Foreign Enterprise Service Corporation or, occasionally, the local Labor Bureau.

The pool of possible employees for a given foreign-invested enterprise is typically restricted to the local area, given Chinese regulations that prevent the free mobility of labor. Nevertheless, foreign companies should feel free to pressure their Chinese partners and local authorities to recruit candidates with specialized technical or managerial skills if none are available in the immediate locality.

### How does the foreign manager measure and reward worker performance?

Foreign firms in the People's Republic utilize various forms of Western motivational techniques in their China ventures, including systematic evaluation of worker performance, promotions, and wage increases tied to productivity. However, Chinese attitudes about foreigners tends to prevent the wholesale transfer of the foreign firm's managerial methods without considerable modification. The extent to which foreign firms are able to guide incentive programs in their enterprises with the Chinese partner depends largely on government permission. Creative approaches should be taken, however, to fostering worker loyalty to your factory. Make the factory as much a part of the local community as possible. For example, you might set up a lounge in the joint venture factory, construct a recreation room, provide entertainment, sponsor classes, provide a library, or install shower and bath facilities on the premises. Safety, cleanliness, and good food should also be part of the joint venture regime.

### INCENTIVE-CREATING GUIDELINES

- Encourage workers not only to believe in the current enterprise reforms, but to apply them in the joint venture, and celebrate their implementation.

- Motivate employees to work hard for raises in bonuses and wages, but be cautious not to single out individuals from the group for exceedingly high or low rewards. Moreover, do not isolate workers, but consolidate them in task groups.

- Reward workers with recognition for being ambitious. Offer upward mobility to workers by training them as versatile managers, teaching them skills that will further their career outside the joint venture.

- Ensure worker satisfaction by helping with housing and welfare.

- Maintain a worker's titular role longer than for a worker in the West. Western workers value being promoted into new positions of authority; Chinese workers don't value changing their working role as much as possessing an honorable title.

- Give the factory interior and exterior a new look. Clean-up working environments, add lighting, renovate workshops, showrooms, and the like.

- Initiate a reward system to encourage workers to voice criticisms and make suggestions.

- Promote a factory philosophy based on the Western axiom: Time is Money.

- Create training programs for young workers based on breaking old habits.

### Who sets workers' wages in a joint venture?

All employees in a foreign-invested enterprise will receive a labor contract that is approved and registered by the local labor bureau. Employees recommended by the local FESCO will need to be registered with FESCO. All salary payments are made to FESCO, which then deducts a commission and passes the remainder onto the employee. The local FESCO authorities should be asked to provide detailed information regarding the transmission of bonuses and other salary incentives for good performance. The foreign company may wish to ask the Chinese authorities to waive their commissions for these transfers.

Salaries in foreign-invested enterprises are required by Chinese law to be a minimum of 120 to 150 percent higher than those paid by Chinese enterprises in the same industry. In addition, employers are required to contribute to a percentage of the employee's wages for welfare, medical, education, pension, insurance and housing benefits. Female employees receive additional medical benefits and protection from dismissal for pregnancy or other health reasons.

### A note on termination of employees

The employment contract for all employees in a foreign-invested enterprise should specify on what grounds the employer can terminate the employee. These provisions will be reviewed and approved by the local labor bureau upon receipt of the contract for registration. Often agreements to transfer employees from an existing PRC employer to the joint venture will oblige the employer to take the employee back upon termination. Some local regulations require the joint venture to reimburse or compensate the employer in such a case. This may be a provision the foreign company wishes to negotiate away in the joint venture agreement.

## CONTROLLING POLITICS IN THE VENTURE

Since the CCP is powerful within the governmental planning entities that wield control over joint ventures, its influence is always felt through the Chinese joint venture managers and members of the ventures' board. Foreign partners have few complaints concerning the party, yet acknowledge that party presence must be recognized. A foreign manager can be certain that having the backing of local and central CCP officials will be an asset to the venture. This support may not be present at start-up and could require informal networking among factory cadres. As a general rule, firms should attempt to convince party members of the benefits that Sino-foreign joint ventures represent to China's modernization. Urge them to perceive the venture as the foreign side perceives it, as a production and profit-making center in which Chinese and foreigners can work together as equals. Party members are skeptical of foreign management of Chinese workers, but cannot be thwarted from initiating a creative incentive system. Enlist Chinese managers to the cause of generating the ground swell of necessary enthusiasm for management changes. During negotiations, consider whether your Chinese partner and factory manager will be tough enough to carry out plans that may conflict with CCP ideologues.

### *Will the Chinese manager be a Party member?*

In most cases, yes. To obtain a position of manager of a state firm—especially one ordained to enter a joint venture with a foreign company—a manager will have to be a member. As such, he/she may have a political agenda which may, at times, override the interests of the venture. You must recognize that the manager might be politically bound to give in to a Party request once in a while, like refusing to fire workers, or reducing production to protect another firm. You should not jump to blame the manager, however, without acknowledging the political constraint, on the manager. In some cases, it is best for you to confront outside government entities yourself to get action, and leave the Chinese manager out of it.

### What role do labor unions play in a joint venture?

As with the Chinese enterprise, the Chinese compel foreign joint venture partners to set up labor unions at their ventures. The participation of workers in the management of a joint venture is organized and channeled through the trade union of the joint venture. Labor unions and FESCO also play key roles in managing Chinese workers in a China venture. Labor unions do not play much of an adversarial role in promoting wage increases or worker safety. Under the auspices of the CCP, the unions school workers in the current political stance. They play a cooperative role throughout the enterprise management structure, monitoring benefits and supervising employee relations. Labor unions readily accept the adoption of foreign managerial techniques in Chinese enterprises and have made reasonable efforts to help workers adjust to them. Sometimes, however, a labor union can become a nuisance to the foreign partner by meddling in the hiring and firing of workers and in the process of implementing incentive programs that it believes infringe on the inalienable rights of Chinese workers. In one of these cases, an obtrusive labor union gladly stepped aside when the foreign partner—C. P. Pokphand (CCP)—set up an office in the factory exclusively for the trade union representatives. CCP gave the union people the office with one simple condition—that they stay out of the management affairs of the joint venture. This rather prosaic solution to union problems in a China venture appears to have sufficed.

### Should expert managers from Taiwan, Hong Kong, or Singapore be hired to run a factory in China?

While expatriate employees are often necessary in the initial period of a venture, particularly for technology-intensive or service-oriented enterprises, the high cost of maintaining expatriate employees has caused many ventures to increase the speed at which they train and revert control to local managerial staff. Foreign companies should actively seek assistance from local authorities to offset or subsidize the cost of expatriate living expenses. Expatriate costs can also be minimized by employing Chinese engineering, technical and management students who have studied abroad and are now returning to China and seeking employment in joint ventures. Regional technical universities and institutes can assist foreign ventures in finding candidates for management positions.

Most firms interviewed in China employ ethnic Chinese to run their China offices and joint ventures in China. With Chinese background and language training, these expatriates can be more effective in dealing with China's socialist bureaucracy. Hiring managers in Taiwan is becoming standard practice for many foreign firms in China. KFCs general managers in China who run its 14 restaurants are from Taiwan. Many of its executives at its China headquarters are Taiwanese as well. Du Pont and Hewlett-Packard have hired Taiwanese managers for their China operations as well. In fact, the founder of Hewlett-Packard's Taiwan operation in 1970, Lee Ting, from Taiwan is the current chairman and managing director of Hewlett-Packard, Ltd. Hong Kong, which coordinates company operations throughout Greater China. The use of Taiwanese managerial skills and expertise by Western firms is an unexpected threat which has grown up alongside Taiwan's growing participation in the China market as a result of warming relations between Beijing and Taipei since the early 1990's. Of course, where Cantonese is spoken, for example in Southern China, a Taiwanese manager will not be effective. One half of the managers who run Shenzhen's McDonald's restaurant are from Hong Kong.

## MANAGING FOR MANUFACTURING OPERATIONS

Foreign managers in China must transform an indigenous system of crisis management into one of preventative management. Many problems can be avoided by considering the past experiences of other firms in China and developing strategy agendas for supply sourcing, quality control, modes of distribution, and repatriation of profits prior to start-up of operations. Foreign firms should present a schedule by which the joint venture board can handle problems before they crop up and resolve them as a unified team within the venture.

By creating a situation in which the board, managers, and departments in charge all collaborate in preventing mishap, rather than waiting for a disaster to occur, the venture will not only survive, but enjoy greater likelihood for prosperity. The following sections deal with solutions, strategies, and formulas that may assist executives in preventing and resolving operational problems.

### *How should I approach the task of managing a plant in China?*

Use "family-style" management methods. Western personnel management may seem cold, clinical, and depersonalizing to the Chinese worker. As manager in Greater China, you need to foster "family oriented" corporate culture in your company by participating in the lives of your workers. Attend weddings. Bring flowers to people who are sick. Participate in religious celebrations and funerals. And never favor your expat colleagues in the company, professionally or socially, to the exclusion of your Chinese colleagues. Treat your workers as family, as Chinese managers do. Ensure that workers enjoy their work by allowing them to socialize during work with each other and you. You can generate worker-manager affinity by creating more than mere economic incentive for your workers to be there. Celebrate holidays together, birthdays, and each new phase of your factory's expansion and performance. Remember also that in China, a long midday break for workers is practiced religiously; in China, the midday break for workers is guaranteed in the country's constitution.

When hiring, keep in mind a Chinese attachment to group. Use a local person to help you hire so to avoid creating intrafirm conflicts between worker factions that are based on kinship ties, school background, regional dialect, and so on. Conversely, don't practice nepotism, either, offering jobs only to the relatives and friends of your workers. To attract good workers you may have to offer employee benefit packages that match, or better, domestic plans. Be frank with your workers if you frown on nepotism, but don't reject the well-entrenched practice altogether. Permit your workers to recommend job applicants who will often be relatives. Say something like, "Merit first and then family members, please."

### How long will it take to make changes in how Chinese workers and managers operate?

"People have habits that you will not easily break," says Domiano Georgino, general manager of the Dynasty Hotel in Taipei. "Like taking a two-and-a-half-hour nap after lunch. You may get it down to one-and-a-half-hours but don't come in thinking you'll change things overnight." An American who manages the expat hangout called the Farmhouse in Taipei, shared an illustrative, if prosaic, case in point about managing for change in Taiwan. "We put out food on the buffet, right? And when a container is empty the Taiwanese cooks go out and get it, and bring it back to the kitchen to fill it up. Then they take it back out to the buffet. It all takes about five minutes and meanwhile the customer has no food to choose from. So I had a new plan. Let's get another pan and use two. When one is empty, bring out the other and just replace it. Takes two seconds, right? All you have to do is buy one extra pan. The Taiwanese react at this. Oh, no, no, no. That's not necessary. We don't need an extra. It works just like we do it.' I even bought them the extra pan. They don't see it! That's the problem working here. It's different." Perhaps the toughest job you will face is getting the Chinese to acknowledge a need for producing at a high level of consistent quality. "I've been to factories where every vehicle being built on the assembly line was different," said Cummins corporate engineer Carl Shaffer to reporter Peter Copeland recently.

### How do I motivate a Chinese manager to lead an effort to promote change?

Most Chinese managers simply lack the extensive managerial skills necessary to effect significant organizational changes in a joint venture. For years Chinese managers spent their time finding ways of satisfying politically motivated party officials and the local welfare interests of their enterprises, instead of concentrating their energies on implementing modern management techniques in their factories to upgrade production performance. One U.S. manager in Shanghai described Chinese managers as accepting of new ways of management in principle, but that they have difficulty putting them into practice. Chinese managers may be able to define a problem, yet the reasons for failure are neither accepted nor explored. They eschew organized meetings in which open discussion occurs concerning management difficulties or operating failures, fearing ostracism from superiors if they are perceived as culpable if a problem becomes known. The U.S. manager went on to say: [The Chinese] don't like to get into a meeting where they have to talk about problems. No one will commit to anything until the problem has been solved. That's been the toughest thing to try to change."

Garreth Chang, president of McDonnell-Douglas China, Inc., admitted that the firm had underestimated the difficulty of implementing management improvements. He said, "You cannot turn a guy in a factory into a manager in a year or two. It takes experience and it's that kind of hands-on experience that we have on the American side that the Chinese lack." Countering management incompetence, Fujian-Hitachi initiated a system of manager and cadre "checking," in which the general manager of the joint venture has the power to promote or dismiss management cadres below him. Twice a year, the company carries out checks on cadres and workers, assessing diligence, ability, achievements, work style, and discipline. Similarly, mid-level cadres carry out checks on ordinary management personnel and encourage, promote, or dismiss them. Appraisals are then rechecked for accuracy to prevent favoritism. The close monitoring of workers and managers has resulted in tight management control, worker loyalty to the joint venture, and increased production efficiency.

## QUALITY CONTROL IN MANUFACTURING

As much as one-third of all goods produced in China are defective or do not conform to China's national industrial standards. As previously discussed, most Chinese factories feature minimal quality-control schemes, and many have none at all. Problems with quality control in joint ventures usually stem from the Chinese partners' unwillingness or inability to step up quality control. Sometimes, the Chinese factory manager (fearing loss of face) does not admit openly to the foreign buyer that a certain part of the manufacturing process of a set of equipment is beyond the capabilities of the factory, or that quality specifications cannot be achieved. This results in subsequent breakdowns in the field. Also, one or more components will be manufactured under the auspices of a separate ministry, making it impossible for the contracted supplier factory to ensure the quality of the entire set of equipment. Simple products generally do better in this respect, such as toys, crafts, razors, textiles, hair products, O-ring seals, and simple components. Complex production projects have been seriously impaired by quality problems, in some cases resulting in failure to export any production at all.

### How is product quality control typically handled in Chinese companies?

China passed a new Quality Control Law in February, 1993 and implemented the law in September of the same year. While quality has not been traditionally a concern under China's state-run production systems, the dynamics of the market in the reform era has placed the issue of quality squarely in front of manufacturing enterprises in the PRC. Detailed standards regarding the new law have yet to be published, but the law generally states the products in China must be safe and that the rights of consumers should be protected. The law deals with the obligations of producers and sellers, potential liabilities, and the rights of consumers. Retailers absorb the bulk of responsibility for quality under the law. They bear the initial responsibility for repairing or replacing defective goods and compensating consumers for damages. Moreover, they are held ultimately responsible for all damages and claims if the producers cannot be found or prosecuted. Foreign-invested enterprises involved in the retail sector should take the appropriate steps to comply with industry standards and procure high quality products from their suppliers.

### What is the best way to increase quality control in a Chinese firm?

You have to initiate a regime of quality control in the factory with a great deal of patience and creativity. North Americans have made it a ritual to criticize Chinese workers as the source of quality problems in their Chinese affiliates. But quality control is a problem of management, not workmanship. Don't expect to implement TQM at the outset. Work in steps, taking sole responsibility for structuring the tasks of production to foster high quality in the end product. Quality problems can be dealt with by segmenting the manufacturing process and putting small groups of workers in charge of each step. Break the process of quality down, making it measurable and workers accountable.

Another problem inherent in quality control in China involves keeping Chinese-style groupism from vulgarizing the quality control procedure. For instance, the quality check person should not be from the same region, family, or social group as the person doing the work to be checked. The inspector is liable to favor someone from his own group, or at least, be reluctant to reject their work based on inferior workmanship. Thus, you have to recruit from an array of villages, families, and social groups, no matter how much your Chinese staff lobbies for recruits from their own group. To control the "mix" of your staff will require almost continuous cross checks of personal background.

To solve quality-control problems, U.S. firms have applied progressive systems of quality enhancement in their China ventures, including quality circles, cross-inspection plans, and multiple quality checkpoint schemes along assembly lines. To a great extent, foreign partners have been successful at raising quality levels in their joint ventures in China as these systems are integrated into production and fully accepted by Chinese workers and managers. Often, Chinese factory managers are given tours of similar U.S. factories to observe the equipment they will be using and/or building. Some firms have entered into contracts with Chinese suppliers that codify the exact specifications of components to be sourced, with clear stipulation regarding rejection of goods on the basis of strict quality specifications. On-site quality-control inspection has become a required added expense for many joint ventures concerned with protecting their brand name reputations. Others have pushed for reject-and-destroy clauses to prevent defective products from entering the Chinese domestic market or export markets with their trademark.

## SELLING FINISHED GOODS IN CHINA

The problem of perceived quality deficiency in Chinese-made products that exists among world market buyers also exists among Chinese endusers. Foreign partners of manufacturing joint ventures in China who intend to sell to China's domestic market discover that Chinese industrial customers and consumers have similar suspicions of Chinese-made goods, and do not regard products manufactured by Sino-foreign ventures as necessarily "foreign-made." In fact, some firms with a manufacturing venture in China continue to sell similar products to China from outside. For example, direct sales constitute a major part of one engine manufacturing firm's business in China even though the company has set up a joint venture there producing the same model that it sells to China. These sales compete directly with the Chinese partner's plant. Since the joint venture factory has such a bad reputation in China, partly because of the low quality of engines previously manufactured there, many Chinese customers prefer to buy engines directly from the American parent company in the United States. This embarrassing situation has forced the two companies to bid competitively against each other for sales in China. Hewlett-Packard countered Chinese customer reluctance to "buy Chinese" by educating endusers and convincing local government officials to add its products to a list of preferred products. This helped to dispel negative perceptions of their Chinese-made computers and instruments among endusers.

### Should you leave domestic marketing activities to your Chinese joint venture partner?

You may be forced to accept the control of the local FTC over the domestic sales effort conducted by your partner enterprise. I suggest removing the FTC, or relegating it to a nonexclusive status, both because the FTC charges a commission and may be still addicted to the supply-side mentality of yesterday's China in which any product available would eventually sell. Times are changing in China from a supply-side economy to one driven by demand. Many foreign partners find that they should not have left domestic marketing solely in the hands of the Chinese, but should have begun development on their own marketing networks from the outset. In the recent past, the scenario worked like this: ministry might acquire a production technology from a foreign supplier—a state-of-the-art package at top dollar, and totally inappropriate for Chinese needs and capabilities to assimilate it. The products produced by the technology are uneven in quality and supply, and must be sold at an inflated price in order for the ministry to recoup its unwise investment. It did this by selling the product at an inflated price to another ministry, which needed the product because of its persistent scarcity and because of rules against, and the foreign exchange cost of, importing it. The buying ministry teamed up with foreign suppliers of technology in the same way, and sold its overpriced products to a third ministry, on down the line. Where did the money come from? Beijing doled out the money, and the ministries spent it.

Now, however, the ministries are being told to control costs and even fund themselves. They are being forced to buy technologies that result in the production of competitively priced, higher quality products. No longer is Beijing impelling ministries to buy products from other state-run entities which cannot offer a competitive product. The result has been the demise of a number of prominent projects which involved the purchase of foreign technology. James Stepanek, a veteran Chain specialist who runs a project management firm in China, wrote about the end of this phase of China's commercial history recently in *China Trade:* "Why [should a Chinese company] buy overpriced commodities made by government factories? Why buy a real Cherokee Jeep that cost US$35,000 when rip-off Cherokee models (made in Beijing, another in Shijiazhung) are now available for under US$9,500? Why spend US$4,500 for a PC assembled at a state enterprise in Shanghai, when smuggled AST computers are everywhere? Why buy a dump truck when you don't need one?" For foreign joint venture partners who have come to count on these "captive" domestic sales, the old days of China's centrally coordinated economy are dearly missed.

As Beijing falls into deepening financial debt and China moves closer to joining GATT, foreign companies which entered China in the pioneer days, linking their fortunes to the power and clout of large state firms, will see their partners lose that clout and face increasingly foreign competition. Many will not survive the transition to lean and mean manufacturing.

### What is the attitude in China toward Western-style training for Chinese managers?

Western business practice and good communication habits can be taught through sustained training. The operative word here is sustained. Management training (as opposed to worker training) can also be a cost-effective way to sweeten a deal. A training package should include information systems, new management techniques, market research, and performance evaluation, among others. Employees at McDonald's receive two months of training and are evaluated with a final examination. They wear badges—copper, silver, and gold—depending in their performance on the job.

The foreign partner can offer the Chinese manager assistance outside their contract in areas of accounting, market forecasting, and organizational planning. Informal training of this sort bodes well in terms of making middle-level people look good to superiors, thus forming strong personal relationships for the future. Should the foreign firm place a monetary value on this contribution? Before offering such packages, delineate what exactly should be given away as a sweetener and what should be part of the total contribution to the venture.

# PART FOUR

## Dealing with the Chinese

# CHAPTER 18

# COMMUNICATING

# WITH THE

# CHINESE

*"Calamity comes by means of the mouth."*

**—Chinese proverb**

*T*o communicate across Chinese culture we need to develop some interactive skills that can help us gain conscious control over our spontaneous, natural communication patterns that only serve as communication barriers in China. These techniques are called *intercultural communication skills*. These skills will help you in communicating, negotiating, and building strong friendships in China and indeed, around the world. Learning to communicate in China may seem a low priority to you, but it's critical. Especially for loquacious Americans who communicate too much during the pitched battle of negotiations. Maybe you know how to be quiet and more savvy. What about getting the Chinese to open up and communicate with you?

## THE ART OF COMMUNICATING THROUGH AN INTERPRETER

If you aren't fluent in the language of your Chinese customer, you will have to depend on an interpreter at all times whether negotiating or socializing. Even if you are fluent, you may find that your Chinese counterparts disguise what they are saying amongst themselves by speaking a dialect of Chinese which you do not know. As Domiano Georgino, general manager of the Dynasty Hotel in Taiwan told me about the language of negotiating in Taiwan, "Both Taiwanese and Mandarin are spoken during business discussions in Taiwan, depending on which you *don't* understand."

Your interpreter acts as a transmitter of your words, ideas, humor, intelligence, and personality. What I have said about building strong business relationships in China may have sounded relatively easy to do; accomplished while communicating solely through an interpreter, such an endeavor is hardly a simple proposition, however. Few foreigners in Greater China understand how to be interpreted well, and this is unfortunate since to be clearly understood you must know how to get your message clearly interpreted. Most people who have problems getting through to the Chinese blame their interpreters. A better approach is to take *responsibility* for getting your message better interpreted.

### What are the secrets of being interpreted well?

First, limit your sentences to 7 to 15 words, maximum. This may seem like a lot of words, but it's not. Write your script out and you'll see what a challenge it is to speak in short sentences. (Practice with the Presentation Script on page 314.) The shorter your sentences, the less likely your audience will lose your train of thought and become fatigued. Second, be redundant. Given that much of your message fails to pass through your interpreter to your audience, and that much of that will be comprehended only hazily because your words have been denuded of their emotionally and culturally conditioned content in the process of translation, it doesn't hurt for you to reiterate important points to check for nods of comprehension. You should also prepare to present seminal points of your presentation in more than one way. Ernest De Bellis said recently to *China Trade* that, "In the West if you repeat yourself, everybody falls asleep. In China, repetition means that you're really serious; repetition is good in that culture. It's incredible how much you repeat yourself to be effective." Observe strictly the golden rule for good speaking and presenting in the West: First tell your audience what you're going to tell them; then tell them; and lastly, tell them what you've told them. Moreover, find and train a good interpreter.

The best way to find an interpreter is through referral. Call your business colleagues and ask if they know of an interpreter they have used before. If that doesn't work, call the American Translator's Association in Crystal City, Virginia at telephone: (703) 412-1500. The organization represents hundreds of certified interpreters and translators for all languages, many with special expertise—microbiological terminology in Cantonese, for instance. They can refer you to a chapter of the organization located in your area or overseas, and send you a personnel directory. When I say "train" your interpreter, I mean to rehearse your presentation with them well before your departure for China. No interpreter will be able to translate all of your technical terms without opening a dictionary; this should be done at home and not in front of your Chinese audience. Moreover, if there is *any* humor, irony, or special verbal twist in your presentation, make sure the interpreter has rehearsed it, found just the right nuance to translate it, and knows the body and facial language in which to deliver it, so that you audience gets your message clearly and responds favorably. Some marketers work with their interpreters for two or three weeks before leaving for China.

Do not speak until your interpreter has finished. Westerners often forget, especially when things get heated during a negotiation, that anything they say that is not heard by their interpreter will not be understood at all on the Chinese side. They often get angry and cut in before their interpreter has finished their last sentence. Of course, the Chinese person across the table senses that the foreigner is angry about something from his gestures and expression, but much of his message is coming across garbled. Another tip: when speaking through an interpreter, look at the person to whom you are speaking and not at your interpreter, which can be more comfortable than looking at a listener who cannot understand your language. Rehearse doing this as part of your pretrip training. Experienced businesspeople in China tend to look at the North American businessperson when they are speaking to him and being interpreted. Not-so-experienced businesspeople will often look at the interpreter.

You can expect your counterpart not to trust your interpreter. And don't trust their's either. Suggest to your interpreter that they break into the conversation to retranslate what a Chinese negotiator has said if *his* interpreter fails to translate something, or if the tone of his statement has been modified by his interpreter in any way. Note also that the oldest trick in the book is for someone to *pretend* that they don't understand your language, when in fact, they can comprehend conversations amongst your team. So make sure you're out of earshot before discussing sensitive topics amongst your colleagues. The trick works both ways, of course. Lastly, have your interpreter debrief you after each meeting. They often overhear utterances on the Chinese side that you should know about.

### SAMPLE PRESENTATION SCRIPT

Read each sentence out loud and then pause as if you were speaking through an interpreter. Notice that each sentence takes 4-7 seconds to say and expresses only one idea at a time. Having your opening presentation scripted in this fashion will get any negotiation in China off to a good start.

— I want to welcome all of you to the Los Angeles area.

— Today I want to tell you about a new technology.

— It is part of the global war against international terrorism.

— In 1989, the world's terrorists attacked 4,400 times.

— That's 12 incidents per day.

— Two thousand of these violent attacks involved the use of bombs.

— Most terrorism occurs in South America

— Terrorism is now on the increase in Asia.

— The name of the technology is *Thermal Neutron Analysis*.

## SPEAKING WITHOUT WORDS

*"An angry fist cannot strike a smiling face."*

**—Chinese proverb**

Chinese communicate less directly and less explicitly. Having originated from agricultural village societies, they communicate in a manner conducive to what intercultural communication pundits call an *implicit* social environment. This means that people communicate with each other assuming that both possess a complete knowledge of the *implied* background information regarding the subject matter that they are discussing. In such groups, much of what needs to be communicated can simply be implied rather than stated explicitly. Communication between people can rely more on body movements (called *kinesics*), facial expressions, eye messages, and other nonverbal signals to get a message across. Nonverbal signals and unspoken assumptions continue to figure prominently in Chinese personal and business relationships. The problem for Westerners is that the Chinese don't always agree on the meaning of nonverbal cues and signals. A smile or a laugh in China may mean embarrassment or disapproval, as well as happiness and approval as in the West. Direct eye contact may be taken as an intimidation tactic by the Chinese while the Westerner is only trying to give the Chinese his undivided attention. Also, it's hard to *control* your nonverbals since they are mostly automatic and spontaneous; sometimes, you simply cannot avoid communicating. Your posture stiffens when you get angry, your eyes widen and your stare gets intense, the volume of your voice rises, your head movements become jerky. Without knowing it, you are *communicating* that you have grown impatient and irritated. During a negotiation in China you will find it much more difficult than in the West to read facial expressions because Chinese tend to control them to such a great degree. On the other hand, Americans tend to wear a remarkable amount of information on their faces.

### Does direct eye contact with the Chinese mean they are being honest or intimidating?

Although they may stare long and hard at foreigners on the street out of curiosity, most Chinese business people will not gaze at you when speaking or listening to you to the same degree that North Americans typically will. In the West, we are taught to look at our parents and superiors when spoken to. Seeing "eye-to-eye" connotes mutual understanding and trust. When a person "can't look you in the eye," he is suspected of being dishonest. In China, NOT looking at a superior directly in the eye indicates obedience and subservience. The Chinese, in fact, consider it rude to look directly into another person's face because it *feels* to them like a threat. So you have to be careful not to misread the Chinese person's lack of eye contact. When a Chinese person doesn't look the Westerner directly in the eye, the Westerner may *feel* that somehow he's not being listened to or that the Chinese person is not interested in what he's saying. The Chinese person must be bored, preoccupied, or worse yet, dishonest. Nothing, of course, could be further from reality. The Chinese *are* paying attention.

### *Can I casually touch a Chinese person—say pat a negotiator on the back as an expression of appreciation?*

You may have to control your natural tendency to touch businesspeople in China as part of the way you communicate non-verbally with them. If you do (unless you are close personal friends), you'll sense the person stiffen and become uncomfortable. Fortunately, North Americans and Chinese are similar in that they rarely touch each other when negotiating as, for example, Latin Americans tend to—tapping someone on the forearm, for instance, to emphasize a negotiating point. However, more than once an American executive has ruined a deal by backslapping a partner at the banquet table or at the conclusion of a meeting. Slapping backs and jabbing ribs just don't travel well in China. So too with opposite sex touching. Chinese men will not touch foreign women under any circumstances beyond the handshake. You should not touch across the sex line either with Chinese business associates of the opposite sex who are not very close friends.

There's also a difference between what experts call proximics and touching. North Americans stand about 18 inches apart when speaking to one another, whether the person is a stranger or a friend. The Chinese stand about 24 inches apart. In other words North Americans tend to crowd their Chinese hosts a bit during initial formal meetings, chasing them around the get-to-know-each-other cocktail party, for example.

### Is it possible to "read" the body language of the Chinese negotiator?

Yes. The Chinese maintain a deep-set aversion to outbursts and aggressive body language; under repressive communist social regimes people in the PRC are reticent to express themselves verbally. For this reason you need to be able to observe what they are thinking and feeling in their nonverbal communication. Positive feelings are often expressed as smiles and nods, nods at one another, note taking, and the thumbs-up sign.

Some tell-tale signs of impatience, nonacceptance, and anger include:

- A sucking sound of breath being drawn through the teeth produces a "sah" sound. This may indicate the person is upset and running out of patience

- The Chinese, whether in China or overseas, may show their negative response or anger by waving a hand in front of their face in a quick fan-like motion. Other signs that your counterparts are uncomfortable, disinterested, or downright ticked off:

- blank expressions with no smiling

- disconcerted and/or impatient smiles and nods

- repeated glances at a clock or watch

- sudden unwillingness to make eye contact

- a cessation of question asking

- an inquiry by a lower-level functionary to your assistant or interpreter as to how long you're presentation will last

- a cold silence is allowed to prevail in reply to your request

Your best response to these signs is to back off and call for a break. Don't become resentful and provoke a pitched battle.

Drop the issue and take it up later, informally, through a go-between.

### How do I communicate in writing with the Chinese?

The Chinese do not expect informal comments in a business letter, so you do not have to start each correspondence with a line about the weather and the kids. Get right to the point and utilize numbered lists whenever possible. That is, if you are asking questions, number them. If you are inquiring about a number of issues, number them in the letter. Number your communiques as well for referencing them later; it works better than using a date when you begin sending more than one fax per day. The writing style should be free of idioms and slang. Also, use the English language only in corresponding with the Chinese.

# CHAPTER 19

# NEGOTIATING

# IN CHINA

*"Everything in China is a negotiation. When you come right down to it, the negotiation process continues after the joint venture agreement is signed. To be successful, you have to make a continuing commitment to negotiation....Even though you have signed an agreement, you still have to continue to reaffirm what was originally decided on."*

**—Ernest De Bellis,**
Former Managing Director
of International Ventures
for Foxboro Company,
Shanghai joint venture—1985-1987

*For the Chinese negotiator, his "face" (mianzi) is his future.*

**—John So,**
Manufacturing Operations
Manager of China Hewlett-Packard—1984-1987

$T$he best way to begin talking about how the Chinese negotiate is to find out how you negotiate; in this way you can find out how different, or similar, your bargaining behavior is from the Chinese.

## WHAT'S YOUR NEGOTIATING STYLE?

Rank each of the following characteristics of negotiating behavior 1 to 10, with 10 being the most valued. That is, if you like "straight and direct answers to your questions," write 9 or 10 in the blank, then tally your score,

> Straight and direct answers to your questions_____
> Small number of key players on the other team_____
> Involvement of your lawyer to assist in contracting_____
> Truthfulness, even if harsh_____
> Time-efficiency_____
> Negotiating specifics of a deal one after another
> until done_____
> Good and consistent eye contact (seeing "eye-to-eye")_____
> General informality and casual behavior during negotia-
> tion_____
> Use of a little humor during negotiation_____
> No third-parties involved to help things along_____
> **TOTAL SCORE:_____**

If your score on the above test was between 40 and 100, your negotiation values are more Western than they are Chinese. The typical Chinese negotiator will usually score around 30-40 on this nonscientific test, while Western executives typically score between 60 and 75. The higher your score, the further you will have to come in order to adjust to the way the Chinese negotiate.

Western negotiating style is to get down to business quickly, become informal quickly, and use heavy doses of the powers of persuasion to carve out a deal that is fair for both sides, (though it is rarely thought to be by either side). In the West, a deal is a deal, not to be changed casually. And deals are typically negotiated by one person, single-handedly, rather than by a group of people working together. The Western style emphasizes straight answers, honesty, eye-to-eye contact, humor, and candor.

## How do the Chinese negotiate?

The Chinese place a great deal of emphasis on information gathering and relationship building in the bargaining process. Question asking makes up the bulk of discussions during the first phases, and they seek to engage the foreign firm in a working relationship that will begin with a first deal and remain in place over time.

They expect the foreign side to inform and educate them about its product line and technology well beyond the level of depth that the foreigner may be accustomed to.

They often play that they "don't have the authority" to approve a deal when in fact they do, and they play that they "have the authority" to approve a deal when in fact, they don't have it. This is an issue of prestige and face. The Chinese negotiator tends to have complete superiority until there is a problem in the bargaining process; then this person has to "talk to his boss" to do anything at all.

They make use of a mediator. Business in China is normally done through personal introduction by third parties, much like an arranged marriage. Unlike negotiations in the West, the introducer is often a go-between who remains involved in the negotiation from start to finish.

They start high and bargain. The Chinese bargaining style is to ask for a high price and expect to compromise. The negotiator on the Chinese side will want to win large concessions from the foreign side, to win respect and face among his superiors. The good news is that the Chinese are quite willing to compromise and make concessions to provide face for you as well.

They want to realize individual benefit in a deal. No doubt about it, a deal in China must result in privileges, income, or prestige for someone or some group, in order to get approved. China may be an ostensibly egalitarian society but individual gain is crucial in achieving closure of a deal.

They use venue and time as weapons. You arrive in China with three days to stay and on the afternoon of the third day they propose a deal and demand a final decision from you. Often the naive foreigner, up against a deadline and anxious about returning home without a contract, accepts the offer.

They will exploit your weaknesses. Should your technology be second best, or your price higher than another vendor, or your company smaller than your competition, the Chinese will seize upon your shortcomings to squeeze out concessions. You should know what are your weak points, which could include: higher price than your competition; lower quality than your competition; unwillingness to share your technology; lack of office presence inside China, and so on.

They use the "orphan strategy" often. "China is a developing country...very poor," the Chinese will tell you. "Your company is large, thus you should help China develop by accepting our proposal." Foreigners need to be cautious when "committing to help China develop," often as part of an initial memorandum of understanding in which principles for the partnership are articulated. The Chinese may hold you to it!

They will cite the "law" to maneuver, often so-called *neibu* regulations—"invisible, unpublished laws"—which tend to surface when negotiations become pitched. The legal framework for commerce is poor in China and changes in it are routine. The Chinese seem unsure at times whether a deal is within the law; on the other hand, they can dissuade a foreign negotiator on a certain clause by claiming that the law prohibits something, or is unclear about it.

They have no qualms about playing off competitors. The Chinese have a way of making you feel you are the only supplier being considered for a purchase, but don't be fooled. The Chinese have a saying about this: "Seek three before buying from one." That is, talk to three vendors before making a purchase. They will not buy from you before appraising your competitors product line. They might not be considering the alternative supplier seriously, but they will, if it bolsters their hand, use your competitor to leverage a better deal from you.

They use status and rank as a tactical weapon. The Chinese are experts at pulling rank on the Western company representative. Halfway through a negotiation a senior official shows up at the bargaining table to announce that a change must be made in the agreement. The official might even ask that the foreign company replace their representative negotiator! This strategy is known euphemistically as "kill the chicken to scare the monkey."

By humiliating the negotiator, the Chinese are sending a clear message to the CEO of the foreign party.

They are extremely conservative in spending foreign exchange. Convertible currency is in short supply among Chinese endusers. As such, they bargain with the intention to lock the foreign side in an equity joint venture or a barter arrangement to reduce their cash burden.

### What is the negotiation process in China?

A typical negotiation will progress through the following steps.

First, pre-meetings will be held that include a small group of representatives; these meetings will be rather informal and entail much question-asking and checking out of the other party. The small working group which participates at this stage will continue to discuss and resolve problems throughout the entire process of the negotiation.

As a second phase, an official negotiation will be held, including selected negotiators who will merely articulate areas of agreement and disagreement between the two sides. Real negotiation does not occur in this formal, very public setting. Use it as a chance to meet outside officials who will have to approve the deal later.

Continuing necessary repetitions of the above steps mark the next phase of a China negotiation. Again all of the tough issues are handled by the small working group in an informal, "roll up the sleeves" atmosphere.

Next preliminary agreements may include a letter of intent and or one or more letters of understanding between the parties. Formal contract signing follows an occasion attended by senior officials from both sides; this is an appropriate time for your company's CEO to be present. Finally, post-meetings will be taken that will include the original small working group in this stage, the finer details of the arrangement will be discussed; be prepared for unexpected requests for changes at this time. Note: If a go-between is utilized, he or she should be present at all meetings.

### What's the best way to make a presentation?

First of all, don't strive for informality during an initial presentation. Make it formal and do not use humor. Prepare to introduce your company (preferably through your own interpreter), and present all of your materials in English, not Chinese. Keep your talk close to the material that you hand out. Give out copies of materials at the beginning of the meeting to everyone present, and leave all materials with the participants to keep. Be careful not to appear protective of any part of your presentation materials, such as a view graph or document; provide copies of everything that you show. The Chinese are easily made suspicious if you don't want to show them everything or appear to be keeping from them selected information. Lastly, keep your presentation short; 30 minutes is on the long side. Twenty minutes is optimal. Gather information about the needs of your counterparts with questions. Give plenty of compliments to your listeners and take notes about what they say; indeed, don't be bothered by incessant note takers on their side.

Present your product in the English language. Brochures and specifications should be drafted in English as well. Remember that most Chinese who you will deal with will speak poor English, but read English quite well. Videotaped promotional material is a different story. You may want to have a short company introduction tape translated and dubbed or subtitled in Mandarin or Cantonese. Beyond that, your presentation can be delivered in English.

Make your presentation as visual as you can with graphics and slides, but remember that the real presentation will occur during informal meetings involving just a few core members from the Chinese side. So you don't need to go into great detail in the formal setting. Most of the attendees won't be experts, anyway. Should you go into scientific detail, you'll see people dozing off. Key point: whatever the Chinese want to know during a formal negotiation, they should already know through pre-meeting discussion with you, and by reading the materials that you have sent them, including answers to questions that they have asked.

### *Should I use a lawyer during a negotiation in China?*

Your lawyer should not participate in the initial phase of negotiations. Keep a lawyer who is versed in Chinese law on standby to advise you as legal aspects of the venture arise, but don't send a lawyer to negotiate with the Chinese or you will jeopardize trust. An outside lawyer will not have become part of the relationship with the Chinese parties, and thus, will wield no power. Moreover, Chinese law is subject to wide interpretation; solve legal problems together with your Chinese partner, using a lawyer—Chinese or foreign—when needed. Moreover use a lawyer as your negotiator only if he/she knows how to structure a business deal. Most can write up a contract to reflect an agreement. Few can forge the actual agreement.

### *Do the Chinese do business using detailed contracts, short contracts, or no contract at all?*

The Taiwanese and Hong Kong Chinese often do deals without contracts among close ties, but that doesn't mean you should not have one. "On the other hand," says Domiano Georgino in Taipei, "if they're going to screw you, they're going to do it whether you have a contract or not." The mainland Chinese generally *do* sign contracts as most arrangements are made between large organizations rather than individual entrepreneurs. This does not mean, however, that your Chinese partner perceives the written agreement as a finite, binding, and obligatory agreement like you might. Chris Beck, a principle with Pacific Tradeworks located in Shanghai explains: "The Chinese don't fully understand international contracts, but they're really important to them. They tend to have no idea what certain international contract clauses mean, but they value highly the formality of signing one." The Chinese put great stock in the act of both sides signing on to a commitment to enter a business deal together—the start of what they wish to be a long-term series of transactions with the contract as a starting point. They value the contract as a point of protocol which commits the foreign party to them; a symbiotic relationship is forged in their minds at this moment, even though the insides of the agreement may not be understood, nor their specific obligations as stated in the contract. When the agreement begins to impinge on them they want to renegotiate, or they ask the foreign side to bail them out. Negotiators must remember that an open and transparent bargaining style is critical. Don't hide anything from the Chinese in small print; you will only regret it later.

In Taiwan and the PRC, two versions of a contract may be signed, one in English and one in Chinese. Problems can, and often do, arise because the two versions cannot be made to match exactly in translation. Conflicts have resulted when each side begins referring to its own translation of the agreement and each seems to say different things. Thus, you should state in the contract that the English version will be the binding version of the agreement, and the one consulted in case of legal action.

### What is the legal system in China like?

In a word, incomplete. Many of the most profitable businesses in China were set up before there were laws in place to make them "legal." Because the government has a controlling influence over every aspect of commercial intercourse with foreigners, the "law" as it applies to a venture is often interpretive, and certainly manipulable by local officials. Moreover, there remains opaqueness in the approval process related to foreign-funded projects; "who needs to sign off for what" is a question nobody in China seems to be able to answer.

The court system in China and Taiwan is fraught with peril for the foreign business arbitrator. All proceedings are conducted in Mandarin. All documents must be in Chinese. Thus you will most likely need a Chinese lawyer who speaks perfect English, which is expensive. The legal system is lengthy and may well result in only a face-saving compromise similar to that which you could have negotiated out of court.

### What is the best bargaining style to use with the Chinese?

First, don't pursue a "quick kill" contract with the Chinese enduser. You will be spending a lot of money entertaining an unrealizable fantasy. Second, don't ask for instant decisions to be made on the Chinese side; this will only aggravate the Chinese and make you appear impatient and insensitive. Send a new proposal ahead of time for consideration. Don't expect feedback during a large conference. In meetings that include people of different rank, it is critical not to ask for input on a proposal since a you might embarrass a high ranking official who simply doesn't have the faintest notion of what your proposal is talking about and is made to feel ignorant. That's bad news for you. Simply submit proposals at formal meetings, or better yet, through the mail. Later, use your go-between to ascertain what is going on behind the scenes rather than blatantly ask the group. Third, don't assume that your counterpart is enthusiastic about doing a deal; to protect face and to prolong a prestige-enriching negotiation with a foreign company, a Chinese organization might not be completely frank about its inability to finance or approve a deal, nor its lack of real interest. Short initial negotiations are best, after which correspondence from the Chinese side will be a true indication of real interest. To avoid wasting time negotiating at the local level on a project that requires central level approval, visit the relevant ministries in Beijing even though a local entity claims to have approval-making autonomy. Be willing to walk away from the deal with a Chinese party which is dragging its feet; China is a costly place to do business and you should have no qualms about presenting your proposals to as many competing Chinese organizations as you can, especially those located in different provinces, in which case one probably knows little, if anything, about the other. On the other hand, don't expect confidentiality in meetings or other communications with the Chinese. A confidential letter to a close "friend" at a Chinese company will likely be shared with other team members there, especially if the enterprise is state-owned. Faxes and telexes may be read by government officials as well. Depending on the sensitivity of a deal to China's national security, foreign representatives can expect their hotel rooms to be searched and their phone calls to be listened in on. During ongoing negotiations, it is wise to discuss sensitive business topics in the hotel restaurant rather than your room.

Remain patient at all costs during a negotiation in China. Moreover, you have to concentrate on controlling your nonverbal communication, especially your facial expressions which the Chinese are keen to analyze and interpret. Show your commitment to China business at every phase of the negotiation. Make it ineluctably apparent that your company is in China for the long run, and that the end-user can depend on after-sales support from your company for years to come. Lastly, pad prices reasonably (15 to 25 percent) to ensure that you can make price concessions to face-conscious Chinese negotiators. You'll be thankful that you did when the Chinese begin to "beat you up on price" nearing the end of the bargaining stage.

## Other Advice for China Negotiators

- Take copious notes during all meetings, and enter every negotiation with a long list of questions to ask; you can con trol the context of the discussion simply by always having the next question at hand.

- Do not except a "standard" contract; engage the Chinese party to write an agreement together with you which reflects the unique working relationship that the two sides have in mind.

- Expect switchbacks and "wild cards" in dealings; sudden additional fees, higher tax rates than expected, a necessary "commission" that must be paid—you need to enter the negotiation expecting the proverbial surprise. The key is to keep your cool and deal with the snag in the informal setting rather than the formal one. This is where a go-between is crucial to soothing nerves on both sides and getting the Chinese to back away from unreasonable demands.

- Be prepared to renegotiate the agreement after it is signed. In fact, be ready to continue negotiating it throughout your working relationship with the Chinese. Remember that the built-in flexibility of a China agreement can work to your advantage as well.

- Identify what their decision pivots on, and concentrate on this point. Attempt to negotiate critical points at the pre-meeting phase; don't offer small concessions in the public meetings or you will eventually lose by attrition.

- Do not cause a loss of face on their side; don't be party to a showdown. Defuse rather than posture. Reiterate rather than badger.

- Generate reward for individuals on their side in any way you can, and play up any senior government connections that you have, which could provide prestige for your Chinese counterparts.

- Don't be stingy in hospitality toward the Chinese. Reciprocate banquets and site-seeing excursions when a delegation visits you in your country.

### *Are there formulas for successful negotiating with the Chinese?*

Win-win agreements are best with the Chinese based on long-term working relationships. Negotiate for an outcome that commits the parties to a true collaborative partnership. Your mode of "bargaining" should be to position your company to actively assist them to achieve their objectives and solve their problems rather than cut a deal. The more flexible you can be in terms of the technology package, training, and financing the better. Expect the Chinese to ask for one last concession at the end of the negotiation. If you don't give in on this, the deal could fold. Plan ahead for this final phase and have a deal sweetener ready to offer if needed. Second, be willing to give in order to get something in return. The Chinese will reciprocate a concession but you may have to initiate the give-and-take process. At the same time, do not forget to enter the negotiation with a best alternative offer in mind to fall back on. Find out what crucial thing the Chinese want in the deal and try your best to accommodate it. Third, maintain personal relationships throughout the negotiation between as many members of your team and those on the Chinese side. Make sure your go-between keeps you apprised of every new development. Fourth, seek high level sponsorship. While negotiations progress make sure you make the requisite visits to local and regional ministries to keep officials apprised of developments also; it is likely that their extra push will help bring the negotiation to a successful close. Lastly, remember the 3 Ps: patience, perseverance, and persistence. Hang in there when things stall. Ask the Chinese to continue the negotiation in the United States and couple the visit with a tour of your factory in the States. Always use nonaggressive tactics during negotiations; when conflicts arise utilize your go-between.

**THE "PROFESSIONAL" GO-BETWEEN.** Go-betweens can be hired as business facilitators in any Chinese country. They help get the goods off the dock, lobby a key man in government for special consideration of a proposal, and use their personal connections to help make the foreigner's business run smoothly. In order to preserve harmony and create consensus, the Chinese tend to "get things done" informally, through one-to-one phone calls and meetings in your absence. Your go-between can move the process on the outside more than you can working inside the formal negotiation. Always pay a go-between "on spec"—when the job is done, then they get paid.

### Is it wise to utilize a consultant go-between from the start, bring in one later or not use one at all?

Where once a few seasoned veterans with genuine experience and contacts ruled the China consultant market, today numerous collections of independent consultants with limited trade experience or "a cousin in Guangzhou" are seeking out foreign companies for representation in China. Equally risky are large multinational accounting and financial services firms that have opened offices in Beijing or other major Chinese cities. Prevented by Chinese law from practicing many parts of their core business, these entities have attempted to compensate for these lost opportunities by advertising themselves as trading and investment consultants. Yet their practical experience in China may be as limited as your own. Typically, consultants should be brought in at the beginning of your exploration process, but remember that many companies have invested a serious amount of resources in China advice when that money would have been better spent on top-notch translation and interpretation services, as well as simply going to the market oneself.

### Who do I select as an effective go-between?

Your success or failure may depend on your choosing the right go-between. The Chinese favor a go-between who has experience in the United States, as opposed to Taiwan or Hong Kong. Forty thousand Chinese students currently live in the United States. These people, once trained in business and fluent in English, are good choices as representatives. The more experience that they have working for a traditional (i.e., large and high profile) American firm, the more respect they will garner in the People's Republic among your Chinese counterparts. Your go-between must speak the same dialect as your Chinese counterparts; there can exist a high level of suspicion of the go-between if he or she speaks a different dialect, say someone who speaks Shanghaiese and is representing you in Chongqing or Beijing. The go-between must also be chosen for his loyalty to your cause; the Chinese side will do all that it can to manipulate your go-between in an effort to subvert your leveraging power. Look for a forthright, independent, thinker. Also, you must find out whether the go-between has family members living in China, Taiwan, or Hong Kong. Should he have family members living in Mainland China, it is possible that the Chinese will use this to compromise him. That is, benefits might be offered to the family as a way to encourage your go-between to work for both sides. Make these inquiries before sending a person to represent you in Chengdu when the person's impoverished family lives there too.

Be careful of sending a "culturist"—someone who has studied Chinese culture, learned the language, but who is not an experienced hardball international negotiator able to deal with large numbers of Chinese players. A culturist by definition is trained to appreciate the interests of both sides; at an early point in negotiations you need all of the leveraging power you can muster. Perhaps during an arbitration a culturist would be an appropriate choice as a mediator.

### Will I have to deal with requests for bribes and commissions?

PRC state officials who have a controlling influence over the approval or disapproval of a deal are normally bureaucrats who are paid a low set wage. An official typically has little motivation to expose himself to the risk of approving a project just because it is clearly a good project. (Why should he put his name on anything if his wage isn't going to rise commensurately with the success of the project?) His alternative is to imprint his chop for a price—in the form of a kickback, a percentage of the deal, or an indirect benefit made available by the foreign partner. The official, however, must feel absolutely confident that he will receive benefits in a "safe" manner, without any risk whatsoever. The Taiwanese, Hong Kong Chinese, and the Japanese are more accommodating, and adept at creatively influencing officials than Americans or Europeans; unfortunately, many deals get approved only after delicately-handled, behind-the-scenes, arrangements have been made.

My own experience dealing with requests for commissions by mysterious Chinese third parties opened my eyes to the systemic causes of corruption in China. My company was representing Science Applications International Corporation in the PRC. We set out to help find buyers in China for the company's airport bomb detection apparatus used to detect explosives in baggage. The device is based on a technology called Thermal Neutron Analysis, or TNA. We solicited a Chinese-American consultant (and old friend) to help get us introduced to the right parties in China. Within a month we had the opportunity to present the product to the director of MOFERT's technology import division. The meeting took place at the Chinese consulate in Los Angeles, the first sales meeting including a foreign firm ever allowed to be held there. MOFERT wanted the technology. The meeting adjourned with warm handshakes all around. A few weeks later we learned through "friendlies" on the inside that MOFERT had endorsed the project and had obtained the endorsement of it from a member of the Politburo. A meeting of planners and airport directors met and decided on a plan to import 5-10 TNA units for use in China's main airports and government buildings, for a total sales price of over $10 million. SAIC was ecstatic, as were we. Next a delegation was formed to visit SAIC and view the technology. An FTC had been put in place to coordinate the importation process—the China National Import & Export Corporation in Beijing. The Bank of China was soliciting financial proposals from potential endusers and linked up with local foreign exchange commissions to work out financial arrangements. The FTC submitted a proposal to the State Planning Commission and it was approved, in part, because of early high level government endorsements. The delegation of FTC representatives and two atomic scientists were in the air headed first to Paris to visit SAIC's competition, and then to SAIC's TNA factory in Santa Clara, California. The deal was picture perfect.

And then my Chinese consultant received a very strange phone call. The call came from a Chinese gentleman in New Jersey who said he was the president of a marketing company which was a subsidiary of the China National Technology Import and Export Corporation in Beijing. He spoke haughtily and questioned the exclusive contract that my company had with SAIC to market TNA in China. He then claimed to be able to "influence" this deal and in exchange would want a commission. My Chinese consultant "played Tai Chi with him" for awhile, trying to ascertain if the man wielded any clout in the deal at all. We concluded that he could not have a tangible positive effect on getting the deal signed, but he sounded aggressive and nasty enough to have a negative effect on the deal if we did not assuage him. Indeed, it was true that his company was a U.S. subsidiary of the Beijing FTC. Why hadn't he been in play earlier? We did not know. We asked what his fees for "marketing" would be. "Fifty percent of your commission from SAIC," he snapped.

I nearly fainted but my consultant continued to play Tia Chi. Through discussion then and later we learned some very interesting things about how China was deeming to set up the TNA purchase.

The New Jersey gentleman was to collect a 50 percent commission on the deal, but the money would not go directly to him. As it turned out, the money would go to the Beijing FTC. Why would the FTC compromise itself by asking the U.S. seller to pay it a commission in order to sell to it? We did a lot of checking through third parties to find out. In the end, we learned that the FTC was limited by government policy to only a 3 percent commission on the deals which it arranged. With thousands of employees and expensive facilities to maintain the FTC had sought another way to pay its bills—by requesting marketing fees from its vendors through its offshore subsidiaries. To our amazement, we learned that Mr. New Jersey intended to agree with us on an inflated price for the TNA equipment *prior* to the formal negotiations with endusers and the FTC. We would *pretend* to give in on price to a certain extent to give the end-users the sense that they were getting a good deal. The government was the ultimate buyer, of course, and would pay any price, as long as no one could report that commissions were being paid to a Chinese entity out of a gouged price. We tried to no end to explain the strange situation to SAIC lawyers and representatives, with the result that they felt exposed to criminal violation of the Foreign Corrupt Practices Act, since the New Jersey company was a subsidiary of a Chinese government-owned firm and thus, its president was viewed as a Chinese government official, and could not legally be paid commissions. We argued endlessly and SAIC finally gave in to the idea of my company doing what was necessary as long as SAIC didn't know about it.

The delegation arrived and were impressed by the technology but did not purchase. The point to make here is that the socialist system in China—in which state-owned FTCs are limited in the commissions rate they can charge—forces many FTCs to seek monies from the side of the supplier, which places all parties in a position of conflicting interest and legal awkwardness. Most U.S. firms, the Chinese will tell you, are not "flexible" when this sort of situation arises. The Japanese suppliers would presumably have gladly given in to the gentleman in New Jersey, negotiated a clandestine arrangement with him, and moved the charade forward toward a signed deal. On the other hand, we were highly uncomfortable with being asked to provide a kickback to the Chinese side with whom we were expecting to negotiate with on a litany of contract clauses. As the manufacturer's representative, our hands were tied to engage in the behind-the-scene negotiation that was suggested. Beyond these problems was the real concern that what was suggested might result in our indictment in a court of law, not to mention damaging SAIC's corporate reputation.

In the end I sympathized with the gentleman in New Jersey and his parent company. They were simply not being allowed to make money. The rational alternative was to engage us to help pay their lighting bills. It was hardly bribery for the benefit of an aggressive Chinese guy in New Jersey; it was company survival for a state-run firm in China. The ultimate victim in this system is the government of China which pays the sometimes enormously inflated prices for foreign equipment. The kickbacks, I have heard from sources inside other deals like the one I've described, range upwards of *two or three times* the original asking price! It's a terrible waste of China's scarce resources. Until the structure of the system changes, one can expect to have to deal, in many instances, in ways I've described in order to land large deals with government buyers in the PRC.

### *How constrained are you by the U.S. Foreign Corrupt Practices Act to influence Chinese decision makers with money or favors?*

The application of the law has recently been loosened under pressure from U.S. business interests who argue that American commercial competitiveness is damaged overseas because companies from other countries can not only pay official "commissions," but write off such payments on their taxes! It remains illegal to pay government officials directly in order to influence a deal. However, "marketing" fees can legally be paid to a company which exists to offer such service as long as that money is not transferred into the hands of government officials.

Beyond fees and commissions, any benefit that you can bring to a Chinese company will play in the decision-making process regarding your product and the attention your business receives. You might offer to upgrade a local factory by bringing in needed office equipment, set up a welfare fund for workers, or sponsor star workers with scholarships for overseas training. All of these perks can nudge a decision maker without money changing hands.

# CHAPTER 20

# ETIQUETTE AND

# PROTOCOL

*T*he following tips are for meeting people in China for the first time, whether at a cocktail party, business meeting, or when formally introduced—suggestions that will divorce you from the stereotypes of foreigners that exist in China and put you on a fast track to being accepted as a foreigner willing to play by local rules of social intercourse.

## MAKING A GOOD FIRST IMPRESSION

A number of differences between the Chinese and Westerners come to surface at first meetings. The Chinese place high value on a person's status in society and social rank, as indicators of how they are going to behave in that person's presence. You need to be aware the you will not be judged, as you might be in the West, on the basis of your clothes, your sense of humor, or other personality issues. The Chinese are impressed by social stature, title, humility, wisdom, brevity, and politeness. Here are some tips for making a stellar first impression in China. First, observe greeting rituals and exchange business cards when meeting people. A specific section discusses how to greet the Chinese. Second, try to remain formal longer when getting acquainted with Chinese, emphasizing your position and function in your company. Don't attempt to get things onto formal ground quickly, the person who exhibits a serious demeanor, rather than a purely affable one, will more readily win the trust and respect of a Chinese.

"Nontask sounding" (also known as small talk) is no waste of time. Seek common ground during initial conversations, like similar schools, technical knowledge, business experience, and mutual business associates. Forge a link. Remember to conceal your personal idiosyncracies until the second or third meeting; don't strive for familiarity in speech, apparel, or posture during first meetings. Don't feel you have to ape your Chinese counterpart; you can be Western and be yourself. Just recognize that personal assessments of you will be based on your status in your company and your position, rather than your congenial and convivial nature.

### What is the proper way to greet business people in Greater China?

Surnames come first in Chinese names, then the middle name, and lastly, the given name. Always use the person's surname, adding to it Mr., Mrs., Miss., or the person's title. A person named Chen Wei Da could be addressed as Mr. Chen or Director Chen, if his business card *(ming pian)* says he is a director. I should mention that in China the term "Tongzhi" [TONG-zuh], meaning "Comrade," came back in vogue as a form of address in post Tiananmen China, for men *and* women, though, since 1992 the title is on the wane once again. Foreigners should not, however, use this title.

Don't be alarmed if a Chinese person adds Mr. or Mrs. to your first name and calls you Mr. Fred when your name is Fred Smith. Throughout China, I am known as Mr. Christopher; feel free to correct the person to set things straight before they make a habit of it. There's a catch here, however. When a Chinese person comes to the West, he or she may reverse their names in an effort to make their name more Western, which mixes up everybody who has just learned that Chinese surnames come first. Often it's best when you first meet a Chinese person in the West and see their business card to ask which of their names is the surname. Moreover, the person may have adopted a Western name for use in the West; a friend of mine named "Zhong" uses "John," for example, for use in the United States.

Don't be surprised or make embarrassing inquiries when the names of Chinese husbands and wives do not match. Chinese women keep their family names when they marry. The origin of this goes back to when gentrified Chinese men kept housefulls of concubines, "borrowing their wombs" to procreate their lineages. The offspring were considered the property of their fathers, not the father's wife, and so sons and daughters took their father's surname rather than their mother's, which they do to this day. The famous Chinese dissident, Chai Ling is married to Feng Cong De. You would not call her Mrs. Feng; you would call her Mrs. Chai.

In Taiwan many people will have Christian names due to decades of Western missionary activity on the island. Thus you are likely to meet people with Western given names added to their Chinese names. A man named Ho Cheng may become Johnny Ho Cheng. He's called Johnny Ho, or Mr. Ho. The same goes for many Taiwanese woman's names.

**MEETING ELDERS IN CHINA.** Elders are revered in China. Show them unlimited respect and remain attentive to them at all times. They often sway opinions about business deals regardless of the cold comparison of product specifications. Stand up when they enter a room and greet them in a traditional manner, before greeting anybody else. Put out your cigarette if an elder enters a room where you are sitting and don't smoke or drink alcohol in their presence without asking their permission. You should not recline in a chair or cross your legs when sitting across from an elder; sit upright with feet on the floor and your knees together. If moving about outdoors with an elder, remove your sunglasses when speaking to them and never raise your voice in their presence.

*What are the specific steps in greeting a Chinese person in a formal manner?*

First, step back from your acquaintance so that 2 to 3 feet separate the two of you. Say "Hello, it is nice to meet you," or the equivalent, in English or in the local language. (See Key Phrases on page 341.) State your name and company. If you have been introduced by another person already, state your name and company again, as a Chinese introducer may NOT state your complete name when introducing you, as is the Western practice.

Next, pull out your business card holder from your shirt pocket or inside coat pocket. Do not store your cards in a wallet in your pants pocket or buried in a purse. Pull out one of your cards and offer it with both hands. Your acquaintance should receive your card with its printing face up to him, upside down to you. If you are introduced in Chinese, pass your card with its Chinese-language side facing up; if you are introduced to a person in English—presumably because the Chinese person you are meeting speaks English—then pass your card with its English-language side facing up. This ensures that you will not offend someone who prides himself on speaking and reading English. Take your acquaintance's card with both hands and continue to hold it with two hands as you read it. Read all of it while showing that you are impressed with the job title of the person you have met. Your expression of impressed surprise is a compliment and a courteous gesture.

Spark conversation from the person's business card, referring to his company, his job function, or the company's location, rather than leaping into an informal Western-style conversation concerning current events, your impressions of the person's country, or a joke you heard recently. Stay close to your cards at the outset. Also, try to avoid asking the person to repeat their name if you did not hear it completely. Read their name out loud from their card and then ask if you pronounced it correctly.

After you have ignited a conversation from each other's business cards, place your acquaintance's card carefully in your card holder for safe keeping. If you've met a group of people in a meeting room you can spread their business cards in front of you on the table. But avoid scribbling notes on the business cards of others and don't fiddle with them or shuffle them disrespectfully. I find it handy to lay out the cards on the table corresponding to the seating positions of the negotiators across the table so I can quickly refer to them by name.

### *What is the proper way to introduce others when socializing in China?*

First of all, introduce two people to each other in Greater China only when there is a clear purpose for making the introduction. Don't introduce high status Chinese to low status Chinese (like drivers, servants, and secretaries), unless there is a clear purpose for doing so. For example: "Mr. Chen will be your exclusive driver during your stay here and I thought that I should introduce him to you." When introducing people in China, Hong Kong, and Taiwan, introduce higher ranking persons before lower ranking, older before younger, and women before men. You can shake hands with both men and women, but do not hug, kiss, or pat a Chinese person on the back in a display of bonhomie unless you are very close friends with the person.

### *Should I address Chinese by their title or name, and should I have a title?*

Use a business person's title in Greater China whenever possible, it being polite to limit the use of "you" as an address, especially with executives, Ph.Ds, and medical doctors. Use the person's title instead—"Dr. Wang," "Director Lui," and so on—even when they call you by your first name. Chinese realize that the Western practice is to address a person using their given name after initial formality wears off, but the practice in China is to address colleagues using the surname indefinitely, which you should do also. Conversely, don't urge an acquaintance in China to call you "Sam" when they want to address you "President Smith" or "Mr. Smith."

Your title should be as specific as possible. Western titles printed on your business card like "consultant," "photographer," "writer," or "engineer" may be considered vague by business people in China. So try to be as specific as possible in your job description. For example, call yourself a "Nuclear Shielding Engineer" instead of "Engineer." Any mystery in your title will only invite misunderstanding of your specific capabilities.

### COMMONLY USED TITLES IN CHINA

| | |
|---|---|
| Comrade | Tóngzhì (Never use as a foreigner) |
| Chairman | Zhǔxí |
| Director | Zhuren |
| Manager | Jíngli |
| Minister | Bùzhǎng |
| President | Zǒngjīnglī |
| Factory Manager | Changzhàng |
| Mayor | Shìzhàng |
| Governor | Shéngzhǎng |
| Chief | Zhōng (Use as easy and acceptable catchall title, for example: Liu Zhong) |

### *Do I need to speak some words in Chinese to make a good impression?*

Nothing puts a Chinese host at ease like an effort by his foreign guest to speak a few words in his language. Try to arrive in China with a command of the key phrases listed below.

### KEY PHRASES IN MANDARIN AND CANTONESE

| | *Good Morning* | *Good Afternoon* | *Good Night* |
|---|---|---|---|
| Mandarin | Nǐzǎo | Nihǎo | Wan-an |
| Cantonese | Jóu Sahn | N'ang | Jóu Táu |

|            | *Please*     | *Thank you*   | *Excuse me*   |
|------------|--------------|---------------|---------------|
| Mandarin   | Chíng        | Shyieh-shyieh | Duay bū qi    |
| Cantonese  | Ching Néih   | Dò Jeh        | Deui M̀jyuh   |

|            | *Yes*        | *No*          | *Goodbye*     |
|------------|--------------|---------------|---------------|
| Mandarin   | Duay         | Bú duay       | Zaì Jīan      |
| Cantonese  | Haih         | M̀haih        | Joi Gin       |

### Must my name be translated into Chinese on my business card?

An irritating formality, but it must be done, and done correctly the first time. It can be a vexing endeavor because some English names sound funny in Chinese languages and many names can't be easily translated at all. There are two different routes you can take in translating your name into a Chinese language: phonetic or ideographic. If your name does not translate well phonetically, that is it sounds poor in the Chinese language, you can translate your name into an idea rather than its pronunciation. For example, the name Eve translates poorly into Chinese because it just sounds bad in Mandarin. Thus, someone named Eve might want to change the meaning of their name and translate it into, for example, "Evening." In Mandarin or Cantonese the use of characters will be employed that carry meanings of their own in addition to denoting phonetic sounds. It is best to have your name translated phonetically first, and *if possible,* employ characters that hold special meanings as well. For example, Sir David Wilson, Former Governor of Hong Kong, has what the Chinese consider "good characters." His name is translated phonetically but within the word for "Wilson," he has changed one character so that his name in Chinese means "To protect everybody's credit." Chiang Kai-shek's name meant "middle" or "right," combined with the characters to arrange or manage a country. Margaret Thatcher's characters mean "distinguished." Singapore's former Prime Minister Lee Kuan Yew's name means to glorify country and/or family.

**Warning:** When translating your name, solicit the services of a Chinese translator whose *native* language is that you are translating into. Otherwise, you're liable to go to the region using an inappropriate translation of your name, which can be terribly embarrassing. As soon as your Chinese hosts hear it, they will want to argue endlessly about how to change it. Get two or three opinions on a translation of your name from other native speakers before going to the printer to order your business cards.

**GETTING BUSINESS CARDS PRINTED.** To get cards printed in Chinese languages, look under "stationers" in the Yellow Pages; you can always find an Asia language printer in the Chinese community of a large urban area. It's NOT a good idea to wait until you get to Hong Kong before having your cards printed, as it raises the chance of errors and quite frankly, is a terrible headache to endure at the outset of a business trip to China. The card should also include the name of your company (in English), your title, address, phone number with country code, and fax number.

# DINING AND ENTERTAINMENT IN GREATER CHINA

Throughout China's convulsive history of revolt and reaction against thoughts, policies, foreigners, and democratic-minded students, Chinese leaders have never once targeted the traditional aspects of their timeless cuisine. China's food epitomizes the unalterable cultural tradition inherent in Chinese wherever they live.

China developed the notion of the "balanced diet" in 200 A.D. Ancient Chinese divided all foods into two groups based on whether they embodied Yin or Yang characteristics. They further classified foods into five "tastes"—spicy, bitter, sweet, sour, or salty. These categories corresponded to the five primary elements of Chinese cosmology (metal, wood, water, earth, and fire). A Tao like balance of both Yin and Yang foods was the ideal in one's diet.

The object of Chinese cooking was to enhance the unique taste of each food rather than mix foods together or disguise their taste with sauces. Variety of dishes and harmony between them were equally important in a meal. Individual dishes were to compliment each other. The best cook was the one who created a dish that brought out the natural flavor of an ingredient rather than manipulate it's flavor with spice or sauce. Regional cuisines grew up in China, such as Cantonese, Beijing, Shanghai, Sichuan, and Mandarin, based on what foods were available in each area and degree of exposure to foreign influence. Chili peppers came to China from the Iberian Peninsula. Even noodles came from the West, and were called "foreign hemp" by the Chinese.

The Chinese had a profound impact on Asian cuisine through the invention of soy sauce made from soy beans, wheat, and salt 2,500 years ago. Called "meat without bones," soy bean products (tofu) became essential in the cuisine of East Asia. From China also came tea to Japan around 800 A.D. and with it, the religion on Buddhism. In the tea ceremony of Buddhism a small number of people ceremoniously ate food and sipped tea.

**CHINA'S CODE OF RICE.** Rice symbolizes purity in China because it is grown with nothing else in the paddy. "Fan" refers to rice, rice muffins, and rice soup in China. A Chinese person eats nearly a pound of rice everyday. In fact, three out of five people on earth eat rice as the main item in their diet. Rice is considered "the sweat of fellow men" so don't leave an uneaten heap of it on your plate when you're finished eating. Rice may be brought out at the end of a banquet with rice soup and rice muffins. This is a way of saying, "although we have dined extravagantly, we still eat rice like common people." Recently, however, the tradition seems to be fading. Nowadays rice may be conspicuously absent from the Chinese banquet table. If you ask your hosts about the custom being discontinued, they will take it that you want rice and it will be brought out immediately. So if you don't want it, don't ask.

### *What are essential table manners for dining with Chinese?*

*Declining Food:* One of the most beguiling verbal misses between Chinese and Westerner occurs when the host and guest talk about their next meal. The Chinese is trained to deny that he is hungry when asked. The Westerner is quite frank about his appetite. So when the Chinese asks the Westerner if you would like to have lunch, the Westerner says, "Yes, I'm starved." This may offend the host and be perceived as uncouth since only a low-bred Chinese would say such a thing. Conversely, when the Westerner prepares a meal for the Chinese and asks whether his guest is hungry, he is likely to hear, "No, I'm not really very hungry." The Westerner feels offended because he has just labored over preparing or arranging dinner. A tip: decline an offering of food once before accepting.

*Eating with Your Fingers:* In general, keep your fingers off food if possible, including fruit which you can spear with a fork or pick up with your chopsticks. One exception: shuck you shrimp with your fingers, from head to tail. Don't eat the skin of fruits. Peel apples and pears as you would a banana. Skins are thought to be dirty; the tradition originates with the use of night soil—human fertilizer.

*Who Pays?* Remember that in Greater China there is no such thing as Dutch Treat. You won't hear the Western-style phrase, "We should have lunch," implying that the cost of the meal may be shared. The person who invites the other out, pays.

*Mind Your Chopsticks.* The Chinese started eating with chopsticks about 4,000 years ago when they began to cook chopped, bite-size foods. Utensils like a knife and fork had been used by the Chinese before chopsticks but soon became associated with earlier, more primitive cooking. Chopstick eating came to be thought more sophisticated than eating with a knife and fork because the chef does not have to do much work (chopping) for the eater who uses cutting utensils. So, for the Chinese, chopstick eating is thought to be more elegant than eating with a knife and fork.

There are a few rules for using chopsticks in China. First of all, the chopstick is a sign of heaven and thus, loaded with symbolism. One chopstick stuck in a bowl of rice is used in a typical funeral throughout East Asia. If you leave your chopsticks upright in a bowl of rice, it symbolizes death. So use the chopstick rest at the side of your plate. (Don't lay your chopsticks on the table after using them, either). Do not point with your chopsticks. We all know the person who rudely points with his fork; pointing your chopsticks at somebody is equally impolite. Many people recommend using the reverse end of your chopsticks for grabbing food from communal plates on the banquet table. I suppose this would be more sanitary but I have rarely seen a Chinese person reverse his or her sticks at any banquet, and thus, I don't either. Obviously, if your hosts do it, you should too. You can signal that you are finished eating by placing your chopsticks across your rice bowl. Another way is to leave food on your plate and put your chopsticks on their rest.

## THE CHINESE BANQUET

The banquet will take place in one of three places: in a restaurant, in the dining room of a company, or the dining room at a hotel. I have never heard of one being given at a Chinese host's home. Usually you will be picked up by your host and brought to the banquet location. Wait in an adjacent room or lobby for all of the guests to arrive before entering the dining room. As the guest of honor, you will enter the dining area first. If you are hosting the banquet, then insist that your Chinese counterpart enters first.

The banquet table will be large with a round lazy susan in its center. Wait to be told where to sit. The guest of honor sits facing the entrance to the dining room on the left of the Chinese host. In ancient times, Chinese princes would sit on the left of the emperor, thus the left is the honored position. Also, the prince sitting to the left of the emperor was to be of higher position than the one sitting on his right. Often, Chinese and Westerners will be seated in an alternating fashion. If the Chinese host's wife is present, she will sit opposite her husband, however foreign wives will usually be seated next to their husbands. If you are fortunate enough to have been invited to an official VIP banquet, expect seating to be prearranged and marked with name cards.

Placed before you on the table you will find a small dish, a bowl, porcelain spoon, and a pair of wooden chopsticks. A waitress will be making her way around the table pouring wine into one of your three glasses. The tiny porcelain shot glass is for the strong toasting liqueur—usually the 120-proof *mao tai* made from sorghum and wheat germ.

Start some conversation with a compliment about the center display. Thinly sliced strips of colorful "Thousand Year Old Duck Egg" are often arranged to render a dragon (symbolizing China) or a fish (symbolizing abundance). You might want to demonstrate your knowledge of the duck egg dish, which is made from eggs that are covered with ashes, lime, and mud and then put in a jar for a month or so. The eggs come out multicolored but none too appetizing. Follow your host's lead, however, if he plucks off a piece of egg from the display and eats it. Recently, economic cutbacks in China have curtailed the big rotten egg displays of the past.

After the wine is poured there will be an opening toast. Sometimes your hosts will order *mao tai* or an equally strong local liqueur to be poured for the first toast. The dinner will not begin until there is a toast. Then your host will motion with his chopsticks for everyone to begin eating; he might say "Ching...ching," (Please...please). Pluck food from the communal plates nearest you. Don't twirl the lazy suzan around looking for something you like. Try everything. Take one or two bites at a time from a plate and put them on your plate. To show your cultural knowledge, find a nice morsel with your chopsticks and place it on your neighbor's plate. He or she will do the same for you. No serving spoons will accompany the banquet dishes so use your chopsticks. In the modern cities, you may find long silver serving spoons part of the table setting. Don't touch these, as a waitress will come around and serve each person from dishes on the lazy susan. In this case, you'll have little choice over what is put on your plate. Later in the meal you can use the spoons to serve yourself more of the dishes that you like.

Don't mix the various foods. Appreciate each dish for its uniqueness. Don't use your fingers except with barbecued ribs or hunks of bony mutton. Remove small bones from your mouth with chopsticks, which can be piled on the small plate. Use the bowl to mix food with rice and to eat from. A large communal fish will be turned over by the Chinese working together with chopsticks and spoons. Remember to pace your eating and drinking by participating in the conversation. You will enjoy ten to twenty different dishes before the fruit comes indicating that the meal is over.

If you plan to stay in China for a week or more, you may want to honor your ethic Chinese hosts with a banquet comparable to the one they have given for you. Solicit the assistance of a facilitator (through your Chinese interpreter) from the Chinese side to help you find the right restaurant. There are four classes of banquets; you can see what will be served by obtaining a banquet menu card from the restaurant. Prepare to pay for the banquet before you eat, usually around $100-$150 for five people.

### Will I have to make a toast and a speech at a Chinese banquet?

You simply must toast the host, and *each member of your delegation* should do so, in order of descending rank, throughout the meal. One unknown is whether to stand up or remain seated when making your toast. This is readily resolved by your host, who will toast you first. If the host stands when toasting you, that's your cue to stand up and be toasted. (Everyone in the room will stand up too). If he remains seated, which seems to be the current trend, then you can remain seated for all subsequent toasts. To toast someone, you will probably have to do so through an interpreter. That's not easy, so you have to warn the interpreter first that you would like to make a toast to so-and-so. Then stand up (if your host did for you) with your drink in your right hand with your hand supporting the base of the glass. Make sure that everyone has a full glass before you toast or you'll be standing there twisting in the wind as a waitress is called out to fill each person's glass. Try to make your toast just after the waitress makes the rounds or request the interpreter to have the waitress fill each glass because you would like to make a toast.

What do you say in your toast? The first rule is to be sincere and not sound canned. Don't focus too much attention on any one person, but you can highlight the capabilities of the key person that has put a deal together or has been instrumental in introducing two companies. A good first toast should be to the *company* that you are meeting. You can modify the following toast to fit any occasion: "On behalf of my company, North American Incorporated, I would like to thank Chinese Incorporated for honoring us with this fine banquet. We look forward to our discussions tomorrow and believe that our two companies can build on the friendships that we share." Then say "bottom's up" in the local language, which should not be hard if you were listening to them when they toasted you. In Mandarin, it's "gambei." At meal's end, the leading member on your team should make a final toast to the host, thanking the Chinese for the banquet, and wishing the Chinese leader "good health."

You might be wondering how to resist the bottom's up part of the toasting ritual, especially if you plan on negotiating with a clear head after a lunchtime banquet. Well, good luck. It's not easy getting a banquet crowd in China not to drink alcohol. But you can try. Although you are required to "gambei" a couple of times, you can "make a deal" with the table to practice "no bottoms up" for the rest of the banquet. I play it up by getting the head man on the Chinese side to shake on it. Make it fun and hold them to it. You can also accept toasts by drinking a few sips out of your cola glass, or wine glass, but be prepared for pressure and prodding to empty your glass of high-octane alcoholic beverage. There really is no easy way out. Just a note on dinner speeches. Sometimes, in a large, multitable banquet, the president on each side will have to stand up and give a short speech to the whole crowd. This is not a toast and you don't have to raise your drink. Use the company-to-company form I gave you above, but elaborate on the future of your mutual collaboration and cooperation. Near the end of a banquet, remember that your delegation should offer one last toast, thanking the host for the wonderful banquet, and wishing him "good health."

### Can I smoke at the dinner table?

Don't smoke at the banquet table unless your hosts do. Most often they will. You will be offered a cigarette whenever somebody lights up. You should do the same for them. Western women should not smoke at the banquet table in China, unless a Chinese woman is doing so. The same goes for drinking alcohol. This may sound chauvinistic and it probably is, but there is little point in bucking the tradition by openly smoking and drinking in China if you are female. Again, follow the lead of the Chinese women who are present. They may turn out to be more liberated than you'd expect.

### Do the Chinese talk business over food?

Chinese attitudes vary over the Western practice of the "power lunch"—talking business over a meal. A good policy for the foreigner is to avoid talking business during a meal unless your host initiates it. All that said, remember that business ideas (as opposed to specifics), will often be discussed at a Chinese banquet. In fact, the occasion is often used to drop subtle hints to the foreigner about the sort of business deal that the Chinese side is seeking. Sometimes you have to be on your toes to decipher what is being expressed, which can be tough if you're feeling the effects of too much local brew. At a banquet in the Xinjiang Province of China, a bureaucrat on the Chinese side asked politely whether the visiting American CEO was interested in, of all things, raisin drying technology. Running a company that specialized in cotton production, the American said "No," and quickly forgot about the question. It was discovered later that the Chinese lacked the approval power to purchase cotton spinning machinery at the time, but were actively seeking to purchase raisin drying technology. The Chinese bureaucrat was giving the American a lead on a significant sale, but the hint was missed.

### *Will the Chinese expect me to participate in nighttime business entertainment?*

As Confucius says,: "It is better to play than do nothing." If you are fortunate enough to have built up a number of business relationships in Greater China, you are well aware of how important it is to maintain these bonds by participating in business socializing. Much actual business takes place at informal drinking sessions. Important introductions can be obtained at a company party. And most importantly, the casual atmosphere of camaraderie that pervades social gatherings gives you the chance to relax, express yourself, and clear away some of the cultural differences between you and your Chinese business partner.

Whether you are invited out drinking, to a singing bar, or to a small party among Chinese friends in your neighborhood, make certain that you attend. Don't shy away from any social event fearing you may have to sing, dance, play the piano, or drink too much. The type and intensity of entertainment that you experience will depend on your standing in your company, the size of your company, and whether you are a buyer or a seller. One thing is certain: the business entertainment that you experience, after the banquet will involve drinking alcohol.

After a Chinese banquet, one of a numbers of things could happen to you. First, you may be invited to company party at the office or in a lounge at a nearby hotel. Most Chinese have small homes that could not accommodate a large party. Many of the people at such a party you will have already met during negotiations. A second possibility is bar hopping—moving from singing bar to singing bar until everyone is inebriated and it's three in the morning. A third possibility is a night at a discotheque, a mode of business entertainment that has gained in popularity especially among younger Chinese business people. Business visitors to some Shanghai bars might be abashed when offered the city's unique service of *tuo yi he jiu*—"taking off clothes accompanying drink." Foreign businessmen with close ties might even be invited to visit one of a proliferating number of brothels in China, many located in hotels funded and operated by the People's Liberation Army. Foreigners are warned that "prostitution, whoring, and pandering" in China is strictly forbidden; more than a few chagrined male visitors have been detained in Chinese jails for weeks.

Depending on how friendly you are with your Chinese host, you may end up avoiding bars and drinking altogether and spend time chatting in a tea or coffee house. A slower mode of business entertainment facilitates communication between partners. The more you can encourage it the better. Whatever it is that you are treated to, the time out on the town with your Chinese host is a time to express otherwise unexpressed ideas to each other.

Don't, however, *expect* to be entertained initially by a Chinese host unless you represent a very large company that the Chinese side has solicited to come to meet them; you should not expect instant VIP treatment. Nobody will be on hand at the airport to pick you up and pay for your hotel room unless you have been expressly *invited* by the Chinese side to visit their company as their guest. Of course, if you place a large order during your first meeting, or indicate that such an order is in the works, a banquet will suddenly be scheduled. The Chinese procedure for initial meetings is representative. The Chinese will not entertain you before being formally introduced to you and conducting an initial business meeting with you at which time they will ask fairly bluntly, "What have you got in mind for our two companies to cooperate in business?" They want to know if its worth dealing with you. They want to hear your ideas about possible cooperation and only then will the ritual of business entertainment begin. If they like what they hear, they will invite you to a banquet that night.

### What is the etiquette for drinking alcohol with the Chinese?

A first rule is not to drink alone. Drinking is a social event and you should use the opportunity to get personal with your business counterpart, expand your network of connections, and show off the real you. Your counterpart will certainly feel freer during a drinking session to show you his or her true self. Your Chinese hosts will drink with you only in groups, so individual opinions and proclivities usually remain concealed, though with ethnic Chinese elsewhere in Asia, drinking is a chance to build trust and knowledge of each other.

Try to appreciate the local brews. Every country takes pride in its drinking beverages. The region's most famous alcoholic beverages are *mao tai* in Chinese areas. Of those, mao tai is, by far, the highest in alcohol content and the toughest to appreciate, whether you are feigning to like it or not. Don't plug up your nose at the smell of mao tai. Remember that these are national drinks that carry deep cultural significance.

Of critical importance is to pace yourself when drinking. So if you are a drinker, or someone with a low tolerance to alcohol, you have to be especially careful. Drink slowly and pace yourself. A good system for any visiting delegation is to keep track *of each others'* drinking so that nobody gets obnoxiously intoxicated or sick, which is always embarrassing and repugnant wherever you are.

Women might want to abstain from the drinking ritual. Chinese women drink less alcohol than do Chinese men. As a visiting woman from the West you may want to follow suit. However, as a general rule, foreign women should follow the lead of the Chinese women present at the function before accepting an alcoholic beverage. And never drink to excess even if the male participants do.

To decline to drink, do so politely. When you want to say no to drinking alcohol in Asia, remember the words of the poet Baudelaire: "A man who drinks only water must have something to conceal." Do not use an oblique "no" in declining booze. Claim it's "doctor's orders" or that you are having some stomach problems. Ask your host to fill your cup with cola rather than something hard.

When drinking with the Chinese, take the opportunity to talk business. At drinking parties, go for business concessions on your contract. If they are available, you'll win them here. This is a good reason to participate in any drinking outing that your Chinese counterpart invites you to.

## CHINESE GIFT GIVING

Reciprocal favor-giving is the cornerstone of "guanxi" connection making. This may sound ironic in a country that prides itself for its egalitarian socialist idealogy; indeed, coercive gift giving was discouraged in China after Communist Liberation. Yet favor-accepting ballooned with the free-market reforms under Deng Xiaoping and the Chinese now expect foreigners to exchange gifts (given to the company, not individuals) when they visit China. Motivate Chinese with gifts. If you need help finding information, getting a phone installed, obtaining an introduction—all of these tasks deserve a gift, to be given before the service is rendered. Do not fail in this or you will not be able to ask the person for a favor a next time. When Chinese need these things they reward those who help them with gifts.

### *What are the basic rules concerning gift giving to the Chinese?*

First, don't give a gift before your host, but wait until the end of your visit. Second, do not open your gift in the presence of the giver unless you are asked to do so. Third, always *refer* to a gift you have received at a later date. This, among other things, helps build continuity in your business relationship. Fourth, never give a gift without alerting your host that you are going to do so; for example, inform your host that you will be bringing over a gift to his office before leaving for the airport. That way, if you are giving to a group, the whole group will be present, which is important. And fifth, give an individual a gift only in private; and give to a group during a scheduled group gathering when everyone in present. Remember that the worst mistake you can make in China is to rob someone of face by giving gifts to their colleagues and forgetting them.

Be prepared for many types of gift giving. Gift giving is a pervasive way to maintain human relationships at all levels of Chinese society. You have to be prepared to give not only to your high-ranking Chinese counterpart, but people occupying lower levels in the hierarchy as well. To be safe, always pack three types of gifts before leaving for China. First, you should bring expensive, "perfect" gifts bought especially for your most prestigious partners. Second, bring food gifts and other middle-range consumer goods (pen sets, paper weights, picture books, high-quality calendars, expensive liquor) for, say, the managers at the Chinese company with which you do business. Third, bring along an assortment of inexpensive novelty items (books, calculators, notebooks, toys, games, cartons of cigarettes) for workers at the factory or the children of your Chinese friends. *A note on corporate logos:* they can appear on small, novelty-type gifts to individuals, or on large gifts given by your company to a company in China. Otherwise use your company logo sparingly so your gifts don't seem promotional.

Gifts should be given to the group; give to the Chinese company, organization, or institution that you are involved with rather than an individual at the company. You can, however, give one substantial gift to the group, and small items to *each member* of the group, like T-shirts, pen sets, or cartons of cigarettes. Your gift may be declined once, twice, or even three times out of politeness, though this Chinese behavior is less common now. The Chinese expect you to humbly refuse a gift once, then accept with thanks. Wrap all gifts. You may want to wrap them in red paper, the color of luck. But remember, no red ink. For a wedding, Mandarin duck pillows make a good (and common) present; they symbolize marital bliss. Be sensitive to the "spiritual pollution" factor when gift giving in Mainland China. Be careful not to give risque clothing, racy fashion magazines, provocative video tapes, or anything else that may be considered morally degenerative. Don't give the Chinese straw sandals (symbol of a peasant), a clock (a homonym for "death") even though the Chinese often do give timepieces), or a green hat (the mark of a cuckold). Don't give perfume or cosmetics to women associates. Chinese women do not all wear perfume or heavy cosmetics yet, forms of adornment which are not completely culturally accepted as of yet. And husbands don't want their wives looking like a million around the office, either. In addition, make-up and perfume are associated with prostitutes. Lastly, if you want to give a gift to someone other that the leader of the group give the gift *through* his or her superior, not directly.

**GIVING GIFTS IN TAIWAN AND HONG KONG.** Where you gave a gift to the group in China, now you can give to an individual in Taiwan and Hong Kong. Beyond that difference, you can simply follow the rules above for giving in China when you give gifts to Chinese people outside the Mainland. In Taiwan, a small gift should be given at the end of your first formal visit. Top-quality tea specially packaged by a local store is a nice gift if you visit a Taiwanese home. Since designer goods are not readily available in Taiwan, and expensive when they are, they make excellent gifts. Just the opposite is true in Hong Kong where every conceivable imported product is available. Western liquors are available as are Western designer goods, at inexpensive prices. Your best bet is to bring a gift made in your home state or town, something that a Hong Kong resident would not have seen before.

### At what times during the year do the Chinese exchange gifts?

Businesspeople in Mainland China exchange gifts twice a year, on National Day (October 1st) and during the Chinese New Year holidays, in February. Foreigners are not expected to send gifts or cards during these holidays; as elsewhere in Asia, give gifts when you visit your Chinese counterpart or when you host a Chinese delegation.

### What should a visiting foreigner give to a Chinese partner as a gift?

Give a gift related to your partner's profession, or better yet, hobby. A good strategy is to add to a collection. You will be surprised how Chinese take note of your tastes and interests. One time, in China, I mentioned that my wife enjoys working with silk. Viola!...ten meters of raw silk appeared as a gift the following day. Also, remember to take note of the birth dates of your associate's children, and their hobbies. You will want to give to them too.

Try to purchase all gifts in the West. Never give a gift that is readily and inexpensively available in China. No "Made in Taiwan" items. Shop for logo recognition. And don't give "oriental" gifts to Chinese like laquerware, porcelain china, statues of Buddha, or jade jewelry. If you are flying blind and know little about your Chinese host, stick with what you know. As an amateur photographer, I might give my Chinese host a Bret Weston print. A music lover might know the best collection of Bach on compact disc. One time I shopped with Denis Fred Simon, a technology transfer expert, for gifts for a group of visiting Chinese scientists. Dr. Simon gave them a number of the best technology books from the M.I.T. University bookstore.

To avoiding sparking a gift war, avoid giving grandiose, too expensive gifts. You don't want to embarrass your hosts by giving a $1,500 silver set and receiving a bottle of maotai in return. Try to reciprocate gifts that you receive with gifts of comparable, or less, cash value. Don't one-up your Chinese business associate by giving a more expensive gift in return. And don't give a luxurious gift *expecting* it will be answered with an equally large gift. Chinese etiquette demands that you always wrap your gifts. Never give a gift unless it is wrapped and accompanied by a card. Don't unwrap a gift *unless you are asked to do so.*

### Should I bring a gift to a Chinese home?

If a wealthy Chinese person has not invited you to his house to meet their spouse, you haven't begun to build up the necessary trust. Americans invite business associates to their homes, partly to impress them. The Chinese don't. When invited to a person's home, you are being invited into a trust-based bond with a business associate. And yes, try to always bring a gift to a Chinese home. Gourmet-quality foods purchased in the West are your best bet. Boxes of chocolate and other sweets work well too. Offer gifts with both hands and don't expect them to be opened in your presence.

## SOME GIFT IDEAS FOR CHINESE

Colorful calendar of the highest quality

Sony Walkmans and Watchmans

Subscription to National Geographic

Photobook of your state or a national park located near your home

Handcrafted item made by the native people in your region

Classical music cassette tapes and Cds

Electronic Chinese-English Translator

# APPENDIX

## China Business Information Sources

*T*he following lists government and nonprofit agencies capable of providing additional, more detailed information regarding trading and investing in the People's Republic of China. For the most part, the information held by these agencies is provided free-of-charge or for a nominal fee to U.S. businesses. The section concludes with selected contact information for Chinese commercial agencies.

### UNITED STATES GOVERNMENT

### Market Research

The U.S. Department of Commerce/**International Trade Administration's Office of the PRC and Hong Kong** supplies basic information to U.S. firms interested in developing commercial relations with China and directs businesspeople to additional sources of information. The office also publishes reports on economic and business conditions in China. Its address is:

U.S. Department of Commerce
International Trade Administration
Office of the PRC and Hong Kong
Room H2317
Washington, D.C. 20230
Tel.: (202) 377-3583

**Foreign Commercial Service Officers** are posted at the United States Embassy in Beijing and at the United States Consulates in Guangzhou, Shanghai, Shenyang, and Hong Kong. The Commercial Officers are able to provide American businesspeople with up-to-date information on local business opportunities and conditions and on the current economic and political situation in China. The commercial sections of the Embassy and Consulates have limited quantities of office and audio-visual equipment available for use by American businesspeople.

Correspondence to the Embassy and Consulates should be sent to the following addresses.

U.S. Embassy
3 Xiushui Bei Jie
Jianguomenwai
Beijing, People's Republic of China
Tel.: 532-3831
Tlx.: 22701 AMEMB CN   Fax: (011-86-1) 532-3297

U.S. Consulate General
China Hotel Office Tower
Room 1262-64
Liu Hua Lu
Guangzhou, People's Republic of China
Tel.: 677842, or 663388, ext. 1293/4
Tlx.: 44888 GZDFH CN
(Attn.: U.S. Consulate)   Fax: (011-86-20) 66-6409

U.S. Consulate General
1469 Huaihai Zhong Lu
Shanghai, People's Republic of China
Tel.: 379-880
Tlx.: 33383 USCG CN   Fax: (011-86-21) 33-4122

U.S. Consulate General
No. 40, Lane 4, Section 5
Sanjing Street, Heping District
Shenyang, People's Republic of China
Tel.: 290038
Tlx.: 80011 AMCS CN   Fax: (011-86-24) 29-0074

U.S. Consulate General
26 Garden Road
Hong Kong
Tel.: 5-211467
Tlx.: 63141 USDOC HX   Fax: (011-852-5) 845-0943

U.S. Commercial Service Officers in the **International Trade Administration's district offices** throughout the United States can furnish businesspeople interested in China with basic information.

The Marketing Publications and Services Division of the U.S. and Foreign Commercial Service's **Export Promotion Services (EPS)** commissions market research on China and publishes the results. The **Event Promotions Division (EPD)** of EPS certifies trade shows and exhibitions in China that meet the criteria of the Trade Fair Certification Program. The addresses for EPC and EPD are:

U.S. Department of Commerce
U.S. & Foreign Commercial Service
Marketing Programs Division
Room H2116
Washington, D.C. 20230

U.S. Department of Commerce
U.S. & Foreign Commercial Service
Trade Events Division
Room H1510
Washington, D.C. 20230

### Financing

The **U.S. Trade and Development Program (TDP)** is part of the International Development Cooperation Agency. It finances feasibility studies and other planning services for major public sector projects in developing countries that are potential export markets for U.S. goods and services. TDP also cofinances, on a reimbursable grant basis, planning services for projects in which a private U.S. investor potentially has equity participation.

About 25 percent of TDP's $20 million budget is directed to projects in China. Since 1983, MOFTEC has served as TDP's principal point of contact in China and now compiles a list of projects for TDP's consideration. TDP chooses the projects that appear to meet its criteria and, in most cases, sends a technical team or definitional mission to investigate the project on site. Upon the mission's recommendation, TDP agrees to fund a full-scale feasibility study.

TDP grants to China are used to pay for the services of U.S. firms chosen by the grantee on the basis of federal competitive procurement procedures. For additional information on TDP's grants to China, write to:

U.S. Trade and Development Program
Director for Asia
Room 309, SA-16
Washington, D.C. 20523
Tel.: (703) 875-4357

**EXPORT-IMPORT BANK OF THE UNITED STATES.** Eximbank lends or guarantees credits to a foreign borrower or to an intermediary to finance U.S. exports. Its current policy is to offer direct loans only when a U.S. company is competing against a foreign bidder who is assisted by a government-subsidized export credit. Eximbank offers China the most favorable interest rates and repayment terms allowed under the Arrangement on Official Export Credits of the Organization for Economic Development (OECD). China has made limited use of the long-term credits offered it by Eximbank and has not used Eximbank's medium- and short-term facilities, preferring instead the concessional, aid-type financing available from other countries and the World Bank. Concessionary or "mixed" credits are offered by Eximbank only on a selective, case-by-case basis to combat predatory export financing by other countries. For additional information on Eximbank's China program, write to:

Export-Import Bank of the United States
Vice President for Asia
811 Vermont Avenue, NW
Washington, D.C. 20571
Tel.: (202) 566-2117

**OVERSEAS PRIVATE INVESTMENT CORPORATION.** OPIC offers loans and loan guarantees to ventures in China (and elsewhere) involving substantial equity or risk exposure and management participation by U.S. companies. OPIC project financing is based on the economic, technical, marketing, and financial soundness of the project, with repayment anticipated from the project itself. Under this direct loan program, OPIC offers up to $5 million at commercial rates to small- and medium-size U.S. businesses investing in China. It also guarantees loans for China investments up to $50 million made by U.S. financial institutions to companies of any size.

OPIC provides political risk insurance to U.S. investors overseas. In China, OPIC provides insurance against the risks of expropriation and war/revolution/insurrection/civil strife. Coverage against the risk of inconvertibility of currency is not available because Chinese law affords no legal right to convert Chinese currency. In the case of disputes between the investor and his Chinese partner, OPIC insures against government frustration of the arbitration process outlined in the project agreement between the partners. There is no difference in the war coverage OPIC offers in China from that which it offers elsewhere. For further information about OPIC, write to:

Overseas Private Investment Corporation
1615 M Street, NW
Washington, D.C.
Tel.: (202) 457-7010

### Licensing

U.S. firms are encouraged to contact the Exporter Services Staff of the **Office of Export Licensing (OEL)** to obtain detailed information on licensing requirements for exports to China. No official determination on licensing can be made before a formal application is filed, but OEL can often provide an advisory opinion on the prospects for approval. OEL's address is:

U.S. Department of Commerce
Bureau of Export Administration
Office of Export Licensing
Exporter Services Staff
Room H1099
Washington, D.C. 20230
Tel.: (202) 377-4811

### Nonprofit Organizations

**The U.S.-China Business Council,** formerly known as the National Council for U.S.-China Trade, is a private, nonprofit organization which assists its member firms in their business dealings with the People's Republic of China in a variety of ways. The Council also publishes the bimonthly China Business Review. Its address is:

U.S.-China Business Council
1818 N Street, NW
Suite 500
Washington, D.C. 20036
Tel.: (202) 429-0340

The American Chamber of Commerce maintains an office in Beijing and can provide information services to visiting American executives attending business meetings in the PRC.

American Chamber of Commerce (AMCHAM)
Great Wall Sheraton Hotel
Beijing 100026
Tel.: 500-5566 x2271   Fax: (001 86 1) 501-8273

### *Investment Service Centers*

Many forward-thinking provinces and municipalities are now providing clearinghouse centers of information regarding potential joint venture investment partners. These centers provide details including the technology or services sought by the entity, its current line of business and contact information. Selected investment service centers include:

Shanghai Foreign Investment Commission
Shanghai Centre
1376 Nanjing Xi Lu
200040
Shanghai
People's Republic of China
Tel:(21) 279 8600

Guangdong Foreign Investment Service Center
Room 2352 Dongfang Hotel
120 Liuhua Lu
510016
Guangzhou
People's Republic of China
Tel:(20) 666 9611   Fax:(20) 666 6960

Investment Service Corporation of Beijing
Federation of Industry and Commerce
32 Zhushikou Xi Dajie
100050
Beijing
People's Republic of China
Tel:(1) 301 1994   Fax:(1) 301 5664

### *Foreign-Invested Enterprise Associations*

As the number of foreign-invested enterprises in China has
increased in recent years, foreign companies have begun to form
associations designed to share experiences and resources regarding China's investment climate. While not a direct source for
Chinese investment partners, these associations can serve as
invaluable aids in exploring investment opportunities and assessing the track record of existing Sino-foreign joint ventures.

China Association of Enterprises with Foreign Investment
Eight Floor, A Block, Poly Plaza
No. 14, Dong Zhi Men Nan Da Jie
Beijing
People's Republic of China
Tel:(1) 500 1188 ext. 3861   Fax:(1) 501 9361

Shanghai Foreign Investment Enterprise Association
Room 601 New Town Mansion
55 Loushanguan Lu
200002
Shanghai
People's Republic of China
Tel:(21) 275 1423   Fax:(21) 275 1208

#### CHINESE GOVERNMENT

### *Commercial Contacts*

The **Chinese Embassy** in Washington maintains a commercial section. Its address is:

Embassy of the People's Republic of China
2300 Connecticut Avenue, NW
Washington, D.C. 20008
Tel.: (202) 328-2520 or 2527

## Customs

Chinese customs regulations provide for suspension of duties on imported goods stored in bonded warehouses. Goods may remain in bond for 1 year, and application may be made to extend this period by 1 year, at the end of which the goods must be reexported or licensed for import, and import duties paid. **PRC Customs'** address is:

General Administration of Customs of the PRC
4 Taipingqiao Dajie
Beijing, People's Republic of China
Tel.: 601-115, ext. 60, 433
Tlx.: 20071 CGAC CN

## Banking

Bank of China, Head Office
17 Fuchengmenmei Tajie
Beijing, People's Republic of China
Tel.: 601-6688, ext. 2004, 601-1829
Cable: HOCHUNGKUO BEIJING
Tlx.: 22254 BCHO CN, 22289 BCHO CN

New York Branch
410 Madison Avenue
New York, New York 10017
Tel.: (212) 935-3101
Cable: CHUNGKUO NEW YORK
Tlx.: 423635 BKCHI NY   Fax: 212-593-1831

## Insurance

Most trading companies in China will offer insurance through the People's Insurance Company of China (PICC). The company's headquarters is listed below, although subsidiary and branch PICC offices can be found throughout China.

People's Insurance Company of China (PICC)
410 Fuchengmenai Street
Beijing
People's Republic of China
Tel:6016688   Fax:6011869

### *Intellectual Property*

Companies interested in registering patents in the P.R.C. should contact the following:

Patent Office of the People's Republic of China
Xuyuan Xi Lu
P.O. Box 8020
Beijing, People's Republic of China
Tel.: 201-9221, 201-4447, ext. 2223
Tlx.: 22541 POPRC CN

Patent Agency
China Council for the Promotion of International Trade
Fuxingmen Wai Street
Beijing, People's Republic of China
Tel.: 801-3344, ext. 1706
Cable: COMTRADE BEIJING
Tlx.: 22041 CPTPD CN

Shanghai Patent Agency
601 Yanan Xi Lu
Shanghai, People's Republic of China
Tel. 385-668
Tlx.: 33486 SPA CN

China Patent Agent (H.K.) Ltd.
16th Floor, China Resources Building
26 Harbour Road
Wanchai, Hong Kong
Tel.: 5-8317199, 5-8317200
Tlx.: 76507 CPALD HX

Foreign companies may register their trademarks with the **Trademark Registration Bureau of the State Administration of Industry and Commerce.** The patent agencies referred to above will generally represent foreign applicants. The address of the Trademark Registration Bureau is:

> Trademark Registration Bureau
> State Administration for Industry and Commerce
> 10 Sanlihe Dong Lu
> Beijing, People's Republic of China
> Tel.: 801-3300, ext. 324

### Marketing

Applications for registration of foreign representative offices are handled by the State Administration of Industry and Commerce (SAIC) or its local branches. SAIC's address is:

> State Administration for Industry and Commerce
> 10 Sanlihe Donglu
> Xichengqu
> Beijing, People's Republic of China
> Tel.: 862-710, 801-3300, ext. 211
> Tlx. 222-431-SAIC CN

# INDEX

# ACRONYMS